Solving Costly Organizational Conflicts

*Achieving Intergroup Trust,
Cooperation, and Teamwork*

Robert R. Blake

Jane Srygley Mouton

Solving Costly Organizational Conflicts

Jossey-Bass Publishers

San Francisco • Washington • London • 1984

SOLVING COSTLY ORGANIZATIONAL CONFLICTS
Achieving Intergroup Trust, Cooperation, and Teamwork
by Robert R. Blake and Jane Srygley Mouton

Copyright © 1984 by: Jossey-Bass Inc., Publishers
433 California Street
San Francisco, California 94104

Jossey-Bass Limited
28 Banner Street
London EC1Y 8QE

Robert R. Blake
Jane Srygley Mouton
Scientific Methods, Inc.
P.O. Box 195
Austin, Texas 78767

Library of Congress Cataloging in Publication Data

Blake, Robert Rogers (date)
    Solving costly organizational conflicts.

    Bibliography: p. 313
    Includes indexes.
    1. Conflict management. I. Mouton, Jane Srygley.
II. Title.
HD42.B58   1984   658.3′145   84-47980
ISBN 0-87589-612-X (alk. paper)

Manufactured in the United States of America

The paper in this book meets the guidelines for
permanence and durability of the Committee on
Production Guidelines for Book Longevity of the
Council on Library Resources.

JACKET DESIGN BY WILLI BAUM

FIRST EDITION

Code 8425

A joint publication in
The Jossey-Bass Management Series
and
The Jossey-Bass Social
and Behavioral Science Series

Preface

Executives and managers are increasingly realizing the critical significance of maintaining a competitive edge. Many know that the competitive edge has been eroding for American industry over several decades. There are innumerable drains on profitability that can reduce an organization's success, and some of these are attracting greater attention now than formerly. One problem that has not received the attention it merits is concerned with breakdowns of cooperation and trust at organizational interfaces. An *interface* is any point of contact between organizational groups at which interchanges are necessary to achieve a desired result. The points of contact are between departments, divisions, regions and involve the dynamics between groups rather than interpersonal relationships. Issues of organizational effectiveness that are present in the interface contacts include information flow, coordination arrangements, and decision making.

Breakdowns at organizational interfaces can be seen in chronic polarizations that erupt into mutual destructiveness. They result in poor decision making, lowered productivity, or internecine warfare and ultimately in reduced profitability. The cooperation needed for success is sacrificed because of the emphasis placed on protecting group pride, prerogatives, and priorities.

Practical knowledge of how to restore trust as the basis for achieving improved cooperation at the interfaces has been

ix

one of the great missing links in the chain necessary for increasing productivity and quality. The theory and techniques of interface conflict solving provide an important management tool for creating and maintaining interface cooperation. (Note: We introduced the term *conflict solving* at an earlier time and use it here in preference to conflict resolution, because it connotes an emphasis on identifying and eliminating *underlying* causes. A conflict-solving approach is thus understood to go to the heart of the problem and not to just work at smoothing over surface differences.)

Trust in another group's good intentions is vital for needed cooperation. Intergroup relations are particularly vulnerable to breakdowns in trust and confidence. Once distrust appears, it feeds on itself as a self-fulfilling prophecy. As group members on each side of a cleavage discuss the situation with one another, they further reinforce convictions about the correctness of their suspicions of the other group. Since such distrust is so widespread, it follows that restoring confidence between groups is of primary relevance in contributing to organizational strength and increased profitability.

Achieving effective cooperation when problem-solving relationships have broken down can be extraordinarily complicated. Managers receive essentially no college or business school instruction or in-house training in how to conduct these relationships to keep them healthy or how to rebuild them once they have eroded. As a result, disruptive relationships are widely present, sometimes severely so, such as when a new product launch is sabotaged, when a strike is called, when a subsidiary is sold as a way of getting rid of problems (as often noneconomic as not), or when a mass firing of almost 12,000 takes place as a desperate attempt to put new people in charge who "can be expected to cooperate," as in the FAA-PATCO deadlock.

The Blake-Mouton Interface Conflict-Solving Model, which is described in detail in this book, aids members on both sides of an interface cleavage to explore the conditions necessary for restoring a sound relationship based on trust and respect. It permits them to deal with the factors that have led to the prevailing distrust and to identify the specific actions for reducing destructiveness and shifting the relationship from what it is to what it can become based on collaboration and problem solving. Designing a plan of implementation strategy and an action program to achieve these results is included as a final step.

The model has been built on thirty years of work with a variety of organizations. It has been widely used and documented by such industrial and government organizations as Exxon, TRW, A. M. Castle, and the Internal Revenue Service, as well as several hundred organizations worldwide, both large and small, ranging from basic chemicals, banks, merchandising organizations, and high-tech corporations to shipping firms. Typical results have included savings in the loading and unloading of ships, the rapid realignment of products, as well as a more rational alignment of personnel policies in the aftermath of mergers, the shift of union–management relations from warfare to problem solving by reducing grievances and achieving an extended strike-free period, reduced machine downtime and better scheduling of maintenance, increased utilization of personnel with significant reductions in overhead through elimination of duplication, increments of productivity in the neighborhood of 50 percent with similar improvement in quality. The kinds of results to be expected are related to the particular problems that have arisen from interface difficulties, but, generally speaking, the results are better use of personnel and equipment and the reduction of expense through the elimination of unnecessary overhead.

Solving Costly Organizational Conflicts is addressed primarily to executives and line managers. It is they who contend with interface difficulties on a day-in, day-out basis. The strategies and tactics for strengthening communication, coordination, and decision making constitute a new management tool that they can use. Human resources personnel—including personnel managers, internal consultants, organization development specialists, and consultants—should find the model of importance because they are sometimes in a position to support line managers in implementing the model.

The genesis of the Interface Conflict-Solving Model occurred when, as professors of social psychology at the University of Texas in the early fifties, we were conducting basic research on intergroup competition and cooperation. We were seeking to identify the conditions that result in the breakdown of cooperation between groups but also to investigate circumstances under which cooperation, once lost, might be restored.

The research was clear and easy to interpret regarding the conditions that promote intergroup conflict. However, none of the techniques investigated for restoring cooperation was very successful. These included such strategies as arranging for members of each group to exchange viewpoints with members of the other group on an informal basis. The premise was that when friendships had been established on a person-to-person basis it would be easier for each group to see the other group's point of view. Creating a spirit of cooperation through persuasive lectures on the importance of mutual understanding and helpfulness spurred momentary readiness to forget old battle lines, but the message was ignored the next time the groups came into contact. Negotiations through representatives to reach solutions to problems between groups frequently resulted in impasses or compromises that were unsatisfactory relative to members' vested interests in the outcome. Designing complex tasks that could only be successfully solved when the two groups actively worked toward common achievement had a more positive effect but still left much to be desired. The limitations in each of these and other strategies for restoring cooperation stimulated additional efforts to think through the conditions essential for reestablishing interface cooperation.

An interesting turn of events occurred in 1957. One of the students who had participated in these academic experiments returned home for Christmas. He explained the experiments to his father, a company president, who contacted us, saying, "We have a number of interface tensions that are strikingly parallel to those my son has described in the experiments in which he's participated. It might help us to know more, to take a fresh look at these tensions and how we might try to resolve them. Would you be interested in coming in to tell us about your findings?"

We saw little reason for doing so, since at the time we felt our understandings for how cooperation at interfaces might be reestablished were still too meager to justify applying them. We acknowledged this limitation, but in spite of this, he encouraged us to visit. We agreed to do so only if we could involve line managers in experiments so that they, too, could experience the phenomenon of win-lose conflict and the difficulties of restoring cooperation as active participants rather than as passive listeners. An intensive experimentation with line managers as participants followed. Although improved understanding and insight about causes of interface tensions could be observed, this did little to bring about improved interface relations in actual settings.

A positive strategy needed to be invented that would permit members on both sides of an interface to investigate the conditions essential for reestablishing cooperation. This led to the Interface Conflict-Solving Model. Through its use, line managers were able to solve conflicts embedded within their operations, thus demonstrating its pertinence for resolving real-life tensions.

A development that eventually contributed to this book but that had not been anticipated now became apparent. We got involved in other activities and did not spend time at the industrial location where the Interface Conflict-Solving Model had been developed and refined. On returning after two years, however, we discovered that a large number of applications—thirty-seven to be exact—of the model had been undertaken without our further help, by line managers themselves. Having been participants in applications where we had provided assistance, they were able to take the model and apply it in an effective way on their own initiative. These and other developments suggested ways of strengthening and refining the model. It has now been tested repeatedly and found to be a sound way to reestablish cooperation between groups after they have been engaged in interface conflict.

How could we make the Interface Conflict-Solving Model available to line managers and describe conditions essential for its successful applications without our being present? Whenever we are involved in conducting an Interface Conflict-Solving

Model, it is our practice to make detailed notes and to write up the project on completion. We hoped these cases would convey the concepts and techniques to other line managers in a manner that would make the strategies immediately useful. We handed several reports of applications, such as those included here, to line managers to study. After we answered their questions, they were able to employ the model as outlined to work through interface tensions within their own organizations, often with a neutral line manager or internal consultant who stood outside both groups providing administrative support. This demonstrated to us that the Interface Conflict-Solving Model can be learned and applied by line managers themselves.

The goal of the book is to describe the Interface Conflict-Solving Model in sufficient detail to enable others to administer it as a working management tool. After we present the model, a variety of examples of its use are provided, including guidelines of do's and don't's for applying it effectively. The model can be employed to restore cooperation at disturbed interfaces in government, business and industry, medical institutions, and universities. It can be applied to interfaces between headquarters and subsidiaries, union and management, operations and maintenance or engineering departments, and in a host of other cleavages. Since the model has been employed extensively throughout the world with comparable benefits, its utility is not limited by cultural constraints.

Chapter One gives an overview of the key concepts and depicts the Interface Conflict-Solving Model as a means for resolving interface differences. Chapter Two is an extended case example illustrating the principles involved and the strategies and techniques of applying them to solving concrete interface conflict on a blow-by-blow basis. An extensive description of the techniques involved—step by step and day by day—is provided in Chapter Three. How to select participants and design administrators and how to increase readiness to participate and commitment to solving interface problems are among the issues examined.

To sharpen understanding of the underlying assumptions about the Interface Conflict-Solving Model, it is compared with an alternative approach to a chronic tension between an engineering group and operations divisions in Chapters Four and Five. Chapter Four describes the actual use of the Interpersonal Facilitator Model in which an intermediary seeks to bridge the differences between contending groups. Chapter Five picks up the problem at a later time and shows how the Interface Conflict-Solving Model was applied in the same situation.

Chapter Six concentrates on restoring cooperation in a situation of union–management conflict. Reestablishing cooperation between a headquarters and the international division of a global organization is depicted in Chapter Seven. Chapter Eight does the same for solving a long-standing conflict between a headquarters and its largest domestic subsidiary. A merger is described in Chapter Nine, where the Interface Conflict-Solving Model is employed as the basis for creating an optimal relationship between the acquiring and the acquired organizations. Chapter Ten answers questions that have been asked about the model by people who have participated in the process or have been considering its use. An annotated bibliography follows.

This applied book makes available a new management tool of practical use to the operating executive. In reading it, you might first think about your own organization. Where are the breakdowns between organizational components? Where do you hear "us versus them" or "If they'd only get with it" or "They are hopeless to deal with" or "They are just fighting to protect their turf"? These phrases point to cleavages and tensions that keep people locked into conflict and prevent needed gains in productivity. Focus your mind on one of these and use it as a basis for testing what is said for relevance in grappling with your own situation. Then read the first three chapters.

Next, you might select the chapter from Chapters Five through Nine in which the case example described most closely resembles the interface conflict in your situation. Read only one case study in any one sitting. Each resembles a short story, and the drama and cast of characters for each can be kept separate and distinct by spacing the reading. After you have selected the particular chapter that bears on your situation most closely, other chapters may help in deepening your understanding of the entire approach.

This may be as far as you need or want to go right now.

But one other possibility you might want to consider is to give this book to others in your organization who are entrapped in the same intergroup conflict situation. By doing so you can test whether it squares for them. If it does, this may be a first step in gaining their commitment to doing something about it. You may want to put the book on the shelf and come back to it later as a reference source when you find another interface conflict in your organization that you wish to address.

There are two additional ways for using this book. Organizational members who are to participate in an Interface Conflict-Solving process have found reading selected portions of the book useful for knowing what to expect and how to make maximum use of the process to achieve successful outcomes. Also, since the person administering the design will find illustrations of different aspects of conducting the approach in various chapters, he or she will benefit from examining each chapter closely as preparation for getting started.

The case examples have been changed in regard to place, time, names, products, and other identifying details, but in other ways they accurately illustrate the theory and strategies of conflict resolution through the Interface Conflict-Solving Model.

We acknowledge with appreciation the invaluable editorial contributions provided by Larry N. Davis and Delores Thomas.

Austin, Texas   Robert R. Blake
July 1984   Jane Srygley Mouton

Contents

10. Questions and Answers About Implementing
     the New Approach   286

     Annotated Bibliography   313

     Design Administrator's Procedural Index   317

     Name and Subject Index   323

The Authors

Robert R. Blake is chairman of Scientific Methods, Inc., a behavioral science firm specializing in education and organization development. He holds a bachelor's degree in psychology from Berea College (1940), a master's degree in psychology from the University of Virginia (1941), and a doctoral degree in psychology from the University of Texas at Austin (1947), where he was a professor until 1964. He has lectured at Harvard, Oxford, and Cambridge universities and worked on special extended assignments at the Tavistock Clinic, London, as a Fulbright scholar. Blake is a diplomate in industrial and organizational psychology, American Board of Professional Psychology, a fellow of the American Psychological Association, and a member of Phi Kappa Phi, Pi Gamma Mu, and Sigma Xi.

Jane Srygley Mouton is president and cofounder of Scientific Methods, Inc., and was codeveloper of the concepts of the Managerial Grid, a widely known theory of leadership. Mouton received a bachelor's degree in mathematics from the University of Texas at Austin (1950), a master's degree in psychology from Florida State University (1951), and a doctoral degree in psychology from the University of Texas at Austin (1957), where she also was a faculty member. She is an associate of the American Psychological Association, a diplomate in industrial and organizational psychology, American Board of Professional Psychology, and a member of the American Association for the

Advancement of Science, Phi Kappa Phi, and Sigma Xi. In addition to her work in executive management and organization development, Mouton has engaged in research on conformity, dynamics of win-lose conflict, and creative decision making.

Blake and Mouton have coauthored a series of books, including *Synergogy: A New Strategy for Education, Training, and Development* (1984), *The Secretary Grid* (1983), *Productivity: The Human Side* (1981), *The Academic Administrator Grid: A Guide to Developing Effective Management Teams* (1981), and *The New Managerial Grid* (1964, 1978, 1984). They have served as consultants with governments, industries, and universities in forty countries. Among many other assignments, Blake and Mouton have served as consultants to seven of the top ten *Fortune* companies, to the federal government, and to the U.S. Senate on the structure and functioning of presidential commissions. Currently, they conduct seminars on interface dynamics for training and development personnel, academics, and educational administrators.

Solving Costly Organizational Conflicts

Achieving Intergroup Trust, Cooperation, and Teamwork

Breakdown of Trust and Cooperation: Causes, Consequences, and Conventional Solutions

Three vignettes provide an initial view of how disturbed interface relations drain profitability, stifle productivity, and result in unmanageable antagonisms.

> *One management's view of its unions:*
> Can we really make progress with the union before the contract expires? They're too tough, too militant; they'll never yield or compromise, but we can't live with the many clauses that make us second-class competition in an increasingly competitive environment. It looks like our third major strike in just a few years is inevitable. I may well be the seventh plant manager to be victimized since they took their stranglehold on us. Every day in down time is worth hundreds of thousands. We can't talk to them—we don't even speak the same language. There's too much resentment and hostility on both sides to solve this ourselves.
>
> *A plant manager thinks about the maintenance and operations departments:*

1

I don't know who's to blame, but I know their failure to get along is costing us considerable money, time, and effort. Maintenance blames operations. "Everything would be fine," they say, "if they would just operate the plants and leave the repair to us." The operations managers say, "If maintenance would only be reasonable, if they'd support us instead of dictating to us, there'd be no problem." We're no closer to resolving this problem now than we were a half century ago. No one cares who's right or who's wrong any more; we just want to see some movement in a positive direction.

A vice-president views his international division:

Why haven't we made the progress envisioned when the Worldtex division was formed three years ago? It seemed that everyone would see the benefits of a global strategy, an integrated approach, and cooperate with headquarters to make the goal of a coordinated, worldwide effort a reality. Instead, trading offices are still operating their fiefdoms as independent entrepreneurs, competing among themselves and resisting headquarters' direction. If anything, things are worse now than they were before.

These are examples of different interface relationships, but each reveals the same underlying problem the union-management example characterizes an erosion of trust in a relationship in which neither group has the authority to control the other and neither can appeal to a higher level to resolve their differences. This relationship parallels that between a supplier and a purchaser or one between a contractor and a contractee.

The second example exemplifies the breakdown of trust between operations and maintenance. It is similar to the union-management situation in that neither of the groups has authority to control the other. In this case, however, both groups are in a position to appeal to a higher authority to resolve differences between them. This illustration finds many parallels: management information systems (MIS) and the user groups, production and research and development (R&D), manufacturing and the marketing system, operations and the user groups, and so on.

The third vignette reveals a problem of distrust between the corporate offices and subsidiaries throughout the world—a relationship in which one group has the authority to control others. This relationship also occurs in many other examples, such as between regional offices and their field locations and between manufacturing headquarters and their plants.

While the costs in terms of lowered productivity, shabby quality, and wasted resources are impossible to determine, they obviously amount to a large drain on an organization's profitability. Even more important is the realization that many of these are not acute problems, yet they are chronic; once disturbed relationships start, they tend to have a life of their own. This adverse impact is not measured in terms of a single event but extends over years and, in some cases, decades.

Thus, tensions arising at any interface can create a dynamic history with significant events of the past recalled and the remembrances shared as each group develops a kind of folklore surrounding events within groups and between groups. Seldom are events remembered precisely as they happened but rather as group members believe they happened, sometimes regardless of the facts. It is not history per se that group members commit to memory but their own perceptions of what transpired and the war stories recounted to embellish them. Soon history becomes a source of guidance and a directional force that shapes approaches to the future. Furthermore, a group's history is transmitted from one generation to another and thus can continue to exert influences long after the events that shaped it occurred and the people who took part have moved on.

How History Preserves Conflict
and Impedes Cooperation

On the positive side, a group's history provides its members with continuity and stability—an anchor in time and space. History helps group members understand where they are and how they got there. Records of the past are useful to group members in charting growth and development and in establishing important patterns and trends. A longitudinal perspective on accomplishments gives greater meaning to assessments of current group performance and provides a context for setting goals and objectives.

Yet for all its positive contributions, history is often a formidable barrier to progress and effective resolution of conflicts at the interface. Whether it transpired yesterday, last year, or a decade ago, history may exercise counterproductive influences on members' perceptions, attitudes, and behaviors.

Once interface conflict develops, the distrust surrounding it is kept in place by traditions, precedents, and practices firmly rooted in history. Through its power over thought, feelings, and action, history makes intergroup conflict resolution all the more difficult. History influences the way groups regard and respond to one another in sometimes subtle, frequently silent, but very important ways.

History limits a group's vision of future alternatives and possibilities to those that individuals believe other members will understand, approve, and accept. Past experiences, distorted by time and tainted with subjectivity, are characteristically accepted as valid predictors of the group's response to various suggestions. Recommendations that are contrary to history may be summarily dismissed, and the individual who proposed them may be censored or temporarily rejected.

In effect, competing, contending groups that develop or inherit traditions of suspicion, distrust, and resentment are blinded to the possibility of a relationship based on trust, respect, openness, and mutual appreciation. While groups are unable to see cooperative, collaborative effort as an alternative and traditionally resolve problems through win-lose situations, relying on power and authority or withdrawal, they are likely to repeat the same patterns, even though the consequences are mutually destructive and undesirable.

Why Interface Conflict Is Common in Organizational Life

The potential for interface conflict is already present in the structure of modern organizations. Structures that combine similar work activities into functional groupings and separate them from others that are different are viewed as effective for maximizing effort and avoiding duplication. Interface conflict is likely to arise, however, when separated organizational components must reconnect and work together to achieve a goal. A group that has an interface conflict with another ought not necessarily be regarded as having "bad" teamwork among its own members. Internally, it may be a high-performing group characterized by high morale. Indeed, its morale may be strengthened by its bad interface relations. The deeper issue, however, is how to achieve high morale and productivity while maintaining or increasing good interface relations.

Even though often attributed to personalities, conflict between functional organizational groups that need to cooperate usually arises naturally as a function of dynamics operating at their interface. Managers tend to take such conflict for granted and know little or nothing about how to resolve it in a truly effective manner.

To understand such natural interface conflict, it is important to recognize that a group is much more than an assemblage of individuals. As a group member, each individual's behavior and conduct is influenced by feelings of membership, including a web of entanglements that must be preserved to avoid expulsion. A key to interface conflict resolution is understanding how such group and interface characteristics influence the attitudes and behavior of organizational members. Then it is possible to apply dynamic solutions that take these interface variables into account.

Interpersonal Versus Intergroup Conflict

Intergroup conflict cannot be understood by presuming it to be more or less the same as conflict between individuals. Performance by a person acting alone is largely determined by that individual's behavior, attitudes, and skills—that is, by what is "inside the skin." While obviously influenced by a variety of factors, individuals may choose to think or act in a given way simply because they want to or feel a need to. When differences or conflicts arise with another person, then an individual is free to react and to change his or her mind on the basis of new evidence and to give or withhold cooperation in keeping with personal desires. If an impasse is reached, it may be resolved by compromise or by yielding to the other person's point of view or by the equivalent of flipping a coin. Whatever the outcome, both agree to abide by the decision.

A group member is not free in the same sense as is an individual acting alone. Rules and standards of behavior—norms—are developed within the group that regulate the behavior of members through sometimes subtle but potent pressures. Significant individual departures from important jointly held group values and attitudes or accepted patterns of behavior are rarely tolerated. Members who think or act differently are either punished, persuaded, or rejected. Seeking to solve interface disputes at the group level as though they were personal disputes between two individuals not only disregards these important dynamics but also may create new tensions that may provide short-term solutions and at the same time disrupt internal group cohesion, producing new and more serious problems in the future.

What are the origins and consequences of such feelings of membership for resolving intergroup disputes? This is an important question. In answering it, we find explanations for why intergroup disputes must be approached for resolution in a manner distinctly different from interpersonal disagreements.

Membership Pride

Members have pride in their groups or else leave them, if that is possible; no one wants to be a member of a group he or she loathes. When individuals feel group pride, they accept the group's values and give their support in helping the group reach its goals. This membership pride can be demonstrated empirically using a nine-point scale, with nine representing the best possible group and one the worst possible group. When asked individually and in private to evaluate their group, members seldom rate it lower than six, or "somewhat better than average." Based on statistical logic, an objective numerical comparison would find an equal number of groups above and below average and result in an average rating of five. Thus, members' evaluations of six or more reflect pride rather than objectivity, referred to as the "sixth dynamic." This evaluation holds true even though members may not be completely satisfied with the effectiveness of their group. "We may have some problems," members reluctantly admit, "but at least we're better than most other groups around here."

The fact that members' judgments of their own group are consistently more positive than objectivity would merit suggests a deeper explanation than norm-based uniformity of opinion. Rating the group on the scale's high end may be an effort to enhance self-esteem. Positive regard for one's group is probably a reflection of members' needs to think well of themselves. Individuals are evidently unwilling to accept the implications of an inferior group rating, that is, "membership in a poor group reflects negatively on me as a person." Members therefore conclude that their own group is "good" and that they personally are good by virtue of their group association.

The implications of the sixth dynamic are important to understand. It means that members are likely to resent external criticism or accusations about their group's performance. The resentment is likely to be keener when it comes from another group with which the first group has direct dealings. To avoid the loss in pride that would come from accepting criticism and accusations as justified or valid, the tendency is to react with suspicion toward the outsiders.

Loyalty Versus Logic

The greater this sense of group pride and identity, the more commitment is displayed to the group's position on any issue. Under conditions of high cohesion, group members often come to place loyalty above logic. Judgment becomes distorted and, no matter what the issue, groups see their own position as valid, right, and just. Contrary positions are viewed with disfavor and as less acceptable.

When looking at their own options or alternatives, group

members see positive aspects and tend to be blind to shortcomings or weaknesses in their own effectiveness, points of view, or
proposals. Therefore, group members are biased in their favor.
The converse is also true. Other groups' positions, proposals, or
points of view that are contradictions or even slightly different
are typically weighed and found wanting. Positive features of
others' ideas are obscured, while negative aspects become glar-
ingly obvious.

Invidious Comparisons Between Groups

Once established, group identity is maintained and further strengthened through attitudes and behaviors that distin-
guish *us* from *them*. This "we versus they" dichotomy occurs in
any number of invidious comparisons. Members of each organization's groups come to the jointly held opinion that we are
better, smarter, harder working, more dedicated, and more honest, than any of them.

This membership group superiority coupled with invidious comparisons with other groups has been demonstrated in its
pure form with young adult college students. As participants in
an academic experiment, students arrive in random order at a
selected central site. The experimenter asks the first person to
sit in a chair near a table at Location A. The second person is
taken to Location B. Person 3 is routed to Location A and is requested to speak with no one. Person 4 is taken to Location B,
receiving the same instruction of silence. Each subsequent ar-
rival is directed in turn to Location C or D until those two
groups are also completed. A questionnaire is then distributed
in each group prior to any interaction. Members are asked to
make a judgment as to which group they believe could do a better job on a subsequent task: Group A or Group B? Members
of Group C make the same comparison judgment with Group
D. Note that these judgments are made prior to discussion
among or between group members and before being informed
about the activity in which they will be engaged.

The generalization is that the students in Group A feel
they will be able to do a better job than those in Group B,

those in Group C better than those in Group D, and so on. Reciprocally, the same finding occurs with members of Group B over Group A, with Group D over Group C, and so on. Members feel more positive toward their own group than toward another group with whom they are comparing themselves. This is true although their "members" have never even so much as shared a word with one another.

A member's impressions or beliefs about "them" are also formed from information provided by others from the internal membership group rather than from in-depth observations of the group itself. Because little is known about the inside situation of another group, opinions are formed on the basis of inferences, attributed motivations, and hearsay.

When cooperation is needed between the groups, each group acts on its assumptions about the other, automatically accepting the correctness of its own opinions and perceptions, even though they may be colored by group pride and invidious comparisons. Since members are confident and comfortable with their perceptions, they are likely to tend to disregard contradictory facts or to reinterpret such discrepancies to make them fit prevailing assumptions. When cooperation is less than expected or desired, rationalizations about "them"—the other group—may include that they are poorly managed, incompetent, or devious or that their own internal problems or faulty operations keep them from performing up to standards or expectations. As evaluations of one's group are enhanced, external groups are downgraded. Perceived inferiority is likely whether the comparison group is lower, equal, or higher in rank or authority. These indivious comparisons work against cooperative, collaborative problem solving.

Win-Lose Competition Becomes the Shared Expectation

When groups are vying with one another, a win-lose mentality characteristic of many interface relationships may come to replace necessary cooperation and problem solving. Each group has a vested interest in its own success, even if one group's gain is at the expense of the other. The desire to win becomes an end in itself. This win-lose competitive motivation can be and often is exploited to encourage increased motivation and effort from group members. Then winning becomes the name of the organizational game, and members are pushed to work harder, faster, longer, or better. Tripping up the adversary group helps clear the way to victory, the all-important prize. These divisive campaigns may significantly hinder future attempts to generate enthusiasm among groups for coordination and cooperation. Once established, a competitive mind-set evokes more distrust, which can lead to increased tension, hostility, and conflict.

The circle is complete when the expectation of further conflict is accepted as given. Neither group can visualize alternatives to continued antagonism and hostility. Each group distrusts the other and seeks opportunities to dominate either through exercising power in the effort to win or by other means, if authority to enforce one's position is not available. These patterns of behavior, once established as normative, are especially resistant to change.

When group members have come to accept their conflicts as inevitable and have developed strategies for coping with them, there is little or no motivation to change. Even group members who might recognize change as desirable probably think it is impossible to achieve. Group members seldom make a conscious choice to preserve a poor relationship; they simply fail to see possibilities and alternatives for improving it. Under these conditions, managers armed with a vague and incomplete understanding of interface dynamics and the controlling influence of history rely on conventional approaches that often fail to effectively resolve conflict.

Conventional Approaches for Resolving
Interface Differences

Common approaches to interface conflict resolution usually disregard the underlying dynamics that generate it and the historical influences that perpetuate it. The result, far more often than progress or change, is generally frustration and failure. Several traditional approaches and the probable outcomes of each are presented and explored here for later comparison with the methodology suggested in this book.

Cooperation by Edict

"Starting tomorrow," the boss declares, "it's going to be different around here. No more bickering, one-upmanship, or game playing—we're all going to get along. I want to see more cooperation and collaboration, and I expect you to communicate this message to your people and require the same of them."

If change were so easily accomplished, interface conflict would soon disappear. In reality, board or executive mandates, though issued with every expectation of immediate compliance, are not sufficient to generate lasting, meaningful departures from the status quo. Top management may act differently for awhile, especially when the boss is present, but will soon revert to established, familiar patterns when the boss is absent.

Mandated cooperation seldom has any impact at all beyond an organization's middle management. Supervisors and wage staff may pay lip service to an executive edict, but group norms and expectations often preclude their adapting to it in practice. Compliance with historical standards and precedents is reinforced and rewarded while change is treated as a deviation from normal.

Negotiations and the Hero-Traitor Dilemma

Conventional efforts to resolve win-lose conflict at the interface may be approached by representatives. Group leaders as representatives sometimes come together voluntarily seeking to negotiate their differences. If leaders can agree on a joint solution to a problem, they return to their groups and impose a new policy or practice that implements their decision. Since the culture of both groups is unchanged, members are unlikely to adapt their behavior at the leader's command or request to improve relationships. In fact, the relationship may deteriorate further because each group views the other as violating a mutually established agreement.

Sometimes members are selected from each group and are

empowered to negotiate a settlement of the differences. Then representatives are members, not individuals per se, and are responsible for their group's well-being. Acting as representatives, they are not freed from the loyalty versus logic dilemma. They may want to agree with the other group's representatives, but feel pressured to win to justify the confidence and trust placed in them. The group expects their representatives to explain, defend, and justify their position and to attack or challenge the position held by another.

When these conditions prevail, the "successful" representative is regarded as a hero. Heroes are rewarded with appreciation, warmth, increased status, and heightened prestige. A defeated representative who capitulates to the other group's point of view is likely to be regarded as a traitor and to face ridicule, loss of prestige, and, in extreme cases, expulsion from the group.

Unfortunately, heroism requires adherence to the group's previously established position. The hero must neither yield nor compromise, but must extract agreement from the adversary. Since both representatives are seeking to become heroes and avoid the stigma of capitulation, negotiations typically reach an impasse. Progress is impossible unless one representative or the other is willing to face his or her group's disappointment, anger, and hostility.

Leadership Replacement

When cooperation between a headquarters–field location has broken down, a common approach to reestablish it is to replace the head of the lower unit, not by an insider but by an outsider. "Parachuting in, that's what they call it. The old boss is gone . . . a new boss is coming, but not up from the ranks or from somewhere else in the outfit. No, he's parachuting in from the outside. And in the drop zone, the troops wait and wonder." The apparent logic of leadership replacement is that a new manager for one or more of the groups in conflict, unencumbered by personal experience with or responsibility for the past, might be able to establish and maintain new patterns of interface cooperation and collaboration. This effort fails to consider the persistent strength of tradition-based culture and practice and the group reaction to an individual who violates its norms. Much of what transpired in the past is inadvertently transferred into the future as the new leader seeks acceptance and approval by adapting, at least to some degree, to the group's expectations.

New members are largely dependent for their understanding of the present on explanations of the past that others supply. In acquiring knowledge of history, the new member is inadvertently and perhaps unwittingly influenced by the biases and prejudices of others. As the new leader (or member) responds to the cues provided by tenured and experienced peers, superiors, and subordinates, the old attitudes, values, and behaviors that the new leader might have changed may instead be adopted as desirable and appropriate.

Personnel Rotation

A common approach to strengthening understanding and collaboration between groups that need improved cooperation is personnel rotation. The hope in moving individuals from one group to another is that direct contact might increase understanding of the way the other group operates and alter negative attitudes through sympathetic views of their problems. Group members who have a deeper perspective of and personal experience with another group are expected to view that external group more positively and lead their own group members to do the same.

This effort seldom creates any real change, because group norms are simply too powerful to alter on an individual-by-individual basis. Any benefits from the exchange will likely fade soon after exchanged members rejoin their original group. If the exchange group accepts an outsider temporarily, positive feelings about the exchanged member are specific to the individual, not generalized to the entire membership. Additionally, to avoid being seen as a traitor, returning members generally feel pressured to return to negative attitudes of the original membership group toward the other group.

Structural Solutions

Problems at the interface are often attributed to faulty organizational structures. With this explanation, the solution is obvious—change the structure and eliminate the problem. So a new organizational chart is created, boxes are shuffled and re-arranged, and old lines are erased and different ones drawn to reflect changed reporting relationships and managerial responsibilities. Past conflicts are expected to disappear as if by magic.

Frequently, however, new conflicts arise to replace the old. Restructuring may not solve problems when the attitudes and feelings are deeply embedded in history; it then merely shifts their location, transferring conflict to a different setting.

Liaison Persons

Another solution often applied to resolution of conflict at the interface involves creation of formal and informal liaison positions. Liaisons then become the point of contact through which each group communicates with the other. Common issues may be considered and recommendations made by designated liaisons, but operating decisions are made at some other organizational level. Although the intent of liaison appointments is to expedite or facilitate agreement, the structure often becomes a troublesome extra layer that further impedes change and progress.

Flexible Reporting Relationships

Matrix organizations and project or product management constitute more flexible arrangements for bringing together human resources that are needed for concentrating effort on solving problems. These may create permanent or new groupings. For example, in matrix organizations, one subordinate may report to more than one manager. Project management may call for an employee to work on one undertaking for a time and then be assigned to another one with different reporting relationships at another time. In a similar way, a product manager may be provided with all the resources necessary to launch a successful product with manufacturing, packaging, and sales all coming together under one manager.

These flexible structures may reduce group-anchored vested interests and shorten the lines of communication between those who need to collaborate in contributing to an overall result. They constitute positive alternatives for reducing or bypassing intergroup conflicts whenever they have practical utility. In many situations they simply do not have functional application because expert personnel usually work more effectively and economically when kept together than when dispersed.

Mediation and Arbitration

Outsiders as mediators, or conciliators, and arbitrators are often relied upon in attempts to resolve interface conflict. Mediation involves the intervention of a third party who first investigates and defines the problem and then usually approaches each group separately with recommendations designed to provide a mutually acceptable solution. Conciliation is applied if the mediator attempts to aid each group to understand and appreciate the position of the other. These efforts may be successful in solving specific problems, but they fail to address the underlying tensions that created the unresolved conflict in the first place or to establish a foundation for ongoing cooperation and collaboration in other situations.

When attempts are made to resolve interface conflict through arbitration, both sides of the controversy are presented to a neutral third party, often under formal arrangements. Once opposing positions have been heard, the arbiter is authorized to make a final decision to which each group is bound. While arbitration shares the weaknesses of other approaches, it has an additional disadvantage in that participants in the conflict relinquish problem-solving responsibility to an outsider.

Interpersonal Facilitator Model

The Interpersonal Facilitator Model involves an outsider as intermediary who becomes involved in the problem and its solution through aiding members of groups in conflict to work on the problem in a more effective way. The intermediary may seek to lessen tensions by separating principals and moving back and forth between them as a go-between, much as in mediation and conciliation. The intermediary takes responsibility for resolving differences by formulating proposals that may be more agreeable first to one side and then to the other. In other words, the basic assumptions of this approach are that problems can be solved by one-on-one contact and that solutions are sometimes facilitated by the intermediary becoming an active agent of defining and resolving the issue.

The facilitator as bridge has been a long time in developing and has many adherents. The concept is inherent to the idea of the honest broker or the lawyer who seeks an out-of-court settlement between conflicting parties, seeking in each case to create a meeting of minds without dictating the terms of the outcome. A critical distinction too frequently ignored in negotiation theory and practice is that the leader may be, and often is, a member of a larger group and acting on behalf of shared rather than solo convictions. Then reliance on the Interpersonal Facilitator Model can unintentionally drive a split between the leader and his or her group or cause resistance to change because the leaders remain loyal to their group-anchored convictions.

Since the principals only learn about what the other principal is thinking or how each is reacting through the intermediary, the intermediary is in a position subject to manipulation. He or she can withhold, release, or interpret facts in such a way to produce agreement that may cause agreements already given to be repudiated when the facts later become known. Agreements reached through the application of a facilitator model are more likely to be improvements within the status quo. A more extended description of the Interpersonal Facilitator Model and a comparison of it with the Interface Conflict-Solving Model is presented in Chapter Four.

In summary, traditional approaches to interface conflict resolution have been useful, but none has focused on penetrating underlying dynamics, relieving boundary tensions and antagonisms, or establishing a basis for continued cooperation and collaboration. In practice, a number of catalytic strategies such as the Interpersonal Facilitator Model were used in the 1960s that came closer to achieving these results. An alternative was needed to generate in each group the motivation and commitment required to escape an undesirable history of conflict and establish new norms of cooperation and collaboration.

The Interface Conflict-Solving Model: Six Steps

Interface participants are key members of each group embroiled in conflict. The group members who participate are regarded by themselves, by others who may not participate, and by the members of the other group as responsible for and capable of making the decisions necessary to bring about change. The critical mass includes all those needed to commit the whole membership to actions and whose voices carry weight in implementing or in vetoing action. In addition, the interface development sessions require group members who are sufficiently familiar with the history of the relationship, current norms, and operating practices to recreate and identify them in practice. Participating group members, in other words, represent a microcosm of the whole, but beyond that can commit the entire membership. An apparent contradiction exists in arranging for people to participate in a process of mutual problem solving when existing frictions and antagonisms between groups reduce any readiness of members to cooperate. Certain minimum conditions are necessary to start this process. One is to gain the commitment of the ultimate level of managerial authority necessary for solving the problem that changes are desirable by shifting existing relationships.

The second condition is that members of both groups are

willing to take part in the activities. This commitment involves no promise that positive consequences will occur but rather the acknowledgment that those responsible will give the process a trial. Additional issues concerned with gaining the commitment of participating group members to an interface activity are described in Chapter Three.

The session begins with an orientation to review the objectives, activities, and procedures. While specifics vary depending upon particular problems and needs, the same basic six-step process is applicable to diverse interface conflicts in business, industry, and government.

- *Step 1: Developing the optimal model*—Each participating group works separately to create a model of optimal interface effectiveness specific to their problems and needs.
- *Step 2: Consolidating the optimal relationship*—A consolidated model of a sound relationship is then generated through the groups' joint efforts.
- *Step 3: Describing the actual relationship*—Actual conditions that characterize the relationship are described by each group separately, with members analyzing historical factors that shaped and influenced the relationship.
- *Step 4: Consolidating the actual relationship*—The groups' individual perspectives are consolidated into a joint picture that accurately and objectively describes the present.
- *Step 5: Planning for change*—Changes to be made in specific, operational terms are jointly agreed upon and described in detail. These result in plans for follow-up by this group and those not present.
- *Step 6: Progress review and replanning*—Follow-up dates are scheduled for groups to reconvene three to six months after the initial session to review progress, critique their current relationship, and plan next steps.

Neutral outsiders are present to ensure that the Interface Conflict-Solving Model is employed in such a way as to maximize the likelihood of a successful outcome. Their role is thus to administer the process, while the group members themselves

are responsible for the content—the specific decisions, the recommendations for future actions, or the conclusions formulated. The neutral outsiders do not need to be external to the
organization. Design administrators may be line managers or human resource personnel from within the organization at least as
high in rank as the most senior managers of the participating
groups but, in either case, are not members of the participant
groups and have no vested interest in any particular outcome.
Technical knowledge of building relationships and the theories
and principles upon which this process rests is critical, as is a
dynamic understanding of intergroup behavior.

Why the Interface Conflict-Solving Model Works

Though the Interface Conflict-Solving Model has been
found to have considerable strength in bringing about successful outcomes, this conclusion is a matter of degree, with some
applications more successful than others. The Interface Conflict-Solving Model works for several reasons, which include
the following points.

Unit of Change

Basic to the success of this process is a new awareness of
what a manager is. Although a manager is an individual rewarded according to his or her effective discharge of assigned
responsibilities, managers are much more than individuals. They
are members of groups, persons whose attitudes and actions are
far different because of this membership.

Changes in the behavior of individuals will be resisted if
any one member acts in disregard of what the others in that
group accept as appropriate or sound. Therefore, it is essential
for all members to change together; this is possible in the Interface Conflict-Solving Model because the criteria of group com-
position that determine who should take part ensure that attendees include persons who have knowledge of the history of the
cleavage, understanding of its present adverse effects, and the
authority to authorize and implement the agreed-upon solu-

tions. Thus, norms that govern interaction at the interface and that are contained within the cultures, traditions, precedents, and past practices of contending groups are subject to change because those whose behavior they influence are present. Efforts to alter group norms on an individual-by-individual basis, as may be made when using the Interpersonal Facilitator Model, may stimulate problems related to member disloyalty, hero-traitor dynamics, and so on. These issues, raised earlier in the chapter, are not created by the Interface Conflict-Solving Model. Since group norms are established and maintained through member interaction, they must be changed in the same way. Members who significantly deviate from group attitudes or expectations may be accused of "selling out" to the enemy and subsequently viewed as traitors. The unit of interface change then is not the individual member or members of one group in isolation from the other but the membership of both groups.

Under conditions of shared participation, members have an opportunity to think about alternatives and to test various solutions for utility and acceptability. Those who previously shared norms of doubt, suspicion, hostility, withdrawal, or competition can view the benefits of trust, respect, collaboration, and cooperation and then change simultaneously in a positive direction.

Comparison of Ideal and Actual Relationships

Creating a model of the ideal frees participants to imagine possibilities that are obscured if their thinking is limited to discussing only the actual problem as it currently exists. Thus, group members are encouraged to work with the possible rather than limit efforts to solely working on the problem. Comparison of the ideal model with what is actual aids in identifying specific and concrete actions that are necessary to solve the problem.

Because the model permits the participants to interact with one another in an orderly and sound manner, groups can focus on and evaluate issues internally and communicate their points of view across groups to permit further evaluation and agreement about the actual problem and the solution.

The Design and Design Administrator

The design provides an understandable framework that enables participants to clarify issues and to identify optimal possibilities for solving them. Since the design administrator's participation is limited to aiding participants to operate within the design, 100 percent of the responsibility for success in using the model is retained by the participants themselves. This sense of control over the outcome increases the commitment of participants to initiate the process and thereafter to make it successful.

Direct Resolution of Disagreements

Disagreements are surfaced in the process of developing statements of the ideal relationship and distortions regarding the actual relationship. When disagreements arise between groups, the design itself provides a structure for solving them. By using the design to aid group members to deal directly with one another in a problem-solving manner, they are far less dependent on an expert for masterminding the process. Additionally, since exchanges between groups are carried out through spokespersons rather than by designated leaders, this also serves to depolarize tensions. Destructiveness resulting from mutual accusations, attacks, and counterattacks also is reduced because the emphasis is not on determining which group is right or wrong, but on finding the facts, uncovering the logic inherent in the problem, and agreeing on sound solutions.

What Is to Be Gained?

As the cases to be reported will show, positive gains from following our model include the heightened satisfaction of those responsible for leading and operating organizational systems, to say nothing of the reduction in emotional despair and misery that can be attained. As one participant said, "Last night was the first good night's sleep I've had since coming to work here eight years ago!" This is an intense reaction, but it is an example of the personal cost from living with constant antag-

onism, hostility, and strife generated as a by-product of unre-
lieved interface conflict.

When the Interface Conflict-Solving Model has been employed, it has produced substantial benefits in terms of profitability and creative problem solving. Dollar amounts can only be
estimated, but they are of an order of magnitude that makes the
expense of the effort look trivial by comparison. We believe the
Interface Conflict-Solving Model is an indispensable management tool for use in the search for excellence.

CHAPTER 2

Rebuilding Trust and Cooperation: Illustration of a New Approach

In this chapter the use of the Interface Conflict-Solving Model in resolving tensions between the operations and maintenance departments illustrates the character of interface problems, how they were approached, and how participants conducted themselves and reacted to the model. Most importantly, it answers the question "So what?" Was the conflict solved? Were the participants more involved and committed to strengthening the effectiveness of work performed at the interface? What were the consequences for productivity, profit, and human satisfaction?

In this particular case study, the consultant as design administrator, or third party involved in administering the process, was Len Cooper, an employee of our company at that time. The example takes place in a plant of Padreco, an oil refining com-

---

An article abridged from this chapter appeared as: Robert R. Blake and Jane S. Mouton, "Improve the Work Flow Between Departments," *Hydrocarbon Processing* (Pt. 1) 62, no. 10 (1983): 135–163; (Pt. 2) 62, no. 11 (1983): 227–260.

pany headquartered in Houston. It illustrates the classic antagonisms that, all too frequently, arise between those responsible
for operations and those who design, service, or repair the
equipment. In the plant, refining activities are separated into
two distinct functional categories, operational and maintenance.
Operations is responsible for work flow from raw materials to
finished products. The maintenance staff is charged with maintaining, repairing, and modifying existing equipment and con-
structing or installing new equipment.

On paper, these functions are considered equal in terms
of status and importance, but, in practice, maintenance responsibilities are seen, at least from an operations point of view, as
support rather than line activities. Although maintenance and
operations staff are intended to function as equals in the field,
maintenance activities are regarded by operations personnel as
subservient to and largely controlled by them. The premium
placed on the seven-day, round-the-clock operations creates a
disparity between the two functions because of perceived importance. Established policies and procedures reinforce and
have essentially formalized the ability of operations to "call the
shots."

Structurally, the operations and maintenance groups have
a horizontal relationship, with supervisors of both reporting to
the production superintendent as shown in Figure 1. Considerable autonomy and independence must be exercised in executing routine duties or solving unanticipated problems, and a productive and profitable effort depends primarily on the operations and maintenance staffs' abilities to cooperate with one
another in pursuit of their superordinate goal.

Evidence of an Interface Problem

An important discrepancy existed between what was intended to be achieved and actual performance. Poor cooperation and lack of coordination between the operations and maintenance groups had historically been recognized as a barrier to
greater efficiency and better cost control. Silvers, the plant
manager, and other members of the plant's refining team, had

Figure 1. Key Personnel in Padreco Plant.

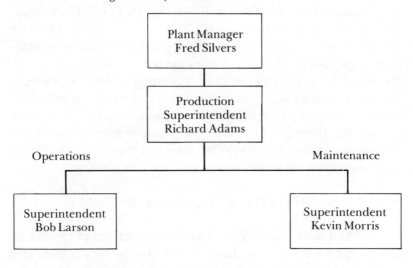

long been concerned about schedule delays, unmet production quotas, equipment failure, excessive downtime, and other chronic problems. They believed that these problems were related less to issues of structure, policies, procedures, or specific tasks than to tensions between the two groups.

Rather than living with and accepting the tensions between operations and maintenance, top management concluded that these problems were subject to resolution through better, more effective management concepts and strategies. Padreco's vice-president of refining and other members of the executive staff gave their guardedly optimistic support to Silvers's proposal that the top team endorse participation by operations and maintenance in a possible approach for resolving their intergroup problems, indicating that a successful outcome would be well worth the investment.

With top management's support, Silvers met with Adams, the production superintendent responsible for operations and maintenance, to gain his commitment to working on the problems. At first Adams felt that, while there might be room for improvement, things between operations and maintenance were as good as they were likely to get in terms of his previous experience; with the lean staffing, the pressure from tight shift schedules, and so on, it was unlikely that there was much room for change. After Silvers pointed out the potential gains to be had from improved cooperation in the face of declining production levels and rising costs, Adams agreed to a next step to test the potential gain. This involved a meeting of himself, Larson, the superintendent of operations, Morris, the superintendent of maintenance, and Len Cooper, the consultant, to review with Cooper the strategy of the Interface Conflict-Solving Model and the commitments that would be expected from each of the departments involved if they undertook such an activity.

Introducing a Way of Approaching the Problem

"As I understand your situation," Len Cooper began in the meeting with Adams, Larson, and Morris, "operations and maintenance need to work together as an effective team for Padreco to achieve improved profitability and efficiency. The problem, at least from a top management perspective, is costly and unproductive conflict. It's clear that problems at the operations-maintenance interface didn't originate with either of you and that they even predate Adams, but the three of you are charged with exploring an approach that can restore a healthy relationship. From what I gather, you both think cooperation between your areas is okay, or at least is par for the course, and the way you're operating now presents no real barrier to getting the job done."

"That's fairly accurate, at least from my angle," Larson (operations superintendent) commented. "Sure, we have our differences, but it's impossible to agree on everything all the time. Basically, I think top management has to look beyond the plant to see our real problems."

"What do you mean?" inquired Adams (production superintendent).

"Just that so much of what happens out there is beyond our control," Larson replied. "It's not our fault when materials are late or the weather is impossible or a tanker's delayed."

"Granted, external factors are a problem," Cooper observed, "but there are almost certainly internal issues and factors that get in the way of a smooth operation. It might be possible to see the real issues between your groups more clearly if the two of you and the supervisors get away for a few days and take a fresh look at cooperation between operations and maintenance."

"I'm not sure it'd do us any good," Morris (maintenance superintendent) said. "I agree with Larson ... most of our problems with operations stem from procedures, policies, working conditions, or contract clauses. They're pretty much beyond our control. How would the kind of meeting you're proposing solve those kinds of problems? We spend plenty of time together as it is. If we can't solve our problems in twenty-four hours of togetherness every day, how would another meeting help?"

"Apparently," Cooper replied, "there's enough evidence of excessive equipment downtime, conflicts in shift scheduling, and inordinate delays in making simple repairs to suggest 'hidden' barriers to production beyond policies, procedures, working conditions, or external influences. These may reside in the relationship between operations and maintenance and in the quality of teamwork existing at the interface between the two groups. If this proves true, results might be significantly improved through an approach designed to identify and resolve interface conflicts and strengthen integration between these groups."

"By Silvers's estimation," Adams added, "output can be increased by something like 25 or 30 percent—if your groups really supported one another in a unified, cooperative effort."

"Maybe Silvers has a point," mused Larson. "We've been struggling with the same concerns year after year even though procedures and working conditions have changed with time."

Morris added, "My people complain about the attitudes of operations people more than anything else."

"Now that you mention it, we do the same in reverse. Our reasons or excuses for not getting a job done usually involve difficulty with maintenance in some way," remarked Larson. "We say work orders are inaccurate, routine maintenance isn't being completed, materials to do a job are underestimated."

Morris said, "I guess we could do something about these problems."

"What do you think, Larson?" Adams questioned.

"We have ample cause to hold maintenance responsible for failure to meet production quotas," Larson said. "From an operations view, they are unresponsive, disorganized, too slow, and often arbitrary in terms of priorities. Even your tool management is so sloppy that when you have the materials and parts and the people to do the job, you can't cut it because you don't have the right tools and equipment to make the necessary repairs. Some mechanics don't return their tools to the tool room so the others, even the competent ones, can't seat a nut if they don't have a wrench. That's the pathetic part. I guess I'm convinced we know what some of the problems are, but we don't get the cooperation needed to solve them. We've tried surveillance, and that resulted in more hiding. The tools leave the guy's locker and show up in a corner under a greasy rag. Nobody ever knows who put it there."

"I think you're wrong. Our people say your people swipe the tools so they'll have them handy just in case, or else they take them home. But, in any event, if that's what your people are saying," remarked Morris, "then we'd better look at our relationship more closely. You're apparently blaming us when something goes wrong and we're blaming you. Somebody's obviously mistaken, and maybe this meeting will help us find out who's right and who's wrong."

"The interface process session we're considering isn't designed to be a win-lose experience or an exercise in right and wrong," Cooper interjected. "During the proposed meeting your groups would focus on what's soundest for both operations and maintenance in the best interest of productivity, not on who's right and wrong or on furthering either party's causes."

"And how do we get agreement on what's soundest and best for all of us?" questioned Larson. "It looks like our views on that are miles apart."

"At least that's one thing I agree with Larson on," Morris said. "But we've had in experts before. They listened to us, told us what our problems were, gave us solutions, and told us how to implement them. Their ideas seemed okay at first, but there was little change or improvement from them. I don't want it to look like I'm negative, but if your approach is more of the same, I frankly don't think it's worth the effort."

"Let me outline the six major activities involved in an Interface Conflict-Solving session," Cooper offered, "and let's see what you think."

"Go ahead," Adams encouraged. "I'm anxious to hear what Larson and Morris and their supervisors can expect from the three or four days you'd need to work this miracle."

"Well, there's no particular magic or miraculous power in the design," said Cooper. "It's a pretty straightforward process, but a powerful one."

At this point, Cooper explained the model described in Chapter One in detail and answered questions. After walking through it, Larson and Morris became challenged by the possibilities and expressed commitment to taking the next steps. Cooper provided group members with preliminary reading and a diagnostic instrument to complete. (Samples of these items are in Chapter Three.)

Beginning the Interface Conflict-Solving Session

When Cooper convened the Interface Conflict-Solving session with Larson, Morris, and the six subordinate shift supervisors shown in Figure 2, he reviewed the objectives and briefly highlighted the planned activities. After introducing himself and explaining his role during the session, Cooper remarked, "I'm here primarily to administer the process and ensure that each activity is clearly understood. Since you're the experts on your history and your current relationship, problem-solving responsibility is necessarily yours, not mine. From time to time, I'll be monitoring each group's discussions and I'll only intervene if it seems a group is straying too far from the task, but I won't influence the content of your deliberations. Any questions?"

"Just one," said Baker (shift supervisor, operations). "It's great to be away from the daily grind and in a really nice hotel, but is it altogether essential to work every night? How about some time off for fun and games and a little relaxation?"

"What we have to do in these next few days is critical to

Figure 2. Participants in the Interface Conflict-Solving Activity
Between Operations and Maintenance.

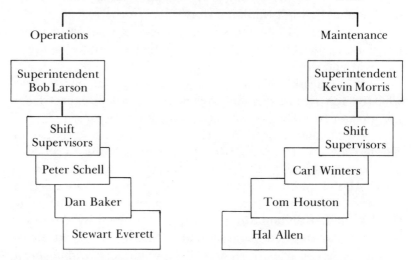

the effectiveness of the entire operation," Larson (operations superintendent) responded before Cooper could answer.

"Let's get serious and give it our best shot," added Morris (maintenance superintendent). "Just because we're away from the job doesn't mean we're on vacation."

"We agree," Winters (shift supervisor, maintenance) chimed in. "We're here to work, not to play, so let's get down to business. This is a real good opportunity to straighten you guys out."

"Wait a minute," said Cooper. "This is a real good opportunity to improve the relationship. We all know what the first order of business is, so are there any final questions?"

"I'd like to know who our leader is for this task," said Everett (shift supervisor, operations).

"Handle the leadership issue within your groups in any way you think appropriate," Cooper replied, "but when you report your findings in the joint sessions, we want to ask you to designate a spokesperson, someone other than Larson or Morris."

"Why's that?" asked Morris. "I'm the boss of this group. Are you demoting me?"

"Because a spokesperson is operating from a shared point of view on behalf of others rather than independently and in his own name, as a formally designated leader is more likely to do," Cooper explained. "Also when a formal boss acts as a spokesperson, members of the other group may be inhibited and may not know whether the leader is representing his or the group's point of view. Does that make sense?"

"Thank you, Len," answered Morris. "You didn't demote me, you just took away my privilege of shooting off at the mouth."

With a smile, Cooper asked, "Anything else?"

"Let's get started," said Everett.

Developing the Optimal Model

The following discussions illustrate both groups' initial values, attitudes, and biases toward one another. Normally there are two distinct subparts to this step: (1) identification of the elements in separate groups and agreement on them in a joint session followed by (2) description of the optimal relationship for each element in separate groups. These two aspects are merged in this case example with identification and description on an element-by-element basis discussed together in each separate session.

Maintenance Describes an Optimal Relationship

"Are we all clear on what we're to do?" asked Winters.

"As I understand this activity," Allen responded, "first we're to identify the elements or characteristics of a sound relationship between us and operations, then we describe the best way for maintenance and operations to relate."

"That's my understanding, too," agreed Houston. "Once we have the list, we indicate the best working relationship for operations and maintenance in terms of each priority element. We don't even touch the actual situation at this stage, right?"

"Then we're all in agreement on what needs to be done," said Morris, "so how should we proceed?"

"Maybe each of us could suggest an element or two for discussion," suggested Allen, "then we can critique the list, agree on which elements are most critical, and create the sound relationship statements."

"I've got an element in mind already," Winters volunteered, "so maybe we can start with it. As I see things, communication is the key to a good working relationship with operations. If they'd keep us better informed of the equipment's condition and let us know as soon as they spot a potential problem, maybe we wouldn't have so much downtime."

"I think you're right," agreed Allen. "They let something go for weeks then expect us to fix it in a day. They need to let us know about a problem as soon as it's spotted when we can make repairs with a minimum of time and effort, not after the equipment goes down and needs a major overhaul."

"If operations would be more open and honest with us," Houston suggested, "I think we'd see a dramatic improvement in the way things get done."

"They'd probably be more honest and more open, too, if they viewed us as equals instead of second-class citizens," said Winters. "They don't talk to us because they don't respect us. Trust and respect are lacking and poor communication is only a symptom. All the promises on earth to 'communicate better' won't do it till we want to communicate better. And we'll only begin to communicate better when we've got a relationship based on trust and respect. I'd like to add trust and respect to our list of elements since I don't think they trust us either."

"I have to agree," Morris nodded. "If operations trusted us and had respect for our abilities, conditions would be a lot different. We'd be working toward a common goal and there'd be real team effort between us. We'd be more than two groups of individuals who happen to be working in the same place at the same time."

"And we'd replace the labels that keep maintenance people on one side and operations on the other," said Houston with evident agitation. "Maybe then maintenance staff could get an equal share of the newer, better offices."

"If I could interrupt for a moment," Len Cooper addressed the group. "I'd like to suggest refocusing on the task at hand. The activity for this stage of the session is creating the model for the soundest relationship between yourselves and operations. There'll be ample opportunity to talk about your frustrations and concerns when actual conditions are discussed later on. For now, focus on what sound practices are, not what they aren't."

Members of the maintenance group nodded in unison.

"Len's right," Morris said. "We've agreed on an element, communication meaning 'true' interchange, not frequency, grammar, or spelling, so let's try to formulate the soundest statement around it."

"How about this?" suggested Allen. "Communication should be forthright and candid and honest, and personal feelings and sensitivities should not be withheld."

"Why the proviso?" asked Winters.

"Well, I want us to start calling one another publicly by some of the names we use to describe operations in private," Allen responded.

"Unless we want a 'free for all,' that's pretty dangerous advice, but if we ever solve the trust and respect problem, we won't need that proviso, because we won't have those feelings. But it's okay to put it in as a reminder of the real problem," Winters conceded. "I think we should add something about two-way communication."

"How about, 'Information flow should be two-way'?" Houston asked.

"Let's get something in about meetings," Morris suggested. "In the future, I'd like to see meetings scheduled periodically and conveniently, not haphazardly with only last minute notification to deal with some crisis. We could say 'Formal meetings should be scheduled in a planned way and should anticipate and deal with important agenda. Informal meetings should be held as needed. Important information needs to be shared.' "

"Sounds good," agreed the others.

"What's another element?" asked Houston.

This description provides the flavor and discussion of the

elements in a sound relationship model continued over the next few hours. The following list presents the results of maintenance's deliberations.

1. *Trust and respect*—Members of operations and maintenance merit equal treatment. Since our groups are interdependent and working toward a common goal, all of us must respect the skill and judgment of the other. People need freedom to speak their minds without fear of reprisal.
2. *Communication*—Information flow should be two-way. Formal and informal meetings should be held as needed and important information shared. Communication should be candid and honest, and personal feelings and sensitivities should not be withheld.
3. *Planning*—Objectives should be clear, and priorities should be determined in headquarters by staff who see the organization from a broader perspective. Availability of material, equipment, and personnel should receive sufficient attention when planning work to be done.
4. *Work orders*—Enough information should be supplied for us to plan, schedule, and execute assigned responsibilities. Initiator should state problems and needs clearly and precisely. Last minute work orders should be avoided.
5. *Training*—Trainers should be assigned to maintenance, which then assigns trainers to operations as needed.

Operations Describes an Optimal Relationship

"What do you say we list all the soundest relationship elements we can think of first," suggested Baker, "then go back and describe them and put them in order of importance?"

"That might be a good way to proceed," Schell responded, "but as many problems as we have with them, we'd probably need a week just to make the list."

"Well, we've only got a few hours," Larson reminded, "so let's get started. I think we need to consider communication and information sharing as priority elements."

"They might be too broad," said Everett, "but I'd like to include cooperation and coordination."

"Could we get more specific?" asked Baker. "How about some examples?"

"Take work orders," Everett responded quickly. "We should follow procedure and request maintenance or repair as soon as we notice an equipment problem. Now when the request gets to them, they evidently determine priorities, mostly on the basis of convenience—who they've got available or whether or not needed materials are in the warehouse. If they delay their response, chances are the equipment will go down—and we'll get the blame, at least from them. With better coordination between us, we could be sure their priorities meet our needs."

"I can't tell you how many times they've given me an earfull on early detection of minor problems and prevention of major failure, but they won't respond in a hurry to anything short of a catastrophe," Baker added. "What we need from them is some consistency between what they say and what they do. If they want 'early warning' and we take the time to comply, then they should get the work done on some basis that makes early warnings pay off."

"I think they resent the control over them a work order represents or implies," Schell suggested. "From their perspective, the work order procedure gives us authority to tell them what to do, and they're obviously dissatisfied with the current setup. As I see it, headquarters should formalize maintenance's support role and establish operations as the line function. After all, we're responsible for getting the oil in and out."

"They do need to be more responsive," Larson agreed. "It might be more workable to implement a system where we establish priorities, since we're more knowledgeable about the overall activities and since we work with the equipment on a day-to-day basis."

"The other problem with work orders," mentioned Baker, "is that we in operations don't always do a thorough job, and, beyond that, they don't always do the job well, either. I think one of us should make an inspection and sign off on their work before a job is accepted as completed."

"That might work well," Everett nodded. "Giving us some kind of approval authority would ensure more adequate

controls and a better system of checks and balances. A procedure like that might really improve coordination."

Refocusing the group's attention on the stated purpose
of the meeting, Larson said, "Let's organize these thoughts into
a soundest relationship statement for a work order element then
look at other aspects of our relationship."

"I think I've got it all," Baker declared. "How about this?
'Operations initiates, reviews, or establishes work order priorities. Maintenance executes in accordance. Work is done to operations' satisfaction.' "

Other members nodded agreement.

"We've dug out a number of elements and understand the
problem of coordination and priority of scheduling work, but I
am not sure we have truly gotten to the root of the problem,"
said Schell.

"I don't think so either, at least not for the long term,"
Baker added. "There is a structural problem here that will continue to plague us unless we face it."

"What are you talking about?" queried Everett.

"I feel like operations people operate the equipment, but
they don't feel they own it." Baker went on, "They don't do
the things they could to keep the equipment in working order.
They don't have the feeling of ownership that causes them to
want to maintain a clean working environment. If they did have
pride, then when they have difficulty with equipment, they
would want to learn how to diagnose the problem so maintenance could get it working quicker."

"All that may be right, but can you see maintenance giving up routine maintenance?" Everett asked. "If they didn't
have all of their routine maintenance, they'd feel they'd have to
give up people."

"How could a person have 'ownership' of his equipment
on a shift schedule?" Larson queried. "He operates it for eight
hours and then it belongs to someone else."

"I'm not sure, but we could work out joint 'ownership'
on a two-shift basis." Baker added, "There's no reason on earth
we shouldn't get more of a feeling of teamwork between operators who work on a single machine. I know a cab company that

has done that and they are having terrific results—on a three-shift schedule, to boot."

"It's a very interesting challenge," said Larson. "We have built-in overlap between shifts, but little use is made of it for all practical purposes, and the log book isn't that great. As long as things are going okay, the shift 1 operator and shift 2 operator have little to talk about. If they were to begin talking and set standards for housekeeping, for alerting one another to trouble spots, and stuff like that, we might see a lot of improvement. The baton is really tossed between shifts now on a catch-as-catch-can basis. I think we could do a better job of getting operators involved in an enlarged concept of analyzing and reporting what is going on for the next shift in a better manner. That's really our management responsibility. But now we need to talk about the maintenance-operations interface and the impact that any change in structure would have on the union contract."

"If we were to bring that up," Everett suggested, "wouldn't the union cry like a stuck pig and accuse us of violating the terms of the contract we have now?"

"I expect they would," said Schell, "but we shouldn't allow that to stop us. If we go to them on a problem-solving basis instead of a bargaining basis, we might begin to explore whether or not the contract definition of routine maintenance compels us to bargain for any changes or whether the contract as written gives us enough leg room to get a better sense of 'ownership' while promoting cooperation with the union. I doubt the union is against anyone having a better sense of 'ownership' of his equipment as long as they don't feel it's our way of exploiting their members. I think we ought to bring this up as a new element when we get back with the maintenance people to test for their reactions to an 'ideal' element that says something like, 'Increased sense of ownership and teamwork in the organization should be implemented as fundamental to effective operations by operators doing routine maintenance, housekeeping, and minor repairs of the kind they are currently capable of doing.' Anyone have any reactions to that way of saying the element?"

"No, but I will tell you what the 'actual' is," said Everett, changing the subject. " 'Operations has little or no sense of responsibility for doing those things that are within their job descriptions and that are essential for keeping equipment in sound operating condition. Furthermore, they feel little responsibility for diagnosing breakdowns in a manner helpful to maintenance.' "

"I think what you say is right," Baker said, "and I think the union has hit us repeatedly with this kind of attitude as evidence of poor management. They may be considerably more ready to agree with this kind of shift in thinking than you think. They're not anti good management, you know."

"We're straying again into the actual," Larson cautioned as he noticed Cooper walking into the room. "Let's get back to working on the ideal."

For the next several hours, operations sorted through a list of elements, discarding some and combining others. The following list includes what operations agreed on as priorities and statements representing the soundest practices.

1. *Trust and respect*—Common goal is sufficient motivation to be honest and candid with one another. Trust and respect arise from everyone doing their part to see that joint objectives are met.
2. *Communication*—Communication should flow both laterally and vertically. Messages should be candid, clear, and straightforward.
3. *Planning*—Operations establishes priorities, but overall plans should be made in concert with maintenance services. Maintenance staff executes the plans in accordance with our instructions. Common goals should be incorporated into plans and objectives.
4. *Work orders*—Operations initiates, reviews, or establishes work order priorities. Maintenance executes in accordance. Work is done to operations' satisfaction.
5. *Training*—Operations needs trainers assigned directly to us for training our maintenance people.

Consolidating the Optimal Relationship

Their group work completed, operations and maintenance met to jointly develop a consolidated model for the
soundest relationship between them. The designated spokespersons, Schell (operations) and Winters (maintenance), presented
each group's separate soundest model. Participants listened attentively and sought understanding of each presentation; questions for clarification or information were encouraged, but
these took place between spokespersons. Evaluative comments
and challenges that might evoke defensiveness or debate were
declared out of line. When the presentations of soundest relationships were completed, the task of creating a mutually acceptable, jointly agreed consolidation of thinking about the
soundest relationship model began.

A list summarizing the soundest relationship model eventually agreed on follows this sample of the discussion during
the model's consolidation. Initially conflicting views ultimately
were reconciled through a process based on open, candid exchange of viewpoints and perceptions. To reduce accusations
and defensiveness likely to be produced by surfacing previously hidden or suppressed conflict, the more formal mechanism
of exchanges through spokesmen Schell and Winters was used.

"We don't have any problem with maintenance's views
on trust and respect or communication," remarked Schell,
"but we just can't agree with your idea of a sound approach to
planning. Corporate strategies are necessarily formulated in
headquarters," he argued, "but specific tactics for implementation need to be planned by those of us most directly involved in
the operation."

"We agree with that formulation in theory," concurred
Winters, "but look at your group's statement of soundest. You're
suggesting that priorities be established by operations, and we
simply can't buy that. Adams hasn't given you people that kind of
authority, and, frankly, I don't think he intends to. You all may
think you run the show, and you usually act like it, but the organizational chart says otherwise—on it, we're equal."

"Maybe the chart needs to be changed then," Schell remarked with a note of sarcasm. "The soundest model we can think of would be to formalize operations as the line activity and identify maintenance as a support function. Procedurally, your people are in a reporting relationship anyway, so it wouldn't be much of a change."

"Could we stop a minute," Cooper interjected, "and critique what's happening? The purpose of this session is to improve the operations-maintenance working interrelationship. Restructuring the organization or moving boxes around on the chart isn't likely to make this interface any stronger or more productive. It seems more progress can be made by exploring ways for all of you to become effective members of two cooperating teams instead of arguing about who's going to be the first team and who the second team."

"But somebody has to have the final say and it's silly to take every detail and squabble to Adams," Schell exclaimed. "If operations is officially put in charge, we can make sure the equipment is taken care of. We have the most comprehensive view of what needs to be done to keep the pumps running, so it's only logical we establish priorities and make the schedules."

"Now look," Winters countered, "you all can't even fill out a work order that provides us an adequate diagnosis or at least a meaningful set of symptoms without underestimating or overestimating time and materials. Putting operations in charge of schedules and priorities would be nothing short of disaster. If somebody has to have the last word, it should be maintenance. Our people are the experts at estimating jobs and knowing how long a machine will be down or where to get a replacement. Without us, operations would fold like a tent."

"It occurs to me," Cooper commented, "that maintenance and operations are sounding like the offensive and defensive squads on a football team. There's no distinction between offensive and defensive team members in terms of ability or expertise. Each squad does its job well at its own position. Unless each squad holds up its end of the game, the entire team loses. The superordinate goal of winning cannot be accomplished."

Schell spoke up after an extended and thoughtful silence, "That's a good analogy. The point is well taken. If the offensive and defensive squads on a football team were as uncoordinated and uncooperative as we've been, we'd surely risk losing every game."

"You're right," Winters acknowledged, "and we'll be the losers if we continue to waste our energies trying to ride roughshod over one another instead of working together. To be winners, we need to pull in the same direction, all doing what we're best at and with the maximum support of the other, with a whole effort that's better than what we'd accomplish separately."

"Let's see how this discussion can be incorporated into a planning statement for the consolidated soundest model formulation," Cooper suggested.

"Okay," said Schell. "Let's say for starters that priorities are determined by what's in the best interest of the overall operation."

"We'll buy that," Winters conceded, "and let's emphasize the importance of joint planning for setting a coordinated direction and mapping out the details of implementation."

"I'd like to add something about long-range planning," Schell noted. "In the past, some of our efforts have been pretty shortsighted."

"Hey," Winters offered, "this is almost amazing. Just minutes ago we'd reached a critical impasse on the planning issue. As long as each side tried to gain control at the expense of the other, we moved farther and farther away from resolution. Once we began to focus on a common objective, improving our relationship, our ideas about the best possible solution immediately came closer together."

"When we moved away from looking at our vested interests in favor of the good of the entire operation, we finally made real progress," said Schell.

"What we've proven," Larson commented, "is that we can work out our differences without resorting to edicts stemming from above. Maybe, if we learn from this experience, we'll become a winning team yet."

1. *Trust and respect*—As interdependent groups striving for a
    common goal, we have mutual respect for one another's
    skills, abilities, and judgments. Differences are resolved
    through openness and candor. Decisions are made based on
    the weight of the evidence, not on personalities or to avoid
    problems.
2. *Communication*—Regular meetings should be held accord-
    ing to a mutually acceptable schedule. Conflict and differ-
    ences should be confronted, worked through, and resolved
    so that the lines of communication remain clear.
3. *Planning*—Priorities are determined by what is in the best
    interest of the entire operation. Joint planning is essential
    to setting coordinated directions and designing strategies,
    approaches, and tactics for implementation. More long-
    range planning is needed.
4. *Work orders*—Work orders clearly specify activities to be
    performed, realistic time frames, and personnel and mate-
    rials needed. Maintenance supervisors get feedback on staff
    performance.
5. *Training*—Trainers should be assigned directly to mainte-
    nance services, but "loaned" to operations on a full-time
    basis. Maintenance has authority to make changes in as-
    signed personnel.

Describing the Actual Relationship

Contrary to what conventional wisdom might suggest,
most groups experiencing interface conflict have less difficulty
in creating the model for the soundest relationship than in
reaching agreement on actual conditions and identifying historical antecedents of current misunderstandings or disagreements.
Faulty assumptions and erroneous perceptions must be voiced,
recognized, and clarified before consolidated statements reflecting agreement on "how things actually are" can be formulated
and compared to the model representation of "how things
might be."

The discussions of the actual relationship proceeded element by element. Major points that emerged from the actual

relationship analysis by maintenance and operations are high-lighted in the joint session discussion that follows. The element of trust and respect that exposed long-standing problems and issues is emphasized to more fully illustrate the process and out-comes of examining the actual interface relationship.

Consolidating the Actual Relationship

Following each group's private assessment of the opera-tions-maintenance interface in terms of mutual trust and re-spect, the groups convened to describe, compare, and clarify their perceptions. Both operations and maintenance agreed that mutual trust and respect were essentially lacking in their relationship, although each pointed a finger at the other as re-sponsible for this. A brief sample of their discussions, which were more freewheeling than earlier ones, reflect how differ-ently these groups viewed the past and understood the present. At this point in the session, the groups had made considerable progress in terms of greater candor and reduced defensiveness; they no longer needed to address one another through spokes-persons.

"It's no surprise to hear you don't trust us," remarked Baker (operations). "Your doubts and suspicions have been evi-dent for some time."

"What's that supposed to mean?" asked Winters (mainte-nance).

"You obviously don't feel that our operations people are qualified to do even routine upkeep on the equipment," Baker answered. "What's more, you seem to consider our maintenance activities as trespassing—like the equipment belongs to mainte-nance instead of to the company."

"We may not own the equipment," countered Allen (maintenance), "but we're certainly responsible for it and we're committed to caring for it like it was our own. And when opera-tions performs routine maintenance, the least you could do is follow the manual and log in the work. Without good records, we don't know whether the equipment's being serviced or not."

"And that's not the half of it," added Houston (maintenance). "When operations services the equipment, you never look beyond the ends of your noses. If something's not quite right, your people need to file a report, not ignore it. We can't trust you because you don't seem to care whether the equipment works tomorrow or not, as long as you get the assigned job done."

"Maybe that's the way maintenance sees things, but I think you're rationalizing and justifying because you're threatened," said Everett (operations). "Your people aren't any better about making notes in the log book than ours are. What about modifications? You know and we know they're supposed to be documented and with copies in the central engineering files, and it's your responsibility—but you don't always follow through."

"If we feel threatened," Morris (maintenance) explained, "it's not without good reason. Operations treats us like second-class citizens, and we resent it. You're not the only professionals, you know, but most of you seem to have that idea. Whenever there's a good position open in operations, for example, you continue to promote from within. We just aren't considered, even though we're qualified by expertise and experience. You'd think we're lepers or worse."

"I'd have to agree with much of what you're saying," Larson (operations) said. "We have put you maintenance people down . . . failed to acknowledge your value and importance to the overall objective. Literally, I can take exception to what you say, but, in truth, I must agree with it. There's no way to be honest and to disregard what you say. We have taken people from maintenance into operations, so you can't say we have a policy of promotion from within, but the spirit behind what you say is clear. We have practiced tokenism, taking in someone every once in a great while, but we've done it to placate the higher-ups and to keep you guys from shouting 'foul ball.' Our explanation to ourselves has been that this is the way to build esprit de corps; you know what I mean, team spirit. But the result has been favoritism over merit, narrowness over breadth, department over organization, and, as bad as anything, operations over maintenance. Maybe this is where we can contribute to ending our deadlock by stopping this practice."

"Thanks, Bill. You've said what we all feel and in an honest way," said Morris. "We would be interested in hearing from others. Do the rest of you take exception to what Bill has said, or do you support it? Where do you come out?"

Several spoke almost in unison to repeat what Bill Larson had said, and it appeared that the emotional logjam had been broken with a rapid movement toward identifying many chronic problems that entangled the relationship.

"You're right," Morris nodded. "We've become distrustful. We've misinterpreted your actions, misread your intent . . . and just generally seen everything you try to do in a negative light. The way we misread your intentions is that we saw your promotion from within as wholly motivated to shut out maintenance without even seeing the possibility that you saw it as a positive program carried out in the interest of building team spirit. I'm not saying we're accepting it as a legitimate, sound way of doing things, just that we had no appreciation that the motivation existed to build team spirit."

"I agree with Morris," added Winters (maintenance). "At least we have a better understanding of your motivation, even if we don't buy it."

"Look, you don't need to keep repeating it; we've got the point," Baker said.

"And half of our real feelings about maintenance were hidden. The other half were fully communicated . . . 'You uncoordinated dummies, can't tell a wrench from a screwdriver. You think a fan belt is what the girl at the topless bar holds her fan on.' These negative attitudes spring from frustration. What we didn't admit to ourselves was that we've done things to frustrate you and then complained to you about it, when in fact half of your problems were related to our own sneaky cleverness in frustrating you. Just because we've got it out in the open isn't going to fix it. No magician on earth can wave his wrench and, 'presto,' provide us with instant service," remarked Schell (operations).

"Well, if magic won't do it, maybe the only solution is better management," said Allen.

Schell spoke up, "We'll agree with you on that. How do we commit ourselves to doing it?"

Winters broke in, "Come on; let's get down to brass tacks. We've said it. You tell us what's wrong with the machine, and we've got one leg up on fixing it. You give us a sense of urgency, that helps us set priorities. You get your gang to commit to routine maintenance, that's fewer breakdowns to worry about. That's good management."

"And if we don't fill out a work order in a satisfactory manner, call us on it. If we don't have the facts at our fingertips, we'll go get them for you. And we'll teach the guy that filled in the work order in the first place that you guys don't have the compound to make invisible ink come out," Baker blurted out.

"When we phone in an emergency, you should let us know a little bit more about your competing priorities. Sometimes we can take short-term actions that at least give us short-term solutions and that can tide us over until you can get your paramedics—I mean paramechanics. Sorry, I didn't mean paramechanics, I meant first-class mechanics or your instrument man, or your Michelangelos, or whatever," continued Everett.

"It looks like neither of us is 100 percent satisfied with the current work order system," stated Larson. "I know we're not always as clear as we could be about what repairs or adjustments are needed."

"And it's difficult to establish priorities under the current system," agreed Everett. "We just haven't devoted enough attention to early detection and prevention because there are so many crises demanding immediate resolution."

"It seems that all our efforts are geared toward putting out the latest fire," said Allen. "Maintenance simply doesn't have the staff to respond to noncrisis requests when there are a dozen 'top priority' orders stacked up."

"We're not sure what the answers are," Morris noted, "but I think we've pinpointed some of the problems. From our perspective, work orders should accurately estimate the size of a job, materials needed, and time required for completion. Since our relationship has been so distant and discordant, you in operations haven't felt that you could call on us for assistance in scoping a job. Without our input, you've guessed about requirements and, in too many instances, you've fallen short or overshot the mark."

"And you in maintenance either overschedule or underschedule, overorder or underorder because our best guesses in operations are so far off," admitted Baker. "Because we've avoided getting together on the front end of a job for analysis and planning, both our groups wind up losing valuable time and resources."

"Right," conceded Houston. "And the power-authority issue complicates things further."

"How's that?" Schell asked.

"As I see it," Houston explained, "operations sees the work order as a means of control, a symbol of authority. We respond in kind, so we find ways to circumvent or short-circuit the system in an effort to prove our equality."

"When the pressure's on," Winters admitted, "we may get careless and harried. As the work orders pile up, we start looking for examples of shortsightedness, delayed reporting, or inaccurate directions, and we get angry and resentful."

"So we could help you by improved troubleshooting and prompt notification of suspected problems," said Larson.

"And we're available," offered Morris, "to assist operations in completing the work order forms more accurately."

"In reality," Larson commented, "there's nothing amiss in the system, per se. The real problem has been our use of the system as a weapon against one another rather than as a tool for cooperation and collaboration."

"From now on," Morris said with evident conviction, "let's be as dedicated to making the system work as we've been to preventing it from working."

"Instead of respecting one another for our unique abilities and contributions, in spite of our limitations and foibles," Houston concluded, "we've blamed one another for problems and issues that can only be solved by our working intelligently together. It's clear, now that we've looked at ourselves more honestly, we've been at cross purposes. We've spent so much time finding fault with one another that neither group has focused on our own mistakes or shortcomings or how to overcome them in ourselves and help you do the same."

"We should be able to do much better in the future," Larson summarized optimistically, "since we won't feel the

need to waste so much time and energy in unproductive pur-
suits and games of 'one-upmanship.' Let me assure you, and I
think I speak for all my staff, we know we couldn't function
without you, so let's all admit that we need and depend on one
another, and that working together more cooperatively will
make it possible to get the job done in a better manner."

"Just to put an exclamation point on that," added Baker,
"well spoken. You spoke for us."

The openness, candor, and objective introspection and
interspection that emerged during this exchange marked a turning point in the relationship between operations and maintenance. Consolidated statements for the remainder of the elements were formulated without the accusatory, judgmental
tones characteristic of earlier discussions and demonstrated the
shift toward a more positive, productive relationship. (See
Table 1.)

Planning for Change

The final activity involves comparing actual relationship
conditions with the soundest model, identifying gaps and discrepancies between the real and ideal, and planning specific
steps needed to put the soundest model into operation. Although some of these steps have already been taken spontaneously, deliberate action planning is a critical part of the process
because this step translates each group's professed commitment
to improved cooperation and collaboration into specific,
demonstrable actions.

For each of their five relationship elements, operations
and maintenance outlined a series of implementation activities
designed to remove existing barriers to a positive, productive
interface and to establish an ongoing, healthy relationship. Target completion dates were set for each agreed-upon step, responsibilities for monitoring and execution assigned, and detailed follow-up requirements outlined. Examples of planned
and executed activities included: adoption of a new planning
approach based on setting objectives and joint identification of
superordinate goals; implementation of scheduled staff meet-

Table 1. Descriptions of Actual Relationship.

Element	Operation's Description	Maintenance's Description	Consolidated Description
1. Trust and respect	Maintenance is a support function and they are not comfortable with the second-class role. Maintenance doesn't trust our maintenance activities and feels they signify a loss of power/control over their own destinies. We don't think they're open and candid among themselves or with us. We are trying to be honest with them. There is very little mutual respect.	Operations does not recognize our importance and expertise. In terms of facilities, we are relegated to second-class status and we resent it. Since they feel they could do as well without us, we do not trust them. Mutual respect exists to some degree on a professional but not a personal level.	There is very little trust and respect between our groups, and this impedes our ability to work effectively together. Maintenance resents operations for its control; operations resents maintenance's grudging compliance and pseudo-cooperation. Neither group really trusts the other's judgment, nor do we demonstrate respect for one another's abilities.
2. Communication	Monthly maintenance reports are not helpful. Meetings are infrequent or haphazard—too little advance notice or preparation. Each of us distrusts the other and therefore withholds needed and sometimes critical information.	Proper organizational channels of communication are circumvented because of personal problems. There are no regular meetings between our two groups. Informal channels of communication exist, but mostly on the basis of personal friendships or preferences.	Communication between us is hampered by lack of trust and respect. Each of us is somewhat secretive with the other. Formal channels of communication must be developed and informal lines of communication established.

(continued on next page)

Table 1. Descriptions of Actual Relationship, Cont'd.

Element	Operation's Description	Maintenance's Description	Consolidated Description
3. Planning	Too little cost consciousness when options are being explored or plans made. Excessive overtime results from poor planning, inappropriate work schedules. Human resources are not being used as effectively as they could be. Plans are shortsighted and crisis oriented.	We have no opportunity to participate in planning meetings where decisions are made that concern us. Work orders are not an effective planning tool. Every problem is allowed to develop into a crisis. Preventive maintenance is not performed by operations staff as consistently and effectively as it should be.	Our plans are not the product of synergistic interaction. Poor planning often leads to breakdowns and production shortages. Priorities are too often based on "fire fighting" rather than on "fire prevention."
4. Work orders	Implementation of work orders is basically satisfactory. Priorities are not always properly set, descriptions of work to be done are not always clear. Time frames are not always realistic. Maintenance blames us if we order the wrong or insufficient material.	Our services are often requested without work orders. Established procedures are not followed. Work orders are initiated without proper planning and independent of expert consultation from maintenance. Directions are often unclear.	Work orders are not prepared with the care and forethought they merit and are not always executed with commitment to standards of excellence. Operations and maintenance need closer cooperation and collaboration to make the work order system operate effectively.
5. Training	Operations is providing on-the-job training to our maintenance staff but we need in-depth assistance. Maintenance seems threatened by our interest in training and need to have trainers assigned to us full time.	Maintenance personnel in operations need better supervision. There is no comprehensive systematic way of assessing training needs. Managers are promoted for technical competence, but receive little or no management development.	On-the-job training is haphazard at best and ineffective at its worst. Technical training is not provided by the best resources available. Managerial training is virtually nonexistent for field managers.

ings; improved systems for on-the-job training of operations staff involved in routine maintenance; more revisions to the work order procedures to further simplify and refine the process while making it complex enough to convey vital information.

Critique

A critique, or learning from experience, is an ongoing feature during the course of the interface sequence, especially in the final session. The following excerpt contains something of its flavor.

The consultant, Len Cooper, asked, "When did the shift from complaining to cooperation take place?"

Taking the ball, Morris responded, "I think I can point it out very clearly; it was Larson's admission that they were masking the practice of promotions from within by a little bit of tokenism to placate top management and to stop us from bitching. We knew he was telling an embarrassing truth that, once admitted, had to produce change. He was being open and honest with us, and that told us he was acting in a trustworthy manner."

"His other guys admitted it, too," added Houston. "That said they wanted to do the right thing, not perpetuate the past."

"Well thanks, Kurt. You're giving me credit I don't deserve. I thought you'd penetrated our cover, so I thought I'd better admit it," confessed Larson.

"Come on, Larson, admit it. We talked about it at the bar last night, and you did it partly because we wanted you to do it. We all saw a chance to get on a better footing and the reaction from maintenance is what we had hoped for. They got off the defensive and became honest with us. Admitting a personal wrong is one thing, but what you did was admit a group wrong, and that's what I think it takes to fix a bad interface."

"I think you've got your finger on it," said Houston. "The moment you admitted a group wrong, we followed up in kind."

"And that," said Schell, "let us know we could trust you people."

"I got to know you care," Everett ventured, chuckling to himself in disbelief.

"I think modeling the soundest relationship was pretty basic," said Winters. "It proved to me we can rise above the nuts and bolts of this thing, so to speak, at least enough to design a blueprint for an effective interface."

Several other issues were discussed, including how to meet with subordinate levels in their own organizations and to get an understanding of and involvement with a new and better way of working up and down both lines. The critique ended with Cooper helping Larson and Morris reconstruct their reluctance at even making a try and only doing so under pressure from Adams.

"We were being our own worst enemies, weren't we?" Larson asked.

"Yes, we were," agreed Morris, "but now I count you as my friend."

"Okay," said Cooper. "See you in six months."

Progress Review and Replanning

At the six months follow-up session, a number of specific indicators of improved relationships had been calculated with results indicating a significant reduction in: (1) downtime for equipment maintenance and repair, (2) budgeted items for tool maintenance and replacement, (3) absenteeism, (4) overtime, and (5) lost time due to accidents.

The work order problem was still not solved after six months, but the amount of helpful information contained in each order from a diagnostic perspective was somewhat better. The successes realized during this period stimulated an enthusiasm for cooperation that was previously absent, and additional improvements not discussed during the interface sessions have been identified for implementation in the next six months.

Dynamics of Change

The motivation to change began when Cooper confronted the principals in operations and maintenance and got their agreement that traditional modes of relating to one another were interfering with an effective, productive interface. After the model for the soundest relationship was developed, old habits, traditions, past practices, and rancid attitudes could be viewed more objectively. The need for change became self-evident once sound practices could be looked at in comparison with actual conditions.

To ensure that the gains from their meeting would be long lasting, the design included a discussion of and programming for ongoing monitoring of the quality of the interface. These included a reexamination of the work distribution for routine maintenance, diagnosis, and the responsibility of operations' relations to maintenance personnel, as well as implications for problem solving with the union regarding contract clauses relating to work assignments. Additionally, specific activities for improvement in the short run were identified and readied for implementation.

With effective operations as their superordinate goal and the newly established candor and openness as the rule rather than the exception, operations and maintenance have been able to resolve their differences in ways that strengthen effective teamwork, mutual collaboration, and valid problem solving. Productivity is up and expenses down.

The results in terms of the bottom-line impact of the Padreco effort were judged to have been successful by any standard. The question to be dealt with here is concerned with the dynamics of change that are exemplified in this study. These dynamics can be viewed from three points of view: resistance to change, readiness to change, and the actual turning point that brought about the reversal of attitude.

Resistance to Change

Resistance to several changes was apparent, particularly at the beginning of the project.

Acceptance of the status quo. The first element of resistance, and one of significant importance in everyday situations, is that the status quo was accepted for what it was. It was judged to be "pretty good," "okay," "par for the course," and,

therefore, participants had little concern about the need for applying additional effort to bring about improvement.

Blaming external factors for the status quo. Another resistance to change came from participants' rationalizing that the
problems preventing improvement in the situation were far beyond their control and that efforts applied within the area free
from external constraints would be unlikely to be productive.
They pointed to weather, tanker delays, and unavailable raw
materials and concluded that because of the importance of
these factors, which were not subject to local control, little improvement could be expected.

Organizational practices. Still a third source of rationali-
zation relates to problems being "caused" by the organizational
systems of Padreco, including procedures, policies, working conditions, and union contract clauses. As long as these could be
pointed to as critical factors in the status quo not subject to
local control, then the status quo was accepted as a given.

Readiness to Change

Other influences in the situation promoted a readiness to
change; these include the following factors.

Headquarters' standards of excellence. The focus on the
problem came from above the parties involved in the problem
on a daily basis. Silvers, the plant manager, had a standard of
excellence for judging operational situations and, as with many
senior executives, always felt that more could be accomplished
than was being realized. He could point to schedule delays, unmet production quotas, and equipment failures as evidence of
existing problems within the control of those operating the
system.

Reliance on involvement rather than coercion. These senior executives might have applied pressure on those who have
the problem at an operating level and, in doing so, induced an
increased resistance to change. But they considered another
route and sought the involvement of the operating personnel
through discussing the possibility that some problems could be
improved. The involvement of the process began with Silvers

(plant manager) discussing the problem with Adams (production superintendent) and suggesting that Cooper (consultant), as a neutral outsider, could facilitate the process while leaving responsibility for problem solving within the initiative of the participants in the problem. Next, Adams and Cooper met with Morris and Larson to gain their commitment to taking another step. This led to the Interface Conflict-Solving Model activity between their two departments.

Breakthrough Dynamics

Several events caused the breakthrough in the Padreco situation.

Ideal/actual discrepancies. Once participants had walked through the designing of the soundest model and had compared it with actual circumstances, tensions about the discrepancy between the two were of sufficient strength to suggest that some action should be taken. In this sense, the identified discrepancies created the conditions for a breakthrough.

Self-acknowledgment of error. The actual turning point that created the conditions for interface resolution occurred when Larson admitted the practice of tokenism in promoting maintenance people. This acknowledgment from someone who had previously denied the accusation represents a reversal of attitude and the start of a foundation of openness and integrity.

Few things are of such importance in the Interface Conflict-Solving Model as the readiness of one group genuinely to acknowledge that it has contributed to the problem in ways that only can be interpreted by the other group as honest and accurate statements. This same dynamic in the context of breakthroughs in collaboration will be seen repeatedly in the following chapters.

CHAPTER 3

&ﾟ&ﾟ&ﾟ&ﾟ&ﾟ&ﾟ&ﾟ&ﾟ&ﾟ&ﾟ&ﾟ&ﾟ&ﾟ&ﾟ&ﾟ

When and How to Use
the New Approach

Now that we have studied the example in Chapter Two, we can step back and review the model in greater detail by looking at specific steps and the rationale for them. The Interface Conflict-Solving Model provides a methodology for examining and rejecting historical practices. A process of ideal-actual modeling produces this desirable, positive result. Some of the background rationale and techniques for applying the six-step design of the model are described next. After this fuller description of the model and its use, we will consider diagnosis.

Who Participates?

Participants are key members of each group in the conflict. Members are included who have authority to make needed changes in historical practices or who can design and implement new, previously untried modes of operation. Generally, participants should be familiar with the history of the relationship in order to recreate and track it.

If the conflict is between divisions, for example, the manager of each division participates with those people who report directly to him or her and sometimes with representatives from lower echelons. In a union-management controversy, corporate and international union-level participants may be included, along with key players from the plant management and the local union.

It is not practical to state any fixed number of participants. Furthermore, there is no reason for groups to be of equal size because voting is not used to determine outcomes. Rather, the intention is for each group to learn to speak as a single voice. Individuals are not participating as isolated representatives, each upholding one vested interest or point of view.

The group should include (1) those who can authorize whatever changes are appropriate, (2) those who know the history of tensions, (3) those who will be involved in leading implementation of change, and (4) both positive and negative opinion leaders. Positive opinion leaders can aid in communicating the spirit of intended change, as well as the mechanics agreed to. Negative opinion leaders can continue to resist efforts for change unless they have a deeper understanding of what is entailed and the stakes that are involved.

Selection of participants, while based on the four criteria just given, is determined by each group. Can one group veto participation by a member of the other group simply because that person is objectionable? Vetoing is discouraged because each group is expected to exercise responsibility for its own membership.

Another aspect of the veto question, however, is of a different character. Can one group ensure participation in the other group of those people the first group considers indispensable to solving the problem? Now the answer is less clear. If one group refuses to arrange for the participation of a member that the other group thinks is indispensable, the first group may be using a tactic to pressure. Alternatively, the second group may be failing to recognize the importance of one of its potential participants to the success of the project. Therefore, it is wise for the design administrator to explore the reasons for inclusion or exclusion of members as the basis for determining how to proceed.

There are special cases involving more than two groups in situations where collaboration has broken down. Two examples give an idea of how this occurs. One involved a headquarters and participants from five different subsidiaries. The core issue related to the degree of centralization of staff services and all six groups took part. Another situation involved a central MIS staff and two major operating divisions whose work involved a high degree of interdependence. In cases such as these, special logistical issues need to be addressed, but the same six steps are followed.

Who Administers the Design?

Line managers who are respected and neutral relative to both sides of the interface conflict may be the design administrators, as well as the internal or external consultants. Maximum success requires that nonmembers coordinate the process while group members assume responsibility for content. Other things being equal, it is better when two line managers or consultants collaborate in conducting the design. When there are two, each can help the other see ways of applying the design more effectively; both may monitor groups together and exchange perceptions or monitor them separately to keep track of progress in both.

The manager-administrator should be of a rank comparable to or higher than that of the highest rank existing in either of the two groups of participants. The reason for this qualification is that those who are caught up in the conflict may strike out and attack the other group. Should this happen, an administrator of lesser rank than the person engaged in such an attack is likely to be brushed aside. Bringing order to the situation is significantly more difficult, if not impossible, when the design administrator is not of at least equal rank to any participant.

When internal consultants provide the administration, some of the same considerations apply as for the line manager. They should be neutral with respect to the problem and their rank should be equal at least to the highest rank represented in either of the two contending groups.

External consultants are preferable for using the design to resolve interface conflicts when participants are of the highest organizational rank. This automatically means that line managers or internal organizational consultants will be of less rank. As such, they are subject to being overruled, or they risk the possibility that confrontation may be seen as insubordination by those higher in the hierarchy. This circumstance may arise when the design is used between a headquarters and a subsidiary or between two groups when a merger is taking place. Both involve the top level, and, therefore, reliance on an external consultant is advised.

Arousing Involvement

People come to accept the inevitability of problems that seem insolvable. The first step is to arouse involvement by looking at the problems anew to see if they are inevitable. When some prospect of improvement is realized, the gap between the actual situation and what is desirable increases motivation to try to do something.

Some degree of commitment is necessary to provide the motivation to make an effort. Even though they may have significant misgivings about the likelihood of a successful outcome, participants on both sides of the interface should, at a minimum, be ready to "give it a shot." The reason is that the process itself releases problem-solving motivation that cannot be assessed prior to participants experiencing the process. Therefore, the commitment critical for making the decision to implement the process is that (1) it is worth a try and (2) we have the ability to make it happen if we want to (which is not the same as committing oneself to make it happen).

Considerations that lead to commitment include the following. People experience pain, anguish, and frustration when distrust and suspicion prevent needed progress from being made in solving interface problems. Participants intuitively understand that things are not "right." One group may see its opposite number as a major impediment to its own performance or progress. Only by getting a better attitude of cooperation at the interface is improvement possible. Therefore, sometimes the suggestion of some prospect of improvement is sufficient to tap motivation and arouse involvement to try to make it happen.

Many times people in a tense interface realize that they themselves have been responsible for some of the frustrations in poor decisions and inadequate cooperation. This feeling of personal responsibility places a burden on persons for exercising responsible behavior toward correcting situations that they themselves may have contributed to developing in the first place.

Involvement in wanting to change is by no means sufficient. An educational step is important so that participants have an understanding of the Interface Conflict-Solving Model, of how it works, who participates in implementing the process, what the outcomes are likely to be, and the risks that may be confronted if failure is the result. Reading case examples like those presented in later chapters or a dry run by an internal consultant of the steps in the design provide a basis of understanding. Many times this step is sufficient to increase the readiness of people to commit themselves to an effort when they see a gap between where they are and the possibility of improved collaboration and a means of attaining a sounder relationship.

The prospect of participation increases commitment. This comes about in two ways as members think about who should take part. Subordinate members see that those who are involved in decision making need to actively participate. Key leaders can see that if decisions to change are made, those who would need to understand what is to be done should be involved. Participants can see that the feasibility of resolution is provided for in the selection of participants if agreements to change are attained. Finally, sheer curiosity about what the other group might propose about what would be ideal in comparison with the actual situation motivates involvement.

Another motivation of a questionable character may exist. One side of the interface may feel self-righteous and see the activity as a way of straightening out the people on the other side. Feeling superior in this way, they are more than prepared to participate, because they interpret the circumstances as arising entirely from the other side. This perception is often ill founded, however, and awareness of the self-deception involved can shock the group that feels self-righteous. We see this illustrated in Chapter Five by the engineering group in its relations with plant managers.

There are several sources of resistance to participating. One is pessimism from previous efforts that have failed. Having been burned by efforts in the past that have gone awry, the readiness to try again is substantially reduced. Another source of resistance is when one side feels that it is in charge; from their standpoint, to participate would only result in a loss of what has already been gained. Sometimes there is a concern for things getting out of hand. This fear is expressed in the following statement: "If we really get what's happened in the past out into the open, there's no way it can do anything but cause further resentment and misunderstanding."

These resistances can be allayed when participants are aided to understand that they themselves are in control of decisions made as the process unfolds. When the design and administration of it are demonstrated, these sources of resistance are likely to be seen as unfounded.

The numerous ways of helping participants consider the possibilities that might result from engaging in an Interface Conflict-Solving Model are dealt with later or described in examples. One way aids participants on both sides of the interface to diagnose the severity of the tensions at the interface or the degree of potential collaboration that is being sacrificed. This diagnostic step involves either external or self-diagnosis to determine the severity of the problem and to increase awareness of it by the participants themselves, followed by discussion to determine whether there is sufficient commitment to move forward. This step is outlined in detail in the section on when to use the interface model later in this chapter.

Another approach involves developing meaningful and realistic expectations about what the process may and may not be able to accomplish in a given setting. This can be done by an internal or external consultant giving a test run of the process and answering questions, first with the key leaders and thereafter with others who might participate. Then the consultant can lead a discussion that focuses on the questions (1) "Do we have an interface collaboration problem with another group?" and (2) "If so, what should we do about resolving it? Do we want to give the Interface Conflict-Solving Model a try?"

The design administrator can also confront either or both

groups with a more objective appraisal of what it might be possible to gain and what might be risked or lost through implementation of the model. Both groups can work separately to explore what they have to gain and what they have to lose by not participating in the activity. When there is a breakdown at the interface, it is rare that this kind of a gain-loss analysis ends on the loss side. If it does, then there is no justification for taking a next step. However, the more likely conclusion is that because so much human energy is tied up in needless conflict that there is far more to gain than to lose by attempting to establish a sounder basis for a relationship.

These approaches to arousing involvement, developing commitment, and testing the feasibility to participate through a dry run avoid pressures, persuasion, or coercion and permit prospective attendees to explore the likely consequences of participating or not participating. Often the groups are sick of the hassle and ready to give anything a try that has some prospect of success. But more often members of both groups recognize that they have little to lose by making the effort. Furthermore, frequently neither group wants to be placed in the position of withholding effort when a constructive proposition is put forward for increasing cooperation.

Outline of the Design

The major steps described in Chapter One are developed in more detail here to illustrate how the activities take place and what each is designed to accomplish.

Orientation to the Session

A general orientation session is attended by both groups to get everyone to think through the objectives of the activity. The objectives that are usefully discussed in an orientation session are: (1) the importance of walling off history so that possibilities can be viewed without the contamination that comes from projecting past events as inevitable in the future, (2) studying the relationship to gain an objective appraisal to replace subjective feelings about what is and what is not true of the present, (3) designing program implementation for solving problems currently existing at the interface, (4) scheduling what would need to be done in concrete terms to bring the shift about, and (5) gaining commitment to follow up as a way of measuring the progress and increasing it if possible, and for unacceptable progress, diagnosing why and planning corrective steps.

The ground rules about how the sessions are to be conducted include such considerations as: (1) interchanges between groups through spokespersons rather than by the designated leaders, (2) the inappropriateness of hostile remarks, jokes, and prods, (3) the design administrator's role of leading both groups through the series of steps rather than acting as a mediator.

In addition, openness and candor are requisite to a successful outcome; while these characteristics cannot be demanded, the consequences of failure to achieve openness and candor between the groups can be clarified. Rank is usually not the determining factor for who says what to whom; participants contribute what they can regardless of who they are or what rank they speak from. Finally, questions are encouraged to ensure fullest possible understanding of what is about to take place.

Step 1: Developing the Optimal Model

As the first activity in this step, the groups identify the most important types of interchanges that occur between them.

Typical instructions (written or verbal) include an intergroup interchange when the performance of one group directly impacts the performance of another or the behavior of participants affects operations or outcomes in another group. The quality of the intergroup relationship is contingent on the effectiveness of the many and various interchanges that take place between the groups.

These interchanges, easy to list in organizations, can be studied and analyzed through systematic examination. Some possible points of operational interaction between groups are listed here.

- Headquarters and field: decision making, budgeting, goal setting, performance evaluation, staff support services.
- Sales and manufacturing: delivery schedules, handling of special orders, quality control, customer complaints.
- Union and management: overtime, grievances, seniority, wage scales, safety procedures.
- Operations and data processing: special reports, costs, data input, delivery.
- Research and development and production: procurement of materials, engineering support, pilot-plant facilities, cost estimating.

The full reality of interdependent, group-to-group relationships goes beyond these mechanical and rational aspects of cooperation. It includes attitudes that underlie and guide behavior, such as *trust and respect* for each other, convictions regarding standards of excellence, and *commitment* to the overall goals of the organization. We use the word *elements* to mean both the important *attitudes* and *interchanges* that are involved in achieving an effective *relationship*.

Once both groups have completed listing elements, the groups meet in a general session in order for spokespersons to exchange with one another before all what each group considers as important elements. This meeting is usually sufficient to result in both groups working on essentially the same elements, which reduces the confusion when the groups reconvene to describe the optimal model from each group's perspective.

Each participating group then works separately to create a description of optimal interface effectiveness for each element. (In everyday language, managers equate the words *ideal, sound,* and *optimal,* so these words will be used interchangeably.) For example, a typical element might be *trust and respect.* The description of one group is, "Mutual trust and respect based on candor and openness are reflected in effective collaboration and cooperation." The description of the other group might be, "Trust and respect come from appreciation for one another's uniquenesses along with recognition of mutual competencies."

Step 2: Consolidating the Optimal Relationship

The groups now come together in a general session for a spokesperson from each group to present to the other group the separately developed model. Questions and requests for clarification are answered at this time to ensure understanding by each group of the other's model.

The next step is to combine these into one consolidated model for a sound relationship to which both groups can commit themselves. Sometimes this happens simply, if the statements for each element are easily combined. The consolidated statement of *trust and respect* from the preceding examples was completed as follows: "Trust and respect for one another are consistently demonstrated through open and candid communication leading to understanding, collaboration, and cooperation. Positions, people, and proposals are accepted at face value."

One approach to developing agreement when statements for elements are close involves using a four-point scale to examine each element of the other team's report. This may occur in separate group meetings held either in the general session area or in private group rooms. Any one of the following four points may apply to any part of the model.

4—"We disagree with the statement for the following reasons."
3—"We wish to ask the following questions for further clarification."
2—"We agree with the statement as rewritten in the following way."
1—"We agree with the statement as written."

After the separate group discussions are completed, the groups reconvene to exchange these findings through spokespersons who explain the thinking behind the numbers. As one team's spokesperson reports, the other team listens. At the conclusion, the other team's spokesperson reacts to the 2's with agreement, if acceptable, and to the 3's with clarification. This activity is completed when as many of the 4's, 3's, and 2's as possible have been made into 1's, reflecting mutual agreement on the consolidated statement. One or two disputed items might remain. These can be set aside as unimportant relative to the main problems and returned to later if they still need resolution.

There are times when several elements in the sound relationship description as one group sees it are different and contradict the description of a sound relationship as the other group sees it. This means that the groups reach an impasse in terms of converting the 4's into 1's. Two things can be done at this point. If the differences are not too great, it might be advisable to continue to work toward a resolution.

If the differences are great and the elements are significant to the relationship, the administrator may call for a shift in design strategy to confront these outstanding issues such as using a theater-in-the-round activity to develop more in-depth understanding by each group of the other's attitudes, rationale, and proposals. See Chapter Nine for an example of this technique; Chapter Ten gives further consideration to design variations.

After agreement has been reached on a consolidated model of the optimal relationship, the key elements are ranked by priority for the next discussion of the actual situation. Placing the elements in order of priority permits both groups to work through the elements in the same sequence in their private discussions and therefore discuss the same elements in a general session should this prove useful before the entire list of elements is completed.

Step 3: Describing the Actual Relationship

Actual conditions characterizing the relationship are described by each group separately, with members analyzing the historical factors that shaped and influenced the relationship. Sometimes it is desirable to discuss the first element at a reconvening to compare how each group used the model. Groups complete that element before subsequent elements are discussed. The benefit of doing this is that it establishes a basis for a more standardized approach so that each group covers the same kinds of points at a comparable level of depth prior to reaching agreement on the description of the actual relationship.

Step 4: Consolidating the Actual Relationship

The groups' individual perspectives are consolidated into a joint picture that accurately and objectively describes the here and now. Sometimes this takes place in a general session through spokespersons' interactions. Other times each group, working separately, discusses and digests the other group's presentation to ensure understanding and secure clarification in order to test for agreement. Thereafter, general session spokespersons work to develop a single list. A consolidation of the groups' individual perspectives into a joint picture that describes the present is the next step, again using the four-point method described earlier, if needed. In doing this, members explore and analyze specific historical factors that have shaped and influenced the relationship.

When those who have experienced it agree about what their history has been and what the present situation is, barriers of the past that have stifled organizational progress and productivity, hampered intergroup communication and cooperation, or frustrated individual and organizational growth and development are pinpointed and targeted for change. Previously unrecognized possibilities, alternatives, and potentials then come more clearly into view.

Step 5: Planning for Change

Changes to be made in specific, operational terms are jointly agreed upon and described in detail. These result in plans for follow-up by this group that also include others not present. Tactics typically employed during this fifth step include counterpart discussions, task force designations, and preparation of work flow charts depicting specific action steps and follow-up plans. When subgroups are used for detailed planning, each reports to the entire group to ensure understanding, agreement, and commitment to follow-up before the plans are completed and follow-up dates are determined. This step is completed when changes in specific, operational terms to be implemented are programmed and scheduled. A final critique of the effectiveness of the effort and its lessons conclude the session.

Step 6: Progress Review and Replanning

Follow-up dates are scheduled for groups to reconvene three to six months after the initial session to review progress, critique their current relationship, and plan next steps. This meeting is conducted in the same organized manner as the first sessions.

Typical Schedule

Although subject to many variations, typically these several basic steps are completed during a four-day work session; Table 2 shows the broad outlines of the process.

It is relatively rare for any of the main activities to be shifted in sequence or omitted. What is common, however, is that the time allotments shown are increased or shortened depending on the progress being made. Not every activity called for in the Interface Conflict-Solving Model is commented on in each case study in this book. Rather, the text concentrates on highlights so emphases on activities vary throughout the illustrations.

This schedule is demanding, but the potential rewards merit considerable expenditure of time and effort. Groups often find it desirable to meet at an off-site location (hotel or conference center) where there are fewer interruptions and greater control over distractions. More complete information about design administrator preparation and guidelines for orchestrating the effort are contained in Chapter Ten.

Now that the design of the Interface Conflict-Solving Model has been described, we can return to the question of when this is a desirable procedure for use to resolve interface conflict. The next section presents several approaches to deter-

Table 2. Typical Schedule of Activities of the Interface Conflict-Solving Model Design.

Day	Morning	Afternoon	Evening
1	Orientation to purposes, activities, and procedures. Separate sessions to describe characteristics of the sound relationship in terms of elements of the relationship.	Joint session for presentation of separately developed models (by spokespersons). Questions raised for clarification.	Separate sessions to permit each group to evaluate the other's model and test it for agreement using the four-point method described in text.
2	Joint session wherein spokespersons present each group's reaction to the other's sound relationship description. Divergent perspectives are consolidated and elements of the agreed-upon model prioritized for discussion.	Groups meet separately to begin preparing their descriptions of the actual interface relationship selecting one or two to begin with.	Work on actual relationship descriptions continued in separate sessions.
3	Spokespersons present each group's description of actual conditions in joint session. Questions are raised for clarification.	Groups separate to discuss one another's perception of actual relationship conditions and historical antecedents, using four-point method as needed.	Joint session to ensure greater understanding and prepare consolidated view for actual relationship regarding each priority element.
4	Separate sessions to prepare an action plan for shifting from the actual to a sound relationship. This may be through task forces, subgroups, or functional counterparts meeting to develop concrete plans for implementation.	Joint session to review plans prepared by each group and reach agreement on next steps regarding task force and counterpart recommendations and follow-up requirements. Actions for immediate execution discussed and implemented. Follow-up scheduled. Critique of entire session.	

mining whether or not the model has utility for specific situations.

When to Use the Interface Conflict-Solving Model

To people who have them, many intergroup tensions are well known, particularly those that cause production breakdowns. Many more are not so readily seen or described by those who have them, partly because the tensions may have become chronic and partly because no dramatic breakdowns can be traced to them. The reduced production attributable to them, while it may be substantial, is not recognized as such. In either case, systematic diagnosis of the real problem may be desirable to increase the likelihood that the explanation of the problem is valid, to assess the readiness to resolve conflicts, and to bring awareness that such tensions exist and provide a basis for moving into a problem-solving activity.

Two different approaches are used in diagnosing an interface conflict. One relies on instruments, the other relies on interviews. These may be used independently of one another or in combination with interviews following the use of instruments to deepen understanding of the dynamics involved.

Instrumented Diagnosis

The instrument can be administered by the manager, a human resources person, or a design administrator to one group at a time to identify the presence of an intergroup conflict that needs attention. For convenience, here this person is called the administrator. First, the other groups with which the group undertaking the diagnosis needs to cooperate are identified. The identification of a potential breakdown in collaboration may come about because the tensions are felt by the members themselves or because higher management has detected such signs as diminished productivity and blame and complaint by one group of the other. Alternatively, one side in a cleavage may approach the other, suggesting that a need exists and requesting the other group to engage in self-diagnosis.

The possible groups are identified in the following example as Groups X, Y, and Z although in practice actual group names are used. The following instrument, including preamble and three steps, is first completed individually by team members.[1]

> *Preamble.* Most sections of an organization are not self-sufficient. Some of the work of each department, division, section, or unit can be undertaken and successfully completed only when it acts in concert with others. For many components, this situation is the rule rather than the exception. Under these conditions, joint effort is essential to the soundest and most effective realization of results. When synergy between groups is present, the cooperation that it makes possible permits members of both groups to work together in such a way as to identify opportunities of being more productive that neither would recognize without the open interaction of the other.
>
> Some intergroup relationships that should be dealt with are *horizontal*. There is a barrier to effectiveness that exists between two groups at the same general level in the organization's hierarchy. Sales and manufacturing, for example, must work together—sometimes in special ways—to meet market demands profitably, with consistent, high quality and with full customer satisfaction. Central purchasing and technical engineering must work together similarly to design new units. Manufacturing and distribution is another example of where closely knit effort is required.
>
> Other intergroup situations are *vertical*. These are, for example, situations between the headquarters, the parent company, and a subsidiary, or a headquarters and a plant manufacturing group, or a headquarters marketing organization and a sales region or district office, or perhaps between general foremen and supervisors at the foreman level. A common feature is that neither com-

---

[1] *Grid Intergroup Development* (Austin, Texas: Scientific Methods, Inc., 1983), pp. 5–8.

ponent can act as if it were completely self-suffi-
cient and independent if corporate objectives are
to be met most effectively. Each, in varying de-
grees, must cooperate, coordinate, support, consult, and correlate efforts with the other.

Interdependent effort is often required, but
is often relatively ineffective. One or more of the
kinds of problems listed below often underlie such
situations.

1. Goals that can be achieved only through inter-
    dependent effort are not recognized, clearly
    defined, or accepted as important.
2. Antagonism, hostility, or apathy, indifference,
    and isolation block joint efforts and make
    needed cooperation far more difficult to
    achieve than it should be.
3. Poor understanding in each group of the cir-
    cumstances facing the other prevents or re-
    duces the ability to take action together in an
    effective way with resulting misinterpretations
    about the amount or kind of cooperation which
    is expected, but not forthcoming.

An endless variety of difficulties in communication, planning, and problem solving result from
the three problems listed above.

The groups with which your group must coordinate effort are X, Y, and Z, and so on (if there
are more than three groups).

Step 1. Describe the degree that your group
needs to cooperate and coordinate with the others
by circling the appropriate number on the following scale.

To what degree does your group need to cooperate and coordinate with the actions of the
other groups?

With Group

X	Y	Z	
9	9	9	Total need for cooperation and coor- dination to get the job done
8	8	8	Almost total need
7	7	7	Moderate need
6	6	6	Somewhat of a need for cooperation

X	Y	Z	
5	5	5	Intermediate between need for cooperation and independent of the other group
4	4	4	Somewhat independent
3	3	3	Moderately independent
2	2	2	Almost totally independent
1	1	1	Totally independent—there is no requirement for cooperation or coordination among us

Step 2. How costly is the lack of cooperation?

With Group

X	Y	Z	
9	9	9	Full synergy between our groups is realized; no further gain in productivity is possible from better cooperation or coordination
8	8	8	Almost full synergy
7	7	7	Moderate synergy
6	6	6	Somewhat more gained from cooperation than lost from its absence
5	5	5	Intermediate between gain and loss
4	4	4	Some loss from lack of cooperation
3	3	3	Moderate loss
2	2	2	Almost complete loss
1	1	1	Antagonisms and distrust completely block critically needed cooperation

If there has been a briefing regarding the Interface Conflict-Solving Model approach, then Step 3 can be used to assess commitment to moving forward.

Step 3. Is an Interface Conflict-Solving Modeling activity a desirable step toward improving synergy with Group

X? _____ Yes _____ No
Y? _____ Yes _____ No
Z? _____ Yes _____ No

Each member working alone completes the scales individually to evaluate the character of the relationship, first with

Group X, then Y, then Z. Thereafter, each member's ratings for
Scale 1, Group X are summarized on a chart. This summary is
followed by discussion leading to a team agreement on the rating. The same procedure is followed for Scales 2 and 3 until a
conclusion is reached by the team regarding whether it is desirable to engage in an Interface Conflict-Solving activity with
Group X. The same procedure is followed for Groups Y and Z,
and a priority is established among the groups in terms of the
need for interface sessions with each one.

The design administrator then contacts the manager of
the group with the highest priority to report the conclusion. If
the contacted group has not already done so, the suggestion is
made that use of this instrument by its members might be the
initial step for determining whether an interface activity should
be scheduled. If Interface Conflict-Solving sessions are scheduled, the managers meet to determine time and place and to select a design administrator (or two administrators) for the
activity.

Is Further Diagnosis Valuable?

The view is widely accepted, particularly in conjunction
with reliance on the Interpersonal Facilitator Model, that diagnosis of the problem by outsiders is a step that should be taken
prior to trying to solve it. Whether further diagnosis of this kind
is desirable before undertaking an Interface Conflict-Solving
Model activity is questionable. If the cost of the interface problem is significantly greater than the cost of the process itself,
there is adequate reason to proceed. The Interface Conflict-
Solving Model should be the central diagnostic activity engaged
in by those who have the problem. With the kind of understanding of the problem that the design induces, participants are
in a position to design the steps to rectify the problem. In this
sense, diagnosis by outsiders, if needed at all, may be more for
the purpose of getting a neutral view of the situation and possibly for establishing confidence that the problem can be dealt
with.

Diagnostic Interviews

If it is decided that further diagnosis is desirable, more tailormade, in-depth diagnostic interviews usually begin at the functional top, moving down through all whose performance is affected by the interface on a day-in and day-out basis. Outsiders who interview may be line managers from other units, human resources persons, or people external to the organization.

Such interviews are conducted on both sides of the interface, but it is important that the reasons for conducting them be understood in advance. Their purpose is to determine if problems of cooperation and coordination are sufficiently intense to call for an Interface Conflict-Solving activity. When interviewees understand this, they can contribute their insights more fully.

Interviews may be conducted by two people talking to one interviewee at a time. One of the interviewers conducts the interview and the other makes notes, listening for discrepancies or untouched aspects that need to be further explored before the situation at the interface can be fully understood.

After several interviews have been conducted, the interviewers can uncover facets of the interface problem that may not have come to the surface earlier. "Testing the limits" involves active queries by the interviewer that call for the person being interviewed to accept or reject or negate them. In other words, when material about the conditions at the interface has been collected, the interviewers can ask questions that evoke such answers as "No, that kind of thing never happened," or "I don't recall any deliberate effort to undermine us."

Interviews should be of sufficient length to get to the heart of the problem, but not so long as to induce trivial or irrelevant information; an hour seems appropriate. Thirty minutes between interviews provide the interviewers with an opportunity to review, consolidate, and record their conclusions before the next interview. This reduces the tendency of what one interviewee reports to blur and flow into what the next person reports. The conclusions reached are "cleaner" and more readily traceable should future events require reexamination.

The interviews are summarized and the interviewers draw their conclusions and recommendations, which may be summarized for the two teams or the two teams' leaders simultaneously as the basis for further decision making.

Summary

Diagnosis of the relationship at the interface between any two groups that need to cooperate and coordinate may be a desirable first step in determining whether an interface or some alternative activity might be a useful approach. Data can be gathered through instruments or interviews, which can be conducted by line managers, human resources personnel, or outsiders. The findings serve as the basis for the decision by each team or its leaders whether or not to undertake an Interface Conflict-Solving activity. Further steps in diagnosis are present within the Interface Conflict-Solving Model itself to help those who have the problem to discover the causes of it as the basis for planning how to solve it.

The Interface Conflict-Solving Model should not be confused with the Interpersonal Facilitator Model; the two rest on fundamentally different assumptions about the character of interface conflict and how to resolve the conflict. The former derives its strength from the diagnosis it permits participants themselves to make, the discrepancies between what is and what is possible that it brings into focus, and the group level of support for change it creates. The design administrator is important but incidental to the result while the design itself is the major factor in bringing change about.

The facilitator is the main factor in the Interpersonal Facilitator Model. Change depends on the facilitator's skill in aiding primarily the leaders on either side of the interface to recognize possibilities. This distinction is so important that Chapters Four and Five have been prepared to illustrate similarities and differences in the two approaches.

Ten key properties make up the design of the Interface Conflict-Solving Model.

1. Active participation by those on either side of the cleavage whose understanding and agreement is essential to support any change.
2. Those who have the problem can themselves learn to diagnose the causes underlying it.
3. Reliance on active participation by members to develop the insights, understandings, and agreements that serve as the basis for problem solving rather than using coercion, compromise, or capitulation.
4. The idea that a complex intergroup relationship can be described in terms of elements.
5. The proposition that *ideal* formulations can be composed and agreed to regarding the soundest relationship between them.
6. Identifying the status for these same elements in regard to the actual relationship.
7. The 4, 3, 2, 1 method of achieving mutual agreement reflecting consolidation of viewpoints across groups.
8. The creation of discrepancies with resultant motivations to close the gap by comparing ideal with actual.
9. Interaction between groups carried out by spokespersons rather than by designated leaders. Shared understanding promoted by everyone involved in the relationship studying the situation and how to change it at the same time.
10. The structure and sequencing of the design permits a line or staff person to implement the process without being actively involved in the content of the activity itself.

CHAPTER 4

Dealing with Line–Staff Conflict: Use of a Conventional Approach

The Interpersonal Facilitator Model is an alternative way of approaching the resolution of conflicts between groups. Because of its natural appeal and the extensiveness of its use, this chapter presents a point-by-point study of one example of how an interpersonal facilitator worked to resolve conflict between line and staff groups. In reading this example, pay particular attention to how the facilitator begins by moderating sessions where group members work on the problem together but shifts his approach to that of an intermediary in his efforts to achieve a satisfactory solution to the problem. In the next chapter, the same setting appears with the Interface Conflict-Solving Model applied at a later date.

As a comparison of key differences in the two approaches indicates, neither should be regarded as the preferred approach to conflict resolution regardless of circumstances. Both have resulted in successes and both have been unsuccessful. The key issue is to identify the conditions under which success is most likely for each of the two models employed.

The Interpersonal Facilitator Model

To expand on what was presented in Chapter One, the Interpersonal Facilitator Model is an alternative to the Interface Conflict-Solving Model for solving disputes across group boundaries. It relies on one person (or two) who provides a bridge, aiding the disputing parties to find common ground. The facilitator seeks to do this in many different ways, but all center on acting as a neutral intermediary or third party with respect to the outcome. He or she helps disputing parties to define their areas of agreement and disagreement and to reduce the latter to the point where the dispute can be regarded as either manageable or solved. The facilitator is crucial for providing a bridge between the two groups by asking questions, arranging and conducting meetings, or dealing through private contacts with the principals and sometimes with subordinates. In addition, the facilitator keeps an orderly exchange, sometimes formulates recommendations or proposals or offers more acceptable language, and sometimes lectures on the consequences of success or failure.

The Interpersonal Facilitator Model is a constructive approach for solving disputes and achieving settlements when the parties are unable to come together face to face. Then the facilitator is in a position to help the disputants to communicate in a controlled manner so that each is able to hear the other and to react by analyzing the problem at hand from the standpoint of how to solve it. It has many applications in business and industry such as when the boss and a subordinate get into a private conflict, when a purchasing agent experiences a personal disagreement with a supplier, or even when two candidates are vying for the same promotion and it is important for them to live with the solution without losing mutual respect. It has also found use in the international scene as a procedure for resolving disputes between nations by a third, who acts as a neutral intermediary.

The following step-by-step application of the Interpersonal Facilitator Model at Consolidated Utilities illustrates the differences between these two models. Sometime after this attempt to solve the problem, we were asked to use the Interface Conflict-Solving Model to deal with unresolved issues. Both of these approaches are reported substantially as they occurred. This chapter describes the chronological events for the first day, how the process was reshaped on the second day, and on through an almost month-long series of contacts.

Background of the Conflict

Interface conflict between engineering and the plant management of Consolidated Utilities, a major utility, was reported by the old-timers as having started with the organization's beginning. As Merrill McFadden, chairman of the board, explained: "For the ten years I've been here, central engineering and the plant managers have waged an ongoing battle over control of engineering activities in the plants. From what I understand from the ancients, this problem was around thirty years before I came, and that makes it an unbelievable forty years old. Most people expect it to continue long after I'm gone."

Among many things discussed in employing a new vice-president of human resources, he said, "This is a nasty situation. I'd like you to take a look at it." The discussion moved on to other points. About a month later it came up again, when Bill Craig, the human resources vice-president, said to the chairman, "I've met several people from central engineering and plant management. It's quite a one-sided problem. Central engineering is not too much involved, feeling it's one of those inevitable tensions in organizational life, and they are trying to be patient. But the plant management group seems to be up in arms. They are infuriated."

"Hopeless," said McFadden.

"That depends," said Craig, "on whether the problem is one of competency or communication. If it is the former, yes, the latter, no."

"I can help on that," said McFadden. "Competency? No way. These people are the cream of the engineering crop—the upper 10 percent of their graduating classes, all of them. So if it's not competency, then how can you help?" McFadden asked.

"Well," responded Craig. "I've been through a lot of hang-ups with unions and in principle this situation is no different. As a newcomer, I am neutral as to who might be right and who wrong, or even why they have a problem. Possibly I can get them together to talk it out. At least it's worth a try."

"Anything," said McFadden. "I'm so sick of it I'm ready to try anything. What do you propose?"

"I'd like to get the principals on both sides together for a day and to moderate a discussion to get the facts out on the table to see what can be done," responded Craig.

"You've got my blessing," said McFadden. "I look forward to what happens, even if you have to bang a few heads together to get their attention."

Participants

Those attending the discussion from central engineering included Walt Reeves, vice-president of engineering, and the key personnel under him. Plant management was headed by Jack Lewis, interplant coordinator, with four other plant managers as representatives also present. Craig represented headquarters as the person in charge, and he was joined by two other senior personnel, the human relations advisers who were assigned to central engineering and to plant management. Although those attending were from two different constituencies, the intended purpose of their participation was to get them to deal with one another as individuals by setting aside vested interests arising from feelings of membership. Other interested parties came in from time to time or were consulted depending on the issue being considered.

Expectations Prior to the Joint Meeting

While discussions took place among Craig, Reeves, and Lewis in setting up the meeting, there was little talk about what would happen except, of course, recognition that the issue was to study how they might achieve a better basis of cooperation. Reeves wanted Craig to take part in any negotiations as a full partner speaking for headquarters. Lewis wanted Craig's help to

mediate short of formulating and presenting substantive proposals, feeling that if operating decisions were to be made, it
would be appropriate for Craig to bring line personnel in to represent their own point of view. No significant concern was applied to this, however, because what Reeves implied by "full
partner" was not clear, and Craig's administering of the Interpersonal Facilitator Model could have satisfied this requirement,
particularly if Reeves understood the bridge concept. Almost
certainly it would have been satisfactory to Lewis for Craig to
have done so.

Having initiated the procedure, Craig created the final
format since others deemed it appropriate for him to introduce
his own strategy and to modify it as needed. He had a plan for
the two groups to meet together during the entire period, but
this happened only once at the initial session, when the depth
of the acrimony became evident in mutual accusations and expressions of disgust, particularly those felt by the plant management group for central engineering.

Craig saw himself as a facilitator, describing his expectations prior to the first day as follows: "My thought was that by
producing a constructive atmosphere for our meetings, these
managers would come to know and understand each other better, and they would trust me to be honest and fair in my role as
moderator, mediator, and active negotiator. I also thought that
without a preestablished agenda, this would increase the likelihood that the meetings could really focus on the main issues
rather than getting bogged down in the protocol of formal
meetings. The other human resources people were to make
everyone feel as much at home as possible and to try to ease
tensions. It was important for them to be there to consult with
me from time to time as the next steps for moving the discussions forward came under consideration."

The Problem of Mutual Trust and Respect

The first session was held in a large room with no table
and with chairs purposely scattered around to break up a we-
they seating arrangement. The random seating was an effort to

help each person feel free and responsible for participating through expressing his own personal convictions. (See Chapter Five, Figure 3, for the participants in this session.)

Craig took a seat near the center and started the session. "As you know better than I, Merrill McFadden has long been concerned about how to improve cooperation between your two groups, and he has asked me to help. This meeting has no agenda beyond (1) what the problem is and (2) how it can be solved. Anyone is free to speak, but to keep things moving forward, I will moderate the discussion. Who would like to start?"

A member of central engineering began. "I'll tell you the problem. Engineering has become even more complicated in each of its disciplines, not only in terms of recent engineering developments but in terms of materials employed and construction techniques that are available. When you couple all of these rapidly occurring changes with requirements from EPA [Environmental Protection Agency], NRC [Nuclear Regulatory Commission], OSHA [Occupational Safety and Health Administration], and half a dozen others, there is no option but for engineering to be centralized and under conditions where we keep ourselves free as much as possible of the risks of malpractice. Plant management doesn't understand this complexity. The developing tendency to put heavy fines on operations that violate commission requirements is bound to teach us all a lesson, and we should have learned it long ago."

"That's not the problem at all," a member of plant management spoke as if propelled out of a cannon. "I'll tell you the problem. We're qualified engineers, every one of us, but we're treated like children who can't be trusted to build a derrick with an erector set. It's demeaning. We manage millions in operating expenses but can't spend $10,000 on an air conditioning duct."

This blast was a bit more than Reeves, the vice-president of engineering, was ready to take. He felt a need to tackle it head on. "Look," he said, "this is the same crybaby talk that we've been hearing for years. We know that you're qualified engineers, and we respect you for the competence with which you operate the plants. We are professional engineers and we spend every day of the week at it. You've got to admit that while practice may not make perfect, it sure contributes to a superior product, and in a real sense that's the reason for the division we have. Let's learn how to make it work, not constantly complain." Reeves trailed off and people sat quietly, no one knowing what might be said that could move the two groups off dead center.

After a moment of silence, Craig took up the slack, saying, "I wonder if anyone from the plant has a reaction to what Mr. Reeves has just expressed."

Greene, from the Keystone plant, spoke up. "I think that the holier-than-thou attitude just spoken by Mr. Reeves is an excellent demonstration of the blindness, deafness, and dumbness of central engineering."

Taylor, manager of the Carswell operation, then spoke, saying, "Whether we're crybabies or not is not the point, Mr. Reeves. The point is that we constantly have to do retro-engineering. Your people leave, the design doesn't work according to specifications, and we're pleased to see you leave because at that point we can take over and make the modifications that are essential for the thing to work. That's the real complaint—not that we want engineering per se. We want functional engineering and we can contribute to it."

Valdez of civil engineering had heard more than he was prepared to put up with. "That's why we say 'crybaby.' If you could have done the work in the first place, they never would have created central engineering. But they created it and you've gotta live with it. It's an efficient use of personnel to concentrate design expertise in one segment and to concentrate engineers on effective operations in other sections. That's the way the structure shows it. There's nothing wrong with it. Let's see how we can make it work rather than crying about a technical limitation here or there."

"All you've done is redefine the problem just as it was," said White from the Aransas plant. "Just because the status quo says that's the way it's been done doesn't mean that's the way it should be done. Unless and until we can get you to look at that, I think the situation is hopeless."

This initial discussion had broken down, but Craig was in no way discouraged; he immediately shifted to get the principals together informally where they might talk without embarrassing each other or antagonizing others. Thus Craig moved away from the idea of moderating a discussion to the notion of a series of meetings between Reeves and Lewis. From the very beginning Craig had felt that trust and respect were not present between them, and he saw the importance of Reeves and Lewis getting to know one another better. He thought this process could be accelerated by creating conditions of informality and ease among the three of them. After their first meeting, he commented, "It's a long way from here to where we need to get if collaboration based on mutual trust and respect is the goal."

In Craig's attempts to achieve mutual respect, he felt a central consideration on his part was to "accentuate the positive." He cautioned Lewis not to overreact when he first heard Reeves's formal statement about central engineering being responsible for 100 percent of engineering and plant management being responsible for 100 percent of all operations. Craig was not free to reveal that this had been told him in confidence by Reeves. Later he said, "We knew that Reeves was ready to make immediate modifications," even though they were minor ones such as recommending an increase in the dollar limit for small equipment purchases by plant managers. Craig also knew that Reeves deeply distrusted Lewis's motives of wanting to decrease central engineering staff and activities, and he tried to help Reeves gain appreciation and understanding of what lay behind Lewis's positions.

As Craig said, "It was clear that a great chasm separated the present feelings from those of mutual trust and respect, and at this point in the game it seemed that such might never be established between the two men. Of the thirty or so days that were involved in this total effort, I was to spend much time defending and explaining each of the vice-presidents to the other. For example, once they were moving toward the door, but I got in front of them to partially block the way. I urged them not to withdraw from these conversations, but to give me another opportunity to use my influence and analysis. I said, 'If you have no confidence in me, then the consequence is that these tensions will remain.' Jack Lewis agreed readily. I looked Reeves in the eye and finally he nodded agreement, but they left without speaking to each other."

Craig as Interpersonal Facilitator

Craig had intended to rely on these face-to-face meetings among Reeves, Lewis, and himself to develop understanding of each other; he saw this as critical. He saw the first few meetings as an opportunity for Reeves and Lewis to exchange points of view, and, in this respect, he anticipated that the process would unfold in a natural way: "I decided to play a minimal role in these early sessions so that these two could become more fully acquainted and have more fruitful interchanges. I already had learned what each had to say. I could have repeated their points of view from memory."

Craig continued, "When the first meeting took place, it produced a buildup of tensions between the two men. This was primarily due to Reeves's presentation of the fixed position related to the 100 percent engineering concept, which I already knew to be entirely unacceptable to Lewis. We didn't make much progress and another session was scheduled."

Craig utilized the same approach at the second session. "When we got underway, I decided to step back from the discussions between Reeves and Lewis because I wanted them to speak with one another on a direct basis. While they talked, I took notes and avoided looking up. Soon they refrained from talking to me or attempting to draw me into the conversation."

The second session began with Lewis's reply to Reeves. "Look, Walt, it's obvious that we have some deep differences. I think you're trying to protect your preserve and won't open up and look at the problem."

Reeves retorted, "That's your definition of the problem, but it's not ours. I've said it and I'll repeat it. I think the problem is that you are unprepared to accept the table of organization, the organizational structure, and the assignment of responsibilities, which has been hammered out over the years and has the wisdom of experience behind it. Specialization of effort is basic to effective industrial organization. We cannot see why you will not buy that."

Lewis felt challenged. "All that would be well and good, Walt, except—look at the facts. The corporation is going down the drain, and a significant factor in the drain on our profitability is from costs associated with goldplate engineering and retro-engineering, to say nothing of the hopeless delays between when a PEA [proposal for engineering assistance] is initiated by us, when it gets on your drawing boards, when it eventually gets into construction, and finally when we retro-engineer the operation. The facts are that we are responsible for drains on profitability, and we are not facing the reality of doing something about them."

Again, this discussion continued to move into the area of accusations and counteraccusations. "Their faces were flushed and the niceties of business protocol were stripped away. They had almost forgotten I was there, and there was nothing to distract me from recording this fascinating debate. The two had a long and hot argument, and it bogged down when each began to repeat himself and to ignore the other. The end of it came when both were talking at once. My attempts to change the subject were futile."

As these meetings progressed, Craig shifted into a more active role: "I had been acting as a referee and made efforts to put them back on track, and occasionally explained what was meant when there was an obvious misinterpretation by one of what the other had said. Later, after they had returned to their offices the fourth time, Reeves drew me in, saying, 'Look, I don't want to talk to that guy any more. If you want to talk to him, you can represent my point of view, but I've had it up to here. I'll be pleased for you to come and talk with me about any progress that you make with Lewis, and I promise to be as constructive as possible in trying to meet their criticisms of us, though I want you to understand that the issue is not one of simply sharing engineering in a 25-75 or a 50-50 way. It's not just to give them some that will solve the problem.'"

With this breakdown, a situation had developed where

the procedure of bringing the two men together to deliberate fixed positions was no longer tenable. At the end of approximately six hours of meetings between the two on different days, Craig summarized the situation: "We had accomplished little so far, except to name the difficult issues and to recognize the depth of the disagreements prevailing with regard to them. Furthermore, there was little or no compatibility between the two men as men, and almost every discussion on any subject deteriorated into an unproductive argument that did little more than reopen old wounds of the past. The last meeting that we held culminated in a deadlock and the breakdown of discussions as Reeves and Lewis fell into angry accusations of one another."

At this point Craig shifted to the go-between strategy, which was to become the arrangement for the exchanges between them for the remainder of the activities during the next month. He proposed that he become the intermediary for formulating positions: "I asked them to give me at least the opportunity to understand as best I could the positions of the two groups in their entirety, to devise my own compromise proposals, and to present my views to both of them."

Craig drafted proposals and continued to work with various members of both departments in this endeavor. Then he met separately with each of the two principals to solicit their reactions and agreement. For example, he expressed his intention to Lewis as follows: "I did not draft this proposal with the idea that either side would alter it substantially. I've tried to keep in mind what plant management wants and needs. My commitment is to continue to try to represent your interests and to negotiate for you with Reeves."

From Facilitation to Accusation

Occasionally Craig used confrontation when he got pushed to the wall and saw the discussion was about to be broken off. This usually occurred when he became angry or fearful that disastrous consequences would result if something did not change. The apparent turning point in Reeves's attitude

came when Craig and he slipped into a win-lose argument because Craig continued to urge central engineering to go along
with some local engineering being conducted in plants on small
projects; the discussion deteriorated. Later Craig said, "It was a
hot argument—unpleasant and repetitive. I stood up to leave
and accused him of being willing to give up peace with plant
management by holding on to an unrealistic, rigid position."

Craig explained, "This strong statement of the possible
losses to central engineering due to Reeves's position with respect to 'territory' had the consequence of making me appear
tilted to the plant management perspective and therefore un-
trustworthy as a person providing the protagonists the benefits
of a 'good office' role.

"In a final effort to persuade Reeves to permit me to
continue these negotiations," Craig continued, "I explained to
him the extremely serious consequences of his unilaterally
breaking off the discussions, that his action would harm the relationship of central engineering with the personnel function and
the corporate offices. He would be violating his personal promises to me and the onus of failure would be on him. I described
the possible future progress between central engineering and
plant management and said that the moderate headquarters' tolerance might be radicalized and result in an enforced shift of
assignments. I told him that it would damage one of my most
precious possessions—his friendship and our mutual trust."
Craig finally persuaded Reeves to stick it out for another few
rounds.

What is apparent is that the sessions were in some way a
special version of shuttle diplomacy, but now over short rather
than extended distances. Repeatedly, Craig was moving from
Reeves's office to Lewis's office or meeting with one in his own
office, followed by another, or carrying notes almost as an emis-
sary so that Reeves and Lewis might review and react to them
either before or after he had met and reviewed them with the
other. In other words, the process that had begun with exchanges between the groups, with order and direction in the
hands of a moderator, had come to involve facilitation through
direct efforts at conciliation, mediation, and negotiation among

himself and the two leaders in direct discussions. Finally, Craig had entered the intermediary role as a go-between trying to find common ground acceptable to both.

Throughout the entire sequence of events, Craig relied on many facilitator interventions to keep the discussions alive and moving. These are summarized in the following list.

1. *Anticipation building:* Before the meetings formally got underway, Craig told Lewis that Reeves was coming forward with the strong statement about the 100 percent engineering proposal. Because of increasing governmental regulations, Reeves felt it important that central engineering retain overall and operational responsibility for engineering and construction.

2. *Discussion controller:* These interventions were intended to control who spoke to whom and in what order in the three-way discussions. "I asked Reeves to begin. . . ." "I then asked Lewis to respond. . . ." "I insisted that Lewis not interrupt. . . ."

3. *Question poser:* "I asked Reeves. . . ." Point-blank questions were designed to get Reeves to give a reaction of "yes" or "no" when he was being evasive.

4. *Procedural technician:* Craig suggested they bring supporting documents so they could check on various points. He also proposed examining hypothetical cases and asked participants to walk through an example and give their reactions.

5. *Tension reliever:* After Reeves's strong initial formulation, Craig sought to break the tension by saying in effect that perhaps it was appropriate for Lewis to accept the position as stated by Reeves and send a memo up to that effect. He wanted to meet with the plant management group after the first meeting to ease their concerns.

6. *Social relaxer:* Craig invited group members to join him for coffee.

7. *In-group communication and critique:* Craig reviewed the damage done with other participants and probed for next steps that seemed wise to others who were not as involved as he was.

8. *Accusative confrontation:* On occasion, Craig was blunt; for example, he said, "I don't feel that I have your trust," to Reeves.

9. *Summarizer:* Craig insisted on recapitulating the questions that had been posed.

10. *Information transmitter:* As go-between for Lewis and Reeves, Craig would convey Lewis's position to Reeves, saying, "Lewis sincerely wants to continue to explore how to make functional use of plant engineers to do local engineering."

11. *Information provider:* Craig related how problems similar to this had been solved in other situations and gave participants the reactions from headquarters to the problem.

12. *Role reverser:* With such questions as "Would you repeat what Reeves just said?" and "Is that a fair statement of what you said?," Craig helped participants consider the other side of issues.

13. *Proposition formulator:* From the beginning, Craig held it as part of his initiative to draft procedures that would allow central engineering to perform a check-and-balance function if plant managers were allowed to do some of their own engineering. In the first meeting of the threesome, for example, he informed Reeves that he would delay suggesting any of his own proposals until after Reeves and Lewis had explored all of their differences.

These are only some of the facilitator mechanisms that Craig felt the need to use to keep the process on track and to make it possible for the participants to seek progress.

Impact of the Interpersonal Facilitation

The division of responsibility for engineering and operations was not altered from this effort, but other improvements in the relationship have been realized. The main result has been a deployment of three central engineering personnel to provide liaison engineering functions to the plants. They are stationed at locations that make them available for consultation, communication, and troubleshooting on a more timely basis; their stations also provide them with firsthand knowledge of in-plant engineering activities. They have been able to reduce tensions and improve services in a variety of ways by removing bottle-necks, solving issues of priority, and getting more realistic, more functional design work done by engineering.

However, the broader issues of how to integrate engineering with operations have not been brought to resolution, and se-vere tensions remain unresolved some five years after the interpersonal facilitation effort was undertaken.

An alternative set of assumptions for how interface prob-lem solving was dealt with in Consolidated Utilities a few years later is presented in the next chapter, which shows that the Interface Conflict-Solving Model was particularly well suited to resolving the problems in Consolidated Utilities. Generalizations regarding failures and successes in using this model are dis-cussed further in Chapter Ten.

A Comparison of the Two Approaches

A comparison of the two models is provided in Table 3, which identifies the main similarities and differences between them.

Sequence of Events

Each model can be characterized in terms of a probable sequence of events from beginning to end as the basis for com-paring the components of each of these two procedures. In both models, the groups are likely to begin by exploring hostile feel-ings and tensions toward each other. In the Interpersonal Facili-tator Model, this ventilation may inflame the other group. It does not do so in the Interface Conflict-Solving Model because the hostilities and tensions expressed are not heard by the other group. In the first case, ventilation comes through as an attack; in the second, it is little more than blowing off steam.

The Interpersonal Facilitator Model may continue with a description of the actual situation in which participants are al-ready locked. It seeks to identify ways of escaping from a bad

Table 3. Comparison of Two Approaches to Interface Conflict Resolving.

Points of Comparison	Interpersonal Facilitator Model	Interface Conflict- Solving Model
	Participants	
Who participates	Top leaders only or primarily	Top group plus representatives of major other constituencies
Contact between groups	Primarily through facilitator; informally	Through spokespersons in general sessions with group integrity maintained
Facilitator or administrator deals with	Leaders (and others) usually on a one-to-one basis	All as members of intact groups
	Issues	
Initial agenda	Perceived tensions and antagonisms	Identifying elements in an ideal or the soundest relationship
What is worked on	Exchange of entry positions re problems to be solved Separately, that is, one-to-one, facilitator or intermediary formulates proposals and counterproposals	The ideal relationship statements created on an element-by-element basis with consolidation through four-point program Monitoring and validation of process design
	Role of Expert	
Activities	Go-between Message carrier Spokesperson Solution proposer	Procedural design administrator Not spokesperson No content role Not solution proposer
Communication between groups	Message passing through facilitator Exchange of written positions	Exchanges through spokespersons, not necessarily leaders, both oral and written
Interventions when impasse reached	Influence members of group one-to-one, starting with easiest to persuade Use of acceptance and rejection to induce movement Fear-provoking remarks	Arranges for direct interchanges between groups through spokespersons

situation. The Interface Conflict-Solving Model continues with ideal thinking, allowing participants to consider what is possible; in this way it creates a framework of expectations to be realized.

The Interpersonal Facilitator Model is likely to shift into private discussions between principals, resulting in the other participants being kept in the dark or else being clued in later when it is more difficult for them to bring their influences to bear. In addition, the principals speak to each other directly, making it more difficult for others to know whether they are speaking from their own point of view only, or from the shared view of the other members. In the Interface Conflict-Solving Model, exchanges between groups are public, thus keeping everyone informed simultaneously. The spokesmen are not the designated leaders, thus ensuring that positions presented by spokespersons represent shared convictions.

In the Interpersonal Facilitator Model, the intermediary may seek to lessen tensions by separating principals and moving back and forth between them as a go-between. Agreements reached through the application of a facilitator model are more likely to be improvements within the status quo. The intermediary in the Interpersonal Facilitator Model takes responsibility for resolving differences by formulating proposals that may be more agreeable first to one side and then to the other. Since the principals only learn about what the other principal is thinking or how each is reacting through the intermediary, the intermediary is in a position susceptible to manipulation. He or she can withhold facts or place interpretation on facts or release facts in such a way as to produce agreement that may be repudiated when the facts later become known.

There is no intermediary in the Interface Conflict-Solving Model. A mechanism is provided for identifying areas of disagreement and agreement and for converting disagreement to agreement (the four-point method described earlier). Short of treachery, one group cannot mislead or deceive the other group. The changes agreed to are likely to replace the status quo with new concepts for working arrangements.

Given these similarities and differences, we can now give

attention to a most important question. When might the Inter-personal Facilitator Model be used and when is it preferable to use the Interface Conflict-Solving Model? A basic issue that might be posed to determine which model to employ is this: "Is this relationship characterized by misunderstandings, mutual distrust, or suspicion, or is it based on mutual respect with misunderstandings, if any, related to day-to-day operations?" If the former, consider *interface*; if the latter, *interpersonal.* Some additional guidelines for answering this question are provided in Table 4, where a comparison is made of when to use each model.

Table 4. A Comparison of When to Use the Two Models.

Use the Interpersonal Facilitator Model When:	Use the Interface Conflict-Solving Model When:
—only two people are involved.	—support of several people is critical to successful implementation of the change.
—personal chemistry blocks discussion between the principals, and others can contribute little or nothing to the resolution.	—all members must have a shared understanding as a condition for effective implementation of change.
—the issue of difference is important but arouses little or no emotions.	—the issue is important or unimportant, but change arouses strong emotions.
—once an agreement is reached, others can be brought around.	—others will feel sold out if they are not included.
—the leader's agreeing to change has no adverse consequences for his or her acceptability as leader.	—the leader's agreement to change places his or her leadership in jeopardy with those led.
—the agreed-on change requires little or no attitude shifting by members of the group.	—a change requires attitude shifting by both the leader and the membership.
—the leaders know the full depth and scope of the problem.	—the leaders cannot possibly know the full depth and scope of the problem.
—those responsible for implementing the change can be expected to do so on the basis of compliance or without agreeing to its soundness.	—those responsible for implementing the change can only be expected to do so by agreement and by understanding of its soundness.

(continued on next page)

Table 4. A Comparison of When to Use the Two Models, Cont'd.

Use the Interpersonal Facilitator Model When:	*Use the Interface Conflict-Solving Model When:*
—a deadline is near and decisions are necessary to prevent a total breakdown.	—participants can be expected to continue to solve the outstanding problems even when the Interface Conflict-Solving Model fails to improve the relationship.
—the outcome is expected to be intermediate between the initial positions of the protagonist groups.	—the outcome is expected to be less favorable to one group than to the other because the insight and logic of the model reduces the unacceptability of the loss.
—a multiplicity of views exists in both groups, and therefore there is no common voice.	—the interface problem is deeply embedded in the culture of both groups, and a decision by any one person is unlikely to be implemented in a committed way.

❦❧❦❧❦❧❦❧❦❧❦❧❦❧❦❧❦❧❦❧❦❧❦❧❦❧

CHAPTER 5

Establishing Cooperation Between Line and Staff: Use of the Interface Conflict-Solving Model

Since the underlying differences in Consolidated Utilities remained essentially as they had been prior to the efforts to relieve them through the Interpersonal Facilitator Model, the company decided that it would be worth a try to see if the relationship might be brought under resolution by the Interface Conflict-Solving Model. In describing what happened, this chapter provides an opportunity to compare the underlying assumptions and operations of the two models under circumstances in which the issues needing to be resolved are essentially the same.

Variations have been introduced into the standard Interface Conflict-Solving Model in its use in Consolidated Utilities. These alterations are worthy of particular attention because they demonstrate that while the model is systematic and coherent, it is anything but fixed and mechanical in its application. Several variations were used because of the frozen attitudes in the engineering group. The first was to combine the descriptions of the sound and actual, or unsound, relationship so that each group could better understand the tensions present in the other. This step was taken after the diagnosis indicated that a

significant gap existed between the perceptions of each group
regarding the desirability of preserving the existing relationship.
A second variation was to use the theater-in-the-round technique to demonstrate that one group understood the proposal
for a sound relationship made by the other before rejecting it as
unacceptable. This method was used when an impasse was
reached in attempting to reconcile the two vastly different descriptions of a sound relationship. This latter variation is of such
basic importance that it might be regarded as a recommended
step in the Interface Conflict-Solving sequence whenever it becomes self-evident that large discrepancies exist between the
two groups regarding the statements of what would constitute
a sound relationship. Without the variations that were introduced, it is probable that the Interface Conflict-Solving Model
might have been no more successful than the Interpersonal Facilitator Model.

Another aspect of this case might be emphasized because
of its unusual character. The outstanding underlying problem was
less one of trust and respect than is typical in the great majority
of cases and more one of the group with greater power wanting to
preserve its territory from invasion by the other. Rivalry at the
interface can also be a major cause of friction and conflict.

We can now return to the story of Consolidated Utilities
introduced in Chapter Four. Use of the Interpersonal Facilitator Model as described in that chapter lessened the intensity of
the interface tensions between central engineering and plant
management for awhile, but the underlying animosities remained much as they had been prior to that effort. Dissatisfied
with the situation, Merrill McFadden (chairman of the board)
contacted the next new vice-president of human resources, Fred
Burke, who had been advanced into his assignment on a rota-
tional basis, having spent much of his career in the power transmission department of the company.

Reevaluating the Situation

"Well, what do you think?" asked McFadden after reviewing the depth and scope of the problem with Burke by tele-
phone. "Is the situation still beyond repair without carting a

bunch of people out of this place and introducing a new set of actors, or can that process you've mentioned before produce results between these two?"

"I know you want me to say it's no use trying, Merrill," Burke began, "because you've lived with it so long. Yet I don't think you would want to ask me about something and just sit still and do nothing. But the truth is, it sounds like a conflict that runs along classical lines. Before reacting more specifically, let me ask a couple of questions."

"Go right ahead," replied McFadden. "I hope I can answer them."

"If it's a long-established problem, what other attempts have been made to overcome it?" Burke queried.

"Ten years ago, we had some utilities consultants in. They recommended a slight change in the structure of central engineering along with some reorganizations of various other departments. All the changes were introduced, but the fundamental difficulties between central engineering and the plants remained as frustrating as ever. Beyond that, about five years ago your predecessor, Bill Craig, had a series of meetings with the two heads, which resulted in the appointment of three engineers to serve as liaison persons in the plants. This helped from a troubleshooting point of view and by increasing the timeliness of response, but the fundamental cleavages remain.

"One more thing," McFadden added. "With changes introduced by the NRC [Nuclear Regulatory Commission] and EPA [Environmental Protection Agency], central engineering has had one of their key people meeting with plant managers and their staffs to explain regulatory requirements. He has used these occasions to explain how they can get the best possible engineering services when they file PEAs [proposals for engineering assistance]. I'm not sure he thinks so, but I've learned from others he did this in a pretty paternalistic manner, more or less telling the 'children' from the plants how to get their attention. I'm sure you know already that the way our procedures are set up, engineering is really in control. They can pocket veto any plant initiative on the basis of engineering requirements. This infuriates the plants. It's what triggered this call, as a matter of fact."

Burke replied, "Your remarks and answers fall in place. My conclusion is the problem is not a resource problem; it's not an absence of communication between central engineering and the plants; and it's not lack of functional coordination being provided by the liaison personnel. What's left when these possibilities are eliminated? It means the ways of work have become institutionalized and the attitudes associated with them have become embedded in Consolidated Utilities' culture. Central engineering seems to like and approve of the manner in which they're functioning even though there are chronic tensions on the plant side."

"It does seem that the plants are chomping at the bit for more opportunities and more responsibilities," McFadden concluded. "They want to do more than just set the dials and switches. They want to practice engineering and are doing so in an underground way. Central engineering has come to take on a police function, and thus their specialists are deeply concerned and complain whenever they discover that local engineering has been introduced in the plant or that retrofitting has occurred after they have completed a project. Central engineering further claims that the plant design now does not resemble the blueprints on file with them as additional proof that unauthorized engineering is being done locally. When the plants shift and make modifications without prior approval, engineering cannot be responsible, and yet it is held responsible for ensuring that plant design is in line with NRC and EPA regulations. The situation is a tug of war. Plant managers are pulling for more engineering freedom and autonomy, and central engineering is resisting giving any ground and constantly trying to take back territory that is being trampled on the sly."

Burke responded, "It sounds as though the conflict between engineering and the plants is serious, but by no means irresolvable. If members of departments are seeking a more permanent, long-lasting solution, a better meeting of minds between them should make it possible. There is another approach that really does help contending groups to dig out the assumptions that are embedded in their cultures and to explore how things might be changed to increase their contributions to the broader corporate interest."

"If we need both groups' commitment in order to make progress," said McFadden, "we may just waste our time by going any further. I know the plants recognize a problem, but let me repeat that engineering seems oblivious to the depth of frustration and resentment at the plant management level. They may drag their feet on any proposal to study the problem again if they think the structure is to be changed. Plant managers see themselves as blocked from doing anything constructive by a bewildering bureaucracy of forms, approvals, disapprovals, and legalistic language that differentiates 'engineering' from 'plant maintenance and operation.' "

"And how do the engineers see themselves, from your perspective?" Burke questioned. "Is the engineering vice-president as concerned about the problems as you are?"

"We've discussed the poor coordination and lack of cooperation between engineering and the plants in several recent meetings," McFadden answered, "so I know that both Edwards and Phillips, our engineering and power generation vice-presidents, are aware that the relationship between their groups isn't working well. We can count on their not standing in the way if we decide to proceed."

"With the acknowledgment of a problem," said Burke, "the effort has a chance of success, and I'd like to recommend we get Bob Blake and Jane Mouton involved."

McFadden agreed and Burke arranged with Blake and Mouton to begin with a diagnosis of where things stood in terms of the current relationship.

"I'd like to get in touch with Bill Craig and possibly the previous vice-presidents," suggested Blake, "and get their reading."

Mouton added, "Like you said, the problem's been around for forty-five years so it would be well to get the viewpoints of the key players on both sides and take a few days to really think through the best strategy to recommend."

"That'll be fine," Burke said. "Just get back in touch whenever you're ready with your recommendations, and we'll run them by McFadden."

When Blake and Mouton contacted Craig, he recounted the details of the Interpersonal Facilitator approach that he used five years earlier (see Chapter Four). Craig added his critique: "I've been a little out of touch for the past year, but I do think it did some good. The liaison engineers are partly interpreters, partly troubleshooters in the sense of tracking down problems causing delays. Sometimes they seem to operate as ombudsmen, taking a complaint from one side, delivering it to the other and often with corrective results. These shallow improvements didn't solve the deeper lying problem. We still have Taj Mahal engineering, which is too remote both in time and in place to be responsive to the real engineering needs the plants have. At the same time, we have professionally qualified engineers in the plants who feel constrained from employing their skills by a needlessly cumbersome bureaucracy.

"Since the cast of characters has changed at the top," Craig summarized, "you may find a new readiness, but I wouldn't count on it too much. I anticipated openness that simply wasn't there when we began to talk about real issues of professionalism, ownership, competency, and that sort of thing."

With much of what was learned from Craig having been confirmed by interviews with Lewis (former interplant coordinator) and Reeves (former vice-president of engineering), Blake and Mouton discussed their next steps with McFadden for studying the current problem with key personnel from both areas.

"From my experience," Blake said, "the most appropriate step is for Jane and me to meet with the members of both groups primarily to strengthen our understanding of specific core issues and the emotions and attitudes behind them."

"As we conduct our interviews, we'll be testing, refining, and tailoring the approach to help ensure a successful session if we have one," Mouton added. "The interviews will help us understand the problems and attitudes better and give us an opportunity to review the Interface Conflict-Solving Model with both groups to assess their readiness and commitment to take a step toward examining their relationship."

Within three days, Blake and Mouton had completed twelve in-depth interviews, six with central engineering staff and an equal number with plant managers. From the interviews, they learned that engineering staff reported feeling overworked and underappreciated. Although the engineers interviewed represented four major disciplines or divisions within central engineering, they expressed strikingly similar generalizations about the nature of the problem. They seemed to listen with little more than passing interest to the possibility of an interface development session. Without exception, each of the engineers reported, "We really don't know what all this fuss is about. Things around here are okay, and even though the plant managers may not think so, central engineering performs a valuable, in fact, indispensable service." Blake interpreted this to mean that the engineers accepted the existence of a problem only because plant management kept resisting the notion of a central engineering organization responsible for 100 percent of the engineering effort. "If plant managers would accept that," one engineer said, "barriers to collaboration could readily be solved."

"Look," one engineer emphasized, "we didn't make the rules, we just follow them. If plant managers don't like the way things are, that's their problem. As far as we're concerned, things are working just the way they should be. We're the engineering experts, so we do the engineering; they're the plant experts, so they run the plants. As long as our jobs are clearly defined and everyone sticks to what they're responsible for, we'll get along just fine."

From the interviews Blake and Mouton also learned that antecedents of the current conflict might substantially complicate the development effort. Each plant manager had a memory of a series of engineering deficiencies. Examples of poor engineering performance, "overengineering," and excessive engineering control were passed routinely from plant to plant, assuming the importance of lore and legend and the veracity of firsthand experience. Although each story was embellished with repetition, plant managers firmly believed the image of central engineering they had created.

Blake and Mouton sized up the situation as they saw it. The plant people had told them that the current relationship included: (1) stunted growth and development of themselves and others as engineers, (2) needless expenses, estimated on an annual basis in the neighborhood of $25 million, (3) "good" engineering that had to be fixed through back fitting to make it work after central engineering had left, and (4) double engineering standards—those authorized and official and those undertaken informally to make the plants operate.

The engineering groups found the present solution to the delivery of engineering services to be intellectually valid and morally right. They felt overworked and underappreciated. In some respects they saw themselves being set up by plant managers as the "fall guys" on whom all engineering problems could be blamed. They felt no reason to spend time exploring the problem except for the possibility that by explaining their rationale to the plant engineers *again,* they might gain increased understanding of why things were done as they were. They finally agreed to participate only because they knew that McFadden thought that a real problem existed and he wanted them to take another look. They acknowledged that tensions existed between the groups, but felt that the problem belonged not to them but to the plant group and that the real issue was to fix them.

Blake and Mouton reaffirmed their conclusion that the Interface Conflict-Solving Model was the best possibility remaining for bringing an end to this conflict. McFadden agreed to meet afterward to evaluate any recommendations that might require higher approval to implement if the sessions were successful. They also arranged for Fred Burke, vice-president of human resources, and Jill Jones, his assistant, to understudy the project.

The Beginnings of Reconstruction

The participants (see Figure 3) convened at a centrally located resort. The general session began with a brief review of the objectives for the session and the methodology to be employed to achieve them.

"It's been our experience," Blake began, "and behavioral science research supports the conclusion, that relationships be-

Figure 3. Consolidated Utilities Participants in the
Interface Conflict-Solving Model.

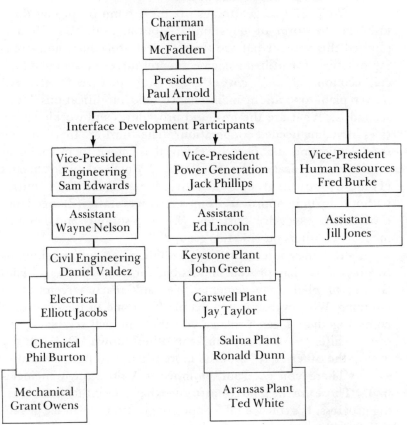

tween groups such as yours are often marred by conflict and
competition. To some degree, you've inherited whatever problems you're currently experiencing from the past. As we see it,
the character of your historical relationship—the traditions,
practices, habits, attitudes, and values you've become accustomed to—is determining what's happening in the present. In
the interface development session this week, two important
questions underlie the way we'll be asking you to work: Is it
possible to stop the flow of history and gain control of it? Can

logic, insight, and conviction replace the historical scenario of the past as the guide for the future?"

"We'd like to get things off the ground by posing three tasks in the form of questions," Mouton said. "The first is phrased this way: 'What are the soundest procedures and working practices for utilizing engineering resources in the most logical, economical, and cost-effective way relative to efficient power plant operation, maintenance, and modifications?' The second is, 'What are the unsound procedures and working practices impeding needed cooperation?' The third is, 'In what way should unsound practices be changed to make them sound or logical, economical, and cost effective? Which of these changes (1) are within this group's authority, responsibility, and control without further approval from executive staff; (2) need approval from executive staff; and (3) need support and commitment from others outside this group?' "

"If I may interrupt, Jane, I think what you're asking us to do is what has proven impossible for us to do," said Paul Greene of plant management. "We can't reach agreement on anything. Whenever any two people from one or the other side come together, I can promise you that one will see black, the other white. One will say 'up,' the other, 'down.' One will say 'right,' the other, 'left,' or, even more often, 'wrong.' "

"There you go, Paul," jumped in Valdez (civil engineering). "Those are the kinds of attitudes that prevent us from making progress. It's true we take opposite positions when we get together and it's true we battle. But the painful truth is that we in central engineering do have a broader or larger perspective, a greater in-depth knowledge of engineering requirements on a discipline-by-discipline point of view as well as from a design point of view. It's true we have experts on NRC and EPA, etcetera. The unfortunate truth from your point of view, I guess, is that when we say right, we're right. When we say wrong to you, we are correct in saying you're wrong."

"Just a second," Blake interrupted. "We know from what we've been told in the interviews that both of you are describing truths about central engineering and plant managers. The difficulty is that by perpetuating these attitudes, as is happening here and now, it only serves to harden the conviction that problem-solving cooperation is impossible. What we would like is to ask you to curb these remarks. We know you feel them and you live with these underlying tensions every day. One of our goals is to see what can be done to reverse these attitudes and to create a spirit of cooperation. So, we'd like to ask you to 'knock 'em off.' I know that you're only doing what comes naturally, and it's fully understandable you feel the compulsion to speak out forcefully with one another. So, we'd like to ask your cooperation in repealing these 'natural' acts for the next few days. It's okay to act unnaturally.

"To ensure that the agreements reached here this week can be operationalized," Blake added, "McFadden and Arnold have been asked to join us for Friday's session. At that time, there'll be ample opportunity to discuss with them whatever conclusions that have been reached, review any agreements reached between yourselves, and outline any proposed course of action."

"But, Bob, I don't think that's a good move," interjected Jacobs (electrical engineering). "It puts us in a corner. That puts all of us under terrific pressure to come to some kind of agreement and we're likely to reach agreements we don't believe in just so we won't have to report failure to McFadden and Arnold."

"Well, you may be right about that, Jacobs," Blake answered. "Let's look at it another way. We have indicated in our talks with McFadden and Arnold that the minimum likely outcome from these sessions is that the two groups come to trust and respect one another. There is distrust at the present time, amply demonstrated in the interviews as well as a few moments ago. Beyond that, however, nothing in terms of promised accomplishment has been suggested. They know it's a tough problem, we know it's a tough problem, and you know it's a tough problem. All that can be asked of the two groups is that they give it an honest shot. Is that okay, Jacobs or anyone else?"

"Yes, that's okay with me. I think it's okay with us," said Taylor (Carswell plant). "I'm eager to get into this thing."

"I've got a question," Valdez (civil engineering) stated. "Are we to respond to the issues based on the way we feel personally or with respect to our corporate roles and responsibilities?"

"As we see it," Mouton answered, "the task is to answer the questions without any restraints, either from the past or present."

"Then everything we do now is fair game, right?" asked Taylor.

"No way," Nelson (engineering) interrupted. "We don't have the authority here to change company policy. All we need is a better way of working within prearranged constraints and limitations."

"I don't buy that," said Dunn (Salina plant). "It's already been agreed we would make recommendations to improve our working relationships and can include ones that are present constraints and yet can be removed by someone at a higher level."

"The ultimate objective," Mouton reminded, "is to design a sound future relationship just as if today were the first day of your corporate lives. A sound, viable future relationship may or may not resemble the relationship you have now, but either way, you're free to think and express yourself in ideal terms, based on convictions, not position. If policies and procedures now preclude optimal productivity and effectiveness, perhaps those policies should be changed. Where these groups lack the authority to change established practices, they can point out these problems in group reports to Arnold and McFadden on Friday for their consideration."

Later, in private, Burke posed a question: "Why did you give them the task of describing the sound relationship and the unsound relationship at the same time? As I recall, in other situations where you have used this model, you utilized a two-step sequence of describing first optimal and then the actual relationship rather than doing both at the same time."

"Well," Mouton said, "Bob and I reviewed our interviews with both groups. We felt that the sound and unsound relationships, as described by the central engineers, would be more or less the same as exists now with little or no unsound practices in existence—not that minor irritations might not be identified, but they certainly would be trivial. By comparison, we know the plant group feels that a very large discrepancy exists between what would be sound and the current practices, which they feel are pretty much unsound. We thought it would be significant to the success of the effort for the central engineering group to be faced with the large discrepancy at the earliest possible time in the sessions rather than simply allowing them to reaffirm the validity of present arrangements."

"But there are other circumstantial reasons, too," said Blake. "Both of these groups have been extensively involved in Grid Organization Development; therefore, they are familiar with working without an outside leader in their groups, dealing with a given task in a manner that they have been experienced with in the past, and so on. In other words, we felt the mechanics were quite well known and understood by both groups and therefore the more complicated task seemed not only to provide a possible early confrontation to central engineering but also to be well within their competence for how to handle it in an effective manner."

Central Engineering's View

The engineering group quickly ratified the status quo and summarized its main properties under the soundest formulation. Under the unsound list, they placed practices that "should not exist" if the plant managers were to live up to the current assignment of keeping engineering work solely in central engineering. They decided to discuss among themselves why they drew so much antagonism from the plant personnel. In other words, the effort was to try to establish clearly in their own minds what was wrong with "them."

"Plant management seems to have the perception," Burton acknowledged, "that engineering bounds aren't defined—that there's no clear, consistent definition of what engineering is and isn't. I think that's a big part of the problem. This constant argument about what engineering is and is not caused me to go out and get the book by Korzybski called *Science and Sanity*. I think he's got a point. We've split one whole operation calculated to produce electricity into two parts: one we call central engineering—they are the planners—and the other we call plant management—they are the doers. We've never been able to agree on how or at what point in the *total* operation the split should be. I never thought I'd be reading a book on philosophy to find out how to do engineering. It's no engineering handbook. It's almost Greek to me; it's on Aristotelian logic. That's where the idea of splits comes from—of splitting things apart and then putting them together again. I guess I'm going to have to keep digging."

"Hey, Burton, knock off this philosophy bit. Let's get back to common sense. We're engineers," said Jacobs.

"The doers want a piece of the planning action and we want to retain 100 percent of planning responsibility," replied Burton, "but interestingly enough we're not eager to share the doing. 'Let the doers do' is our motto. But this split between planning and doing is what causes so much trouble everywhere. We know that if we let them do just a little planning, they'll want to do more, and if we let them, soon enough our work will be strictly limited to the NRC-EPA stuff and we don't want to be confined to that. So we hold on to this rigid planning-doing split, and that's what seems to keep everyone in a constant state of agitation."

"Sure enough, the split causes difficulties, but without the split, we'd be in greater difficulty. Not all engineers can plan and not all engineers can operate. It's a functional separation of unique abilities. I think our problem is to refine and sharpen the split. The ultimate would be central engineering does 100 percent of engineering and plant management does 100 percent of operations. Then there's a clear definition and no confusion, and we can move forward in harmony," proposed Valdez. "It's not a 98-2 or a 95-5 split; it's a 100-0, 0-100."

"Well, what's the confusion?" remarked Nelson. "Anytime a plant manager initiates an engineering activity, we're responsible. That's the way things are—and the way they *should* be! That's a sound definition of the relationship."

"But as engineers," Edwards commented, "we see ourselves as solving people's problems on paper. If somebody in a plant has a leaky faucet, all he knows is he's got a problem, and all he wants is a solution—the leak stopped. People in the plant couldn't care less about the design of a better system on paper. If you need to replace a faucet, that's an engineering problem, but if you need to replace a washer, that's a maintenance problem. In the latter case, maintenance is plumbing, but if you replace a faucet you may be confronted with changes in water pressure, relocation of pipes, and so on. That's not plumbing, that's engineering."

"As far as I'm concerned," Owens observed, "engineering is bounded by those things defined in the various codes, and that's simple enough. The problem I see is that there's no procedure in this company to ensure standardization among plants. That's an unsound practice and a big problem. Be sure to get that one up."

"It's not that there aren't guidelines or procedures," Burton countered, "it's just that the plant managers don't feel obliged to abide by them. They pride themselves in being unique— different. They won't make the effort to do things by the book."

"You're right," said Nelson. "The problem of uniformity and standardization in the plants is like states rights in politics. Each plant sees itself as a state, and managers feel that they have been granted states rights to operate with considerable independence and autonomy. It's a matter of prestige, to do things their own way, in their own plant."

"Maybe we ought to write down that there's no enforcement of prescribed uniformity among plants," Jacobs suggested. "They're given too much authority by management. I've got a good example, too," Jacobs continued. "We put single phase electricity in three plants in a row and had a very good system going. The fourth plant we went to wanted three phase, just because. They could have used single phase, but they just wanted to be different."

"It's clear that we need centralized standards," Edwards agreed, "but what often happens is that we get so involved in defining what projects require central engineering support and determining who calls the shots that poor decisions are made. Take the Carswell plant, for example, where we installed two

100 percent turbine plant-cooling pumps. What the plant manager wanted was 100 percent capacity all the time, so engineering decided to put in two pumps with 100 percent capacity,
each acting as backup to the other. The plant says we made a
costly mistake—that two pumps, each with 60 percent capacity
would have worked just as well. And if we'd studied the problem objectively, and looked at the tolerance of the pumps, I
think we'd have found that the pumps could be pushed to 100
percent capacity if one or the other went down, and so the
plant managers were technically right."

"You've got a point," agreed Owens. "Between us we
can agree on what gravity is, but we can't agree on what we
mean by 100 percent pump cooling. I think one of their real
gripes is that we're not responsive to them. Rather than just taking a PEA that says give me another pump, we take their need
for a pump and prescribe something entirely different. We don't
go to them to find out what their real needs are."

"I'm not going to argue that point," Valdez conceded,
"so long as we remember why an engineering department is
needed. With the changes and developments in new technology
and materials, a centralized engineering function is critical. The
system we have now provides the best use of Consolidated Utilities' technically competent resources."

"We just can't afford to rely on plant management when
the demands of sophisticated technical expertise are becoming
greater than ever before. Let's get that point down on paper before we go on," said Owens. "Write up there under *Soundest
Practices,* 'Central engineering provides the best use of available
technically competent resources.' "

"Yes," said Valdez, " 'and without duplication of effort'
—that's a sound split."

The flavor of this discussion shows that the engineering
department was satisfied with the way in which the engineers
provided resources to the plants. They continued to review
sound practices performed by central engineering in terms of
providing a system of checks and balances, ensuring uniformity
across plants, being able to keep up with regulatory changes and
new developments, and so on, as indications of their professional

contribution to the company. Unsound practices revolved primarily around the fact that plant managers were engaging in plant modification without securing engineering approval and doing so in a manner that hid their activities. The engineers continued to believe that if plant management would just live by the lines drawn on the organization chart and set down in the manual of procedures everything would be okay.

Table 5. Central Engineering's View of Sound and Unsound Practices.

Sound Practices	Unsound Practices
1. Division of engineering responsibility between the plants and central engineering is sound, that is, all "engineering" is done by central engineering.	1. Plant managers get involved in engineering on a plant-by-plant basis in disregard of the need for standardized procedures.
2. Accountability for plant management activities is well defined.	2. Plant managers do not always know regulations and therefore fail to meet them.
3. Central engineering provides the best use of available, technically competent resources with duplication of effort avoided.	3. Outside contractors sometimes receive disparate treatment; plant managers cannot adequately estimate expenditures where complex engineering is required.
4. Central engineering provides a system of checks and balances to ensure safety, compliance with applicable regulations, and equity in contracting for outside resources.	4. Lack of uniformity among power plants because bootleg design work done in plants.
5. Design practices are uniform throughout Consolidated Utilities.	

Plant Management's View

"If you look at the instances of overengineering, Valdez is almost always responsible," commented Greene.

"I agree. Anything Valdez touches is overengineered," Taylor echoed.

"Remember my water cooler?" White asked. "All I wanted was to put the refrigerator next to the water cooler, but engineering got involved in running the wiring. Because the water cooler was within a few feet of the control box, they wanted a major structural overhaul to shore up the electrical conduits of the building. Their report to headquarters, remember? They warned Arnold that in the event of a seismic-level earthquake, the refrigerator *might* fall over, hit and break the water cooler, get water in the control box and short out the wiring. . . . They'll never live that one down."

"It's really a case of needing a Band-Aid," Greene quipped, "and getting open heart surgery. We're responsible for the patient's performance, but we can't choose our treatment; we don't even get to sign the okay sheets authorizing the surgery. Malpractice, that's what I call it!

"And when they are involved, the pain level is so high that their help just isn't worth it. Their PEA must have 476 boxes, hoops, and hurdles. I've put on extra people just to process the paperwork."

"Well," said Lincoln, "one of our problems is we just sit around and complain to one another and not to engineering."

"I agree," Phillips nodded. "There's no good system for follow-up. When engineering does a job for us, they almost never know whether or not we're satisfied, except by accident. Instead of helping them get better, we let them go on making the same mistakes over and over."

"You've got a point," Dunn conceded, "but it sure would help if they'd do the job right to begin with. They designed the turbine deck so slippery that with one drop of oil on it, our people could break their necks."

"But we know how to fix that problem," Lincoln countered, "and all we do is complain about it."

"Maybe so," Taylor asserted, "but it's not our job to do engineering. It's their deck, not our deck. If they want the whole pie, then let them be responsible for consequences. I have plenty to worry about if I just do what I'm supposed to."

"As I see it," Greene offered, "the only thing central engineering does is run up our costs and slow down our operations. Every capital item over $10,000 needs their approval, and frankly I don't see the necessity. What do they know that my engineers don't know? 'Central' doesn't mean 'brilliant,' and 'plant' doesn't mean 'stupid.' In fact, what do they know that we don't? We're all engineers by profession, and while we may not be up on the very latest developments, we certainly know more than enough to determine what our plants need. As a matter of fact, we're overtrained."

"That's the way I feel," White said. "I remember how it was when plant managers had the final say over their own operations over at Aransas. We didn't need some pedigreed professional pencil pusher to tell us what we couldn't do. We sure moved a lot faster then, and we got things done just as well or better without all the fancy formalities and procedures that we have to live under here."

"About the only thing I can say for them," Dunn admitted, "is that they really have been responsible whenever I've had a major problem or emergency. When it comes to a catastrophe-type thing, they're tops. If routine could be handled as smoothly and efficiently as the extraordinary, there'd be no problem."

Missing Dunn's point entirely, Greene said, with a hint of sarcasm, "If we didn't have central engineering at all, we wouldn't have a problem either."

After a moment's silence, Dunn said, "We've got enough already to get started on our newsprints. What do you want to put up? I'll write whatever you want. We could do both sheets at once, okay?"

Phillips started: "I'd say that plant managers should have the initiative and decide when and when not to involve central engineering, particularly on modification and certainly on repair items. How about that for a starter? They ought to be a staff service, and their services ought to be made available on request."

"You know," White said, "they'll say the exact opposite. They'll say we can't see the forest for the trees. Forest means NRC, EPA, and God knows what else while trees mean water coolers, slippery decks, and air conditioning ducts."

"Then why can't we put down as an unsound practice,

'Central engineering retains ultimate authority to tell us every-thing but how to set the dials and switches'—and even then, they set the limits," Taylor proposed.

"That's pretty good going," Greene pondered. "I like that. It's the old 'who's got the ultimate say' thing, and we've got no meeting of minds between us and them." Table 6 sum-marizes the discussion.

Table 6. Sound and Unsound Practices According to
Plant Management.

Sound Practices	Unsound Practices
1. Plant managers having option of when and how to involve outside resources in engineering activities.	1. Central engineering has public- and pocket-veto power over all capital expenditures.
2. Central engineering's respon-siveness to plant managers' re-quests for crisis or emergency assistance is excellent, that is, they are able to circumvent channels and cut through red tape in a quick and responsible manner.	2. Plant managers have no options —central engineering must re-view and approve even the smallest items.
	3. Exclusive use of central engi-neering runs up construction and related costs, due to over-engineering and poor reviews of outside consultants.
	4. Central engineering is not re-sponsible to plant managers, who can accept or reject the final product.
	5. Plant managers set higher stan-dards when central engineering does a job than if and when we do it ourselves.
	6. Procedures for obtaining engi-neering assistance are too cum-bersome.
	7. Central engineering keeps stan-dards under cover and doesn't let us have them to do our own checks.

Putting Problems in Order of Significance

When the groups convened to present the separately developed descriptions of sound and unsound practices, the question arose of who would begin. "Heads it's engineering," Blake suggested.

"Could you turn that around? That's the way it's been. That's the problem we're trying to solve," came a voice from the plant manager group amid chuckles of laughter.

Mouton quipped, "We don't want to pin the tail on the central engineers either, so is there some mechanism of fate other than the coin?"

The engineering spokesperson, Burton, stood and addressed the plant management group. "We'll go first," he said. With little embellishment, Burton summarized central engineering's conclusions.

Next, Taylor presented the plant managers' analysis, commenting on each major point as he went. In explaining plant management's view of central engineering's responsiveness to emergencies or crises, Taylor remarked, "When we've really got to get something done in an emergency, we can call the liaison engineer, say the magic words, and he short-circuits the system and gets us immediate response. We'd like that same kind of service as a matter of routine."

"Then why don't you use the emergency route more often?" asked Burton.

"If we cry wolf once or twice," Taylor answered, "we're afraid you'll stop responding to our real emergencies. It's not that you people won't give us the help we need, it's just that there's such a high price to pay for it."

"We need some flexibility," Taylor summarized at the conclusion of his presentation. "As plant managers, we have authority to spend $500,000 or more on operations or maintenance, but we can't authorize $10,000 if it involves 'engineering.' That's the trouble with the definition of 'engineering.'"

Mouton said, "That gives us the overview of the two sets

of conclusions regarding sound and unsound practices for the fullest possible effective use of engineering resources. Before we take another next step, I wonder if there are any questions for clarification. Let's spend a few minutes around each table to find out what each group wants to ask the other through Taylor and Burton."

After a brief group conference, Burton began. "We'd like to have a better understanding of what you mean by the remark, 'That's the trouble with the definition of engineering.' I think we're pretty clear, and we really don't know what the trouble is. Any design work is engineering."

Taylor responded: "I can give you an example that we discussed earlier in our group of the way we have to bend the meaning of engineering to fit the practical reality of getting on with the job. One of us described what happened when his plant wanted to change a two-inch pipe for a three-inch pipe for carrying steam on the auxiliary line. Central engineering put an outside contractor on the job, and his design was going to cost us $80,000. We told them we decided not to do the project, then bootlegged it later as a repair just to get you out of our hair. The problem keeps coming through to us as a rejection of our intelligence. All too often, though, we recognize that it's related to remoteness. You substitute a product of inferior quality that gives us a second-rate solution when we could have had a first-rate product. Anything else we can clarify?"

"Yes," said Burton. "It's related to the pocket-veto item. We don't approve or disapprove your budget. That's done upstairs. Why do we have a pocket veto?"

Taylor said, "There are two ways you cancel something that you don't think should be done. One way is to sit on it long enough. The deadline for budget review for one year passes and we have to wait until the next. By then, we look for another way or say 'to hell with it.' The other way is to price it out of existence. As an example, one of us wanted to build a little shed to cover a motor that was just sitting out in the open getting wet. The central engineering people said the shed would have to take the force of a hurricane so that it wouldn't blow away. We could have just gone down to Ted's Sheds and bought a simple aluminum building, but engineering wouldn't let that be done. The elegant structure was too much for our yearly budget so we chose not to build it. So now the $300,000 motor is rusted, and pretty soon, it'll have to be replaced. Any more questions?"

At this point, Mouton asked the groups to meet separately again to review one another's lists of sound and unsound practices and to identify the five most significant questions about their relationship. After an hour's consideration, the groups reconvened to reach agreement on the priority items interfering with a healthy, productive interface and needing further study if any significant improvement in their relationship was to be achieved.

Dunn presented the plant managers' list of priority items first, without comment; next Valdez gave the engineering presentation. Then Mouton asked whether there were issues of clarification, and each queried the other's items. It was relatively easy to get beneath the symptoms and examples that inflamed the relationship and to pose the four neutral questions in the following list as pinpointing the core issues.

1. At what level of risk/difficulty will central engineering rather than plant management become involved in the engineering of the job and who will make that decision?
2. What is the problem with plant managers doing "engineering" and central engineering having an adequate review (not veto) and appeal process?
3. How can central engineering streamline our procedures to better match the technical needs of the plants?
4. How do we make sure projects are taken to completion and there is acceptance by the operating group?

"The first and second questions are essentially different ways of phrasing the same issue," said Blake. "The third question is probably unanswerable until the first two are dealt with. The fourth question is also intertwined with the other three since it relates to the same issues but at the end of the sequence. That is, when has engineering 'completed its engineering' and when should the plant assume responsibility for what engineering has provided? Viewed in this way, all four statements come back to a central question: 'How could engineering resources be mobilized and applied in the interest of optimal plant operations?' "

"Bob, I don't think we're any further ahead than we were when we came," commented Nelson. "You have just asked the $64,000 question."

"That is the $64,000 question," replied Blake. "But it's no longer under the table. It's out in public view. Tomorrow and the day after activities can be oriented toward resolving these issues. It seems that an appropriate place to start would be with each group answering the question that has received the highest priority for discussion: 'At what level of risk/difficulty will central engineering rather than plant management become involved in the engineering of a job and who will make that decision?' "

Solving the Key Relationship Issue

Both groups convened early the next morning, apparently ready to go to work. Engineering started from a premise of 100 percent responsibility for central engineering, essentially rehashing their earlier arguments. They explained how plant management should operate based on zero engineering by plant engineers. The positions developed by the two groups were still 180° apart.

Engineering's Discussion

"Let's examine the statement of the dilemma very carefully," urged Valdez. "I don't see that we have any choice here but to endorse the existing mandate under which we currently operate as sound and correct."

"That's right," Nelson confirmed. "Engineering is engineering and it should be done in the engineering department. It's just that simple to me, and I think we need to make it clear to plant management."

"But don't you think there are ways we can use their expertise in the plants?" asked Edwards.

"The real crux here," Jacobs asserted, "is not that they want a share of the engineering responsibilities—they want to run away with the whole thing."

"They're bright, ambitious people," Burton agreed, "and they understandably feel that they are competent to do their own engineering, but there's no way we can operate effectively as an organization with each plant essentially doing it's own thing. I tell you, give them an inch . . . and what? The game is over. We'll all be reassigned to the plants, not just the liaison resident engineers."

"Besides," Owens noted, "a centralized department has a much broader perspective and an obviously higher degree of technical expertise than any plant can possibly have."

"We also know more about the standards and codes and can keep up with the constant changes and amendments," added Valdez. "No plant engineer has that kind of detailed knowledge. Because that kind of knowledge is essential, each plant will begin to expand, and soon each will have small engineering departments with four disciplines, and maybe not so small, rather than one strong central engineering department. To release any responsibility for engineering to the plants would be the heights of stupidity."

"I know we're rehashing the same old stuff, but the logic is inescapable. We have a centralized engineering function," said Nelson, "so that plant managers can concentrate on their basic mission without their attention being diverted from their main game to our main game. What would happen is that we'd have the worst of both possible worlds. No, no, it just couldn't work. It's really beyond me that plant managers can't see how much time and work we save them. It's so ironic to hear them say we take more time away than we provide."

"It's like the airline industry, if you really look at it," Jacobs noted. "Airline pilots don't modify their airplanes, they just fly them. Why can't the plant managers be that reasonable?"

"Let's remember that plant managers are power-driven

people," Owens offered. "It's just as natural for them to want to expand their empires by incorporating engineering as their responsibility and having it report to them as it is for frogs to come out when it rains."

"I'd say the plant managers display a traditional 'macho' mentality regarding risk," said Burton. "They do have some engineering skills, and when there's a lull in their operation, maybe they get interested in doing some engineering. The problem comes when they can't separate a risk-taking attitude from management situations where it's appropriate to engineering situations where it's not."

"And just because someone is willing to jump out of an airplane at 10,000 feet doesn't mean it's the soundest thing to do," Jacobs stated.

"You know," said Valdez, "I know they think I'm a purist, but I tell you plant managers are a bunch of short-cut artists. Give up 1 percent of engineering and you open up Pandora's box. And what do you find? Dangerously engineered projects. I'm telling you, the greatest risk is to give them any responsibility for engineering. I don't think I overengineer, but I'd a hell of a lot rather overengineer than underengineer."

"Let me intervene here for a moment," Mouton said, "to describe an experiment that might have some pertinence to what you're doing. It concerns a propaganda study conducted by the armed forces. The study focused on how to get people to change their minds when they held strong convictions. The experimenters developed a position they wanted people to adopt, then prepared different messages. One message was what's called one-sided propaganda, where only the advantages of adopting the position were proposed. The other was called two-sided propaganda where the pros and cons of the desired position were presented, but there were more pros than cons. The interesting finding was that which message was more successful depended upon the educational level of the recipients. The people who had less than a high school education were much more persuaded by just a one-sided message. People who had more than a high school education, that is, college level, were much more likely to be convinced when they saw both sides of the issue discussed in the presentation."

"What you're trying to tell us," said Edwards, "is that we're making a one-sided propaganda message."

"Well, it's something you might want to consider."

"You're probably right," Owens conceded. "Let's try looking at the issue from the other side."

"Maybe centralized engineering is so ingrained in our thinking," Jacobs suggested, "that we can't see any other option. We might need to seriously reexamine our assumptions that central engineering is right just because it's so."

In response to this plea by Jacobs for greater objectivity, central engineering added to their list the disadvantages of central engineering presented in Table 7. Try as they might to look

Table 7. Central Engineering's Perspective.

Advantages of Central Engineering		Perceived Difficulties by Plant Management	
1.	Duplication of effort is avoided.	1.	Not responsive to individually perceived priorities.
2.	Uniform standards are maintained.	2.	Little jobs take too long and little jobs cost too much.
3.	Budget accountability is preserved.	3.	Corporate meddling—pocket-veto power.
4.	Responsibility for engineering is pinpointed.	4.	Communication difficulties.
5.	A central department has a broad perspective across all engineering disciplines.	5.	Corporate design standards are inflexible, that is, plant managers don't want a Cadillac when a Honda three-wheeler is all they requested.
6.	A consistently high level of expertise is available, that is, up to date regarding code knowledge, and so on.	6.	The engineering department just doesn't understand their operating problems.
7.	Aids plant management to keep their attention on operations.		
8.	A clearing house for knowledge of problems in various plants and solutions that may apply to all plants.		
9.	It provides sound checks and balances against unsound engineering practices.		

at the other side, the end result was a further reinforcement of the position they already had embraced. Note that their discussion of the benefits derived from central engineering took three and one-half hours, seven times longer than their thirty-minute exploration of potential disadvantages.

Plant Managers' Discussion

When the plant managers convened, it was apparent that they wanted to complete the project, but they apparently had little confidence that it would have much effect on the ultimate way in which engineering was undertaken in Consolidated Utilities. The first few minutes were dull. It was difficult to find a way of moving productively into the discussion. Finally, Greene said, "Look, let's do it, let's make a stab at it this way. Let's take some project we all are familiar with, one that's within the scope of our own plant capabilities. Let's find one that's irritating because of the manner in which it's being done. If we can find a problem that meets those criteria, then we can track through how we think it should be done."

"I'll give you one to try on for size," said Taylor. "Building a paint shed. I need a paint shed right now. We have the new standards with regard to the maintenance of equipment and facilities, and we have been requisitioning paint from warehousing but we don't have any place to put it. So we have a can here, a can there, and a can elsewhere. We got some of the cans stacked out in the open. It's a mess. It takes away from housekeeping. We lose track of various paints, so we overstock. When we get ready to do something we find we're understocked. It's a mess. If we had a paint shed, we could gather the materials necessary for doing a paint job whenever we assign personnel to that, and we could be orderly and productive."

Dunn interrupted, "I know, and if you put a paint shed in your budget, the plans would have to be drawn by engineering. They would build it in such a way as to make a sizable dent in your next year's capital budget. But I can give you my word that it would stand up through the next tornado, the next hurricane, the next earthquake, the next volcanic eruption. It would be built on piles driven ten feet into the ground with double heavy steel reinforcements.''

"The foundation would cost five times more than the facility would be worth to me," said Taylor. "I'd rather not worry with it than to suffer the frustration of getting them to do it. I could go to Sears and solve it in an hour."

"Well, that sounds like a pretty good project then."

"Let's take a crack at it. What's the first step in an ideal model?"

Greene replied, "The first step is for the plant manager to initiate a description of what is needed."

"And run out a projected budget," Taylor added. "Then he would know what he wanted and what he thinks it would cost."

"Okay, let's go on," Lincoln ventured. "There are a few other things he might have to do, like getting prices and so on, but let's identify the second step. What would happen next, if we had the option of either doing the design and construction of the paint shed ourselves or asking them to do it?"

"I can imagine," said Greene, "that we would send the description to central engineering for them to evaluate whether regulatory considerations are involved and for them to inform us about whatever codes and standards are applicable for this kind of construction. After all, we don't have access to reference manuals. They could provide this to us almost as a librarian provides books to a reader."

"Yes," agreed Dunn. "They could provide us a package of relevant data regarding needed specifications."

"Hey, I like that," piped up Taylor.

A rising enthusiasm among the plant managers could be detected as they began to see a feasible model for assuming responsibilities themselves and yet consulting with and gaining the advantages that a central engineering organization can provide. A ray of light broke through the clouds of despair.

"Afterwards," Greene said, "we could test whether we have the engineering resources locally to design and supervise the job. What this tells me is that if we didn't, we'd route the project to engineering with a PEA. If we did want to do it, we'd work up the specifications in terms of local engineering and their package and route it to them for their review and approval."

"Hey, that really is brilliant," said White. "You know what it does? It permits us to do the things we have the resources for. It gives them a review that ensures uniformity of standards. It's obvious that none of us are so overmanned with engineering talent that we'd be able to do more than just the small types of things anyway. Furthermore, the kinds of things we could do are the problems they find dull and they dilly-dally on."

"That's terrific. It provides a way of integrating central engineering standards with local initiative. It truly does have the potential of optimizing engineering resources," Dunn concluded.

From this, the group developed a flow chart that eventually showed each of the major decision steps through which such a project would pass and what the interplay would be between central engineering and plant management for deciding at each point who should retain responsibility for carrying the project to completion.

Having seen the possibilities with regard to a small project where the ultimate responsibility remains within the plant, the next step was to take a major project and test how it would work on the same flow chart. They walked through a project involving the installation of a new generator. This project involved considerations regarding location, the electrical systems that came from the generator, transmission of the electricity produced into the network, and so on. It quickly became apparent that a project of this magnitude was the sole responsibility of central engineering to design and execute. The plant did not have the disciplines needed in any depth, to say nothing of labor resources for carrying it out. In a test of this project against the flow chart, a couple of additional loops were introduced that enabled a decision to be made quickly that the plant had no business concerning itself with the engineering for such a major undertaking. The flow chart idea became an important aspect of the next joint session.

Joint Discussion of Each Group's Proposed Solution

The joint discussion was begun by Nelson's review of the fifteen-point summary of advantages and perceived difficulties that led to the conclusion that the current 100 percent central engineering system was sounder than a plant-by-plant engineering approach.

Nelson continued, "We examined the weaknesses and complaints that have been brought up leading to the conclusion: The formula is valid, but we acknowledge the legitimacy of some of the complaints about central engineering relative to pocket veto and flexibility, assignment of priorities to big and little projects, and so on. We do find instances in which each of these complaints are justified. We propose to try to improve our relationship by reexamining what we may be doing that reduces the effectiveness of the liaison engineer and by concentrating our attention on what we can do and what you can help us do to eliminate these complaints.

"After all," Nelson paused, "central engineering knows the history, construction, and operation of each plant from a design orientation. We think the company's engineering activities are much safer in the hands of experts than with people who only do engineering as a hobby."

Though no one from plant management offered a rebuttal, it was clear that they deeply resented the hobby definition placed on their engineering activities. At the same time, one could observe smiles and winks between various plant managers as they foresaw how the flow chart would resolve the difficulty regarding plant participation.

Mouton suggested that the members of each group talk among themselves and review what they had just heard in order to give plant management an opportunity to share and digest their reactions to the engineering proposal and to give the engineers a chance to critique their presentation before moving on to consider the plant solution.

The tone of the engineering group was one of victory. Valdez said, "I think we really got the point through. They didn't have a single question."

Burton added, "You did a masterful job, Nelson, of making that presentation. If we ever need a voice in headquarters, I hope they'll send you."

By comparison, the plant managers' discussion was of quite a different character. The gist of it was caught in the following comment.

"If that's the kind of improvement in the relationship that they are prepared to offer," came the comment from White, "we're in a lot of trouble."

"Those guys really don't understand us," complained Taylor. "They're out of it as far as our problems and needs are concerned. Frankly, I'm not sure we'll ever be able to agree on what's best for all of us as long as their primary concern in engineering is protecting their turf and building their empire."

"They want to put salve on the itching skin oblivious to the underlying infection that is spreading throughout the plant management body," added Greene.

After these internal group discussions, the general session exchange was continued.

"We've depicted our proposal in this flow chart," said Lincoln. (See Figure 4.) "Basically, what we're saying is that it's possible to simplify our current procedures, make some needed changes in the way we look at engineering, give the plants greater flexibility, and still retain engineering quality and regulatory compliance." Lincoln walked through the flow chart. "Any questions?"

"But what about company policy?" Valdez insisted. "We don't have the authority to redefine engineering or to challenge headquarters' procedures on capital expenditures."

Lincoln answered, "We think it's a sound recommendation anyway. If headquarters studies the proposal, it'll be seen as a solution for mobilizing engineering resources, not as a rejection of the centralized approach. At every major decision-making point on engineering issues, we've built in your review and approval. We're merely suggesting that plant engineers be authorized to do the jobs they've been trained for, with full review and consultation and checks and balances. When something comes up that we can't handle, the flow chart automatically throws the problem into central engineering."

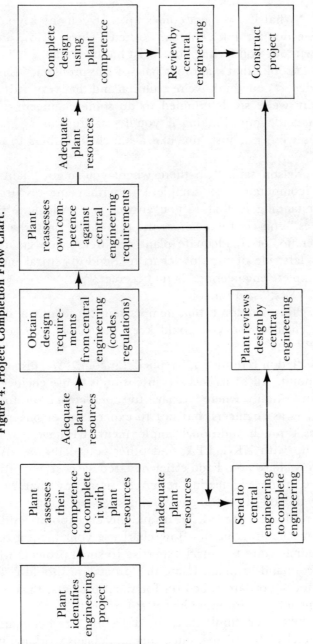

Figure 4. Project Completion Flow Chart.

"What if a project comes up that you think you can do, but we don't think you can?" asked Valdez. "How do we say 'no' without you feeling your wrist has been slapped?"

"Look, that's another part of the problem," Lincoln responded. "You think we're children and that very attitude may be why we're so determined to do some engineering. We can understand your thinking if you'll just trust us as equals and tell us why, not just 'no' like a bunch of fathers to us dumb kids."

Nelson said, "Up there where you've got 'Plant assesses their competence to complete it with plant resources,' my understanding is that if you answer yes—'Adequate plant resources,' you continue across the top of the flow chart. If you answer no, or 'Inadequate plant resources,' you go down the lower left side of the flow chart to 'Send to central engineering to complete engineering.' Is that correct?"

"Yes," said Lincoln.

"But wouldn't that tempt you to go out and employ more engineers so you could keep the job in your own back yard?"

"I don't think so," replied Lincoln. "We discussed this very point. All of us feel our intention is to use engineering opportunities only where we have the competence and to develop ourselves as engineers, but not to expand our engineering capabilities through additional employment. We have no desire to keep up with NRC, EPA, and other considerations. We think the flow chart would add efficiency, reduce cost, and utilize our limited plant engineering resources in a way that would improve the use of central engineering's services for projects where they really are needed. We think the checkpoints and the review mechanisms in the flow chart use your highest resources by adding your technical expertise to small projects while giving us a hand in them. Using this procedure should reduce the man-hours you are called on for small projects, thus releasing your man-hours for more important projects."

"We even think that," said Taylor, "rather than adding personnel to the plants, once this model gets working, it would permit your liaison personnel to be drawn back into central engineering where they could operate as real engineers rather than as a buffer to us. This would result in a net overall reduction in the number of people engaged in managing engineering."

The separate sessions that followed to consider the plants' proposal led to the conclusion that the two groups were as far apart as ever.

The Separate Sessions

The character of the meeting of the central engineers was impressive in what it revealed. Although the flow chart was clear, logical, and structurally sound, the thought of "giving up" anything labeled "engineering" to the plants was so threatening to their vested interests that it was not examined for feasibility, but instead was rejected as giving up territory and power. "Just what you'd expect from a bunch of plant managers." "Yeah, give them an inch and they'll take a mile," said Jacobs. "Now they've asked for the moon and if they don't get it, they'll feel like a bunch of deprived little boys that had a candy bar taken away from them." Central engineering had become such a self-justifying organization that any member who could recognize merit in the flow chart would be branded as a deviant because of the existing frozen attitudes blocking any suggestions that might appear to threaten their vested interests. The word *engineering* belonged to them as well as all activities that might be construed under that term. For all practical purposes, their minds were closed to considering any changes from the current status quo definition of their department.

The tone of the meeting was distinctly different in the plant management group. It was characterized by such comments as "I don't think they understand it" and "It seemed from their questions that they are so wedded to their ways of operating that they are blind to alternatives. They won't even open their eyes to look." Their attitude was that it was probably a mistake to have come to this meeting; they should have known better. By way of summary, we heard remarks like those of any defeated group: They complained but did not exercise initiative any more, they had come to live with what seemed the "inevitable," but they still resented it and felt rankled by it.

Breaking the Logjam

It was about time to bring the activities of the day to a close. The interface had arrived at an impasse that had to be resolved if any success were to be accomplished. Since the end of the day was at hand, Blake and Mouton had an opportunity to review with Burke and Jones what they had learned and to try to reshape and crystallize the issues to bring as much insight as possible to bear on the next steps.

Jones, in a despondent mood, said, "I'm not sure this one has an answer, Bob. The engineers seem to be blind to the limitations in the manner in which they are executing their engineering functions. No matter how many complaints are made by the plant managers, they go by unheeded. The symptoms are treated as causes. They are willing to work on each one of the symptoms but they refuse to recognize the underlying illness."

"Well," said Blake, "I can't help but agree that they are operating that way. My only reluctance is to accept the conclusion you draw, that is, that we have come to the end of the line."

"Then where do we go from here?" Burke asked.

"There seems to be another angle to the problem. I'd like to try to put it in words," Mouton said tentatively.

"Go ahead," said Burke.

"Okay, here's the way I see it. The central engineers fail to see any difference between what would be sound and current practices. They are one and the same, and no one can break ranks and examine the merit of the flow chart because it threatens their vested interests. Yet we hear the plant managers say that what is sound to the engineers is intolerable to them. They are a smart group of people, too. It defies logic to believe that two sets of competent people can be at such odds regarding a sound relationship between them. It's obviously membership pressure at work distorting judgment."

"The flow chart makes good sense," Blake added. "I was

struck that the central engineers were unable to admit any wisdom in it. The only way that they are going to be able to convince the plant managers that it isn't sound is to show them why it won't work. Rejecting it out of hand is the same management by paternalism as in the past."

"At least that sounds good in theory," said Burke. "But it's one thing to want to get a deliberate examination of the flow chart by the central engineers and quite a different thing to get them to do it if they won't open up with each other."

"I have a thought," said Blake.

"What?" asked Mouton.

"We use a fishbowl, a theater-in-the-round exercise. Let's flip to the positive side and ask the central engineers to review and explain to themselves how the system could work if it were imposed on them. They don't have to buy it. They don't have to complain about it. They don't have to do anything except to explain it to themselves while the plant managers listen. This can give the engineering group the opportunity to evaluate the logic in the flow chart design. It gives the plant managers an opportunity to hear the discussions and to know whether what is said is how they intended the flow chart to work. As a second step, if it's necessary, we can ask the plant managers to the fishbowl to critique the interpretation of the flow chart offered by the central engineers while the engineers listen."

"That sounds possible," said Mouton. "It meets all the needs for opening up understanding and for closing the gap if distortions remain. It permits us to do so without the engineers repudiating the flow chart or giving it their endorsement at this point. It lets the plant management group learn what's wrong with it, if it won't work. Sounds good. Let's look for the negative features."

"What's wrong with it?" asked Blake.

"The only limitation I can see in it, I guess," said Mouton, "is that we may have to push the central engineers to do it."

"I'll tell you what I'd do," said Blake. "I'd say, 'As the monitors listening to your discussions, we would like to challenge that you have given serious consideration to the flow chart option. We don't think that you do understand it well enough to test it as a viable plan. You're rejecting it out of hand.' "

"At that point," said Burke, "Burton might speak up or Owens, anyone from central engineering, and ask 'Why do you think we don't understand it?' "

Blake responded: "I'd answer it this way: 'Because we didn't hear you attempt to take a project through it to see how it might work. If you had taken a project and walked it through this system and had tried to envisage the decision-making points and what would happen and what would not happen, we would have thought that you have a good feel for it. What did happen is that one of you said, "It's hypothetical, it won't work, let's forget it, let's not waste our time trying to analyze the damn thing any further." And that became the reaction of your group at that point.' That's how I'd deal with it. But what kind of reaction would that get?"

"I think it's okay," said Mouton. "I think that note you put in, of taking a project through the flow chart to test how it would work is the kind of step that's bound to be seen as sensible. If they can prove it won't work, then what do we do?"

"We reverse the process," answered Blake, "and get the plant managers to do a fishbowl for the same task. You know, 'How could the central engineering design be made to work?' Unless there are some unexpected developments between now and then, I'm ready to get us started in this direction in the morning," he concluded.

Closing the Gap

Blake opened the morning session: "We spent some time last evening reviewing progress to date. From our standpoint, it seems that the engineering and the plant manager groups are now confronted with a deep dilemma. First I'd like to outline the dilemma and then offer suggestions that might test whether a breakthrough is possible given this impasse.

"The dilemma is that there are two different ideals that go against one another because each group rejects the solutions proposed by the other. This impasse brings us to a dead halt unless we can find some way to explore more deeply the fundamental issues. Is that a clear statement of the dilemma? If not, how do you want to change it?"

Taylor said, "That's it."

Valdez added, "Yeah, I am in complete agreement with Taylor. This is the first time it's ever happened." Turning to Blake, he continued, "The real dilemma though is you won't let us agree to disagree."

"As outsiders we're in no position to judge which if either is best, but it is our job to help you answer the question, 'Why can't two groups of sensible people who do know the situation agree on the best way to handle it?' " replied Mouton.

"We may end up by agreeing to disagree, but I'm not there yet. Let's take the next step," said White.

Blake and Mouton outlined the next step, repeating what they had discussed the night before. With a little laughter and jokes, the participants moved into the altered seating arrangements, with the engineers on the inside and the plant managers observing.

"Look, Bob, we're good engineers but that doesn't mean we're good actors," commented Nelson.

Valdez said to Lincoln, "Look, I'm only doing this on the assumption you can separate bad acting from good engineering. I can hear you back at the plant saying, 'He's a lousy engineer because he can't act.' "

Lincoln responded, "Thanks a lot. I'll remember that."

In a few minutes the rearrangements were completed, and Valdez assumed chairmanship of the central engineering group in the fishbowl by saying, "Okay, fellas, what project should we nominate to test how the model could work?"

As the engineering group began analyzing the plant managers' flow chart, their initial stance was to criticize every step and point out its problems and limitations. One of them finally refocused the group on the real task.

"Look, we're still explaining why the plant managers' approach won't work, but the task asked us to explore how their proposal, given our willingness to help, could be successful."

The logjam seemed to break open. "Okay," Jacobs said, "if we'd do this first step of the plant identifying the engineering project their way, it'd really take a burden off our shoulders."

"And if we'd try this third step here of specifying all the design requirements," Owens pointed out, "we'd reduce the entire existing PEA process by four steps. That would eliminate half the bureaucracy we're struggling with now."

"You know," Nelson admitted thoughtfully, "it really *could* work. Maybe it's not such a bad idea after all."

In no time the engineers were pointing at the flow chart and excitedly showing how minor corrections or revisions would satisfy engineering while simultaneously providing the plant managers with an acceptable solution. Enough controls and influence points had been built in to reassure them of the continued importance of the engineering experts. They saw themselves as surrendering no functional control and in fact gaining considerably by adopting the plant solution. Both groups were now seeing the merits of plant management's proposal.

Engineering had developed a degree of ownership for the agreed-upon solution by virtue of the slight revisions they added to the plant managers' original work. Now a free interchange began where the ideas and opinions were no longer colored by membership. The focus had shifted from a "who's right" to a "what's right" basis for planning and decision making. Very quickly, both groups agreed that the flow chart solution was sound and viable and that 90 percent of the proposed changes could be implemented without further authorization or approval.

The integrated design for utilizing engineering resources was then readied for the final session with McFadden and Arnold. The flow chart was further refined and polished, goals and objectives of the approach specified, and a thorough and complete rationale developed. Their major work satisfactorily completed, both groups expressed determination and commitment to continued development and periodic checks on the soundness of the flow chart way of cooperation between central engineering and the plants.

"I think we've learned an important lesson," Phillips concluded as the preparation for Friday's session was ending. "The real blockage was not in what constitutes engineering and operations but in our definition of 'we' and 'them.' The flow chart provides a basis for working a problem between *us*. We have a 100 percent job to do, not 100 percent engineering and 100 percent operations to do. The flow chart provides a common goal that permits each group to make its best contributions." He concluded, "The better the flow chart works, the better our relationship and our results."

With the time remaining, the groups designed a one-way follow-up to evaluate their progress in implementing the flow chart and to further refine their procedures. Each group also discussed how it planned to go about getting the personnel below them involved and committed to making the flow chart work.

Reporting to Top Management

Friday's session began promptly at eight o'clock with McFadden, Arnold, and the interface development session participants in attendance. The session was planned to present the description of the Interface Conflict-Solving activity as well as their recommendations to Arnold (president) and McFadden (chairman). The central engineers suggested a key contribution—they would present the flow chart model because it was a departure from their previous position that all engineering design work should be kept within the engineering department. They thought there would be a greater impact on McFadden and Arnold if the engineers thus demonstrated their commitment to the recommended shifts in procedures.

"This group," Blake began, "has been at it for four days. It's been a tense and difficult situation." He continued, "The basic problem is to try to stop the flow of our history and to try to answer the question, 'Is there a better way than how we have been doing it?' Our history had come to take on a life of its own and control both people and outcomes. Under its grip, we felt compelled to shape the future to resemble the past. The goal in these Interface Conflict-Solving Model sessions has been to stop the flow of history and to model the future based on the soundest thinking possible."

Lincoln then described the groups' daily activities and results during the week, and Nelson presented the groups' agreed-
on recommendations. Walking through each step of the flow
chart, Nelson reviewed the potential cost savings, gains in productivity, and increased efficiencies and reduced conflict.

After a series of questions and answers, Lincoln concluded, "The significant thing about this recommendation, as
we see it, is that it's merely a more efficient, effective version of
how to utilize all engineering resources."

"There are, however," said Nelson, "four things we need
from top management before we can finalize our plan of action." After describing top management's contribution to the
solution, Nelson concluded, "We feel that the approach we've
outlined represents the best use of the company's specialized
resources. It's going to take a lot of work and a lot of commitment, but we're convinced that it can work!"

"It's obvious you've made real progress," McFadden
noted, "and I can only say that I'm anxious to see the approach
you've developed begin paying dividends for Consolidated Utilities. Whether it's easy or difficult, it'll definitely be worth the
effort."

"You'll have complete support from my office," pledged
Arnold. "We'll be following what happens with great interest,
and I know we'll be pleased with the results."

"And this ends a forty-five-year-old saga and offers all of
us the hope of a more profitable and more rewarding future,"
McFadden added to the delight of all.

Summary

Grouping those who have one kind of specialized skills
together and separating them from others who have different
skills is the classical way of acknowledging specialization of effort and of reducing the need for any one group or individual
to acquire more diverse skills. This logic for delineating line-
staff responsibilities in accomplishing highly technical activities
was formulated in modern times and continues to represent an
essentially standard organizational practice. Increased effectiveness and leaner organizations should result when individuals are

doing the work for which they are best qualified by education, training, or experience. What this formulation requires for successful implementation, however, is an awareness of the deleterious effects that can result from splitting a whole activity into artificially contrived parts. In addition, an understanding of the interface dynamics involved when two groups must coordinate their activities is essential for achieving effective cooperation.

Without utilization of these two understandings when segregating people into groups based on specialization of effort, the bureaucracy and red tape that develop in most line–staff relationships can interfere with an organization's ability to get the job done in an optimal manner. While an organization may not grind to a halt, operations become more difficult, complicated, and frustrating than would otherwise be the case, with the result that the organization's members are less than optimally motivated and satisfied.

Problems experienced in Consolidated Utilities are typical of those experienced by some technically oriented organizations that separate essential operational activities, centralize them into a support function, and remove them from direct line authority. By investigating the tensions and antagonisms between central engineering and plant management, we see from this example how problems at the interface between line and staff groups arise and intensify through a split between planning and doing that is excessively rigid; the results are feelings of superiority and inadequacy.

Consolidated Utilities' application of the Interface Conflict-Solving Model demonstrates that once line–staff conflict is objectively analyzed, its historical antecedents explored, and negative consequences identified by those who have the authority to make changes, previously contending groups can learn to work productively together to develop sound solutions to their interface problems. However, this achievement resulted from treating the identified antagonisms as symptomatic of a deeper source of problems that were causing them. The solution in this case involved members of the groups who had to live with the split between planning and doing in rethinking the terms of the division between them that could result in their doing a better

job with greater professional development and increased satisfaction derived from work experiences for both. An optimal
model for a more functional specialization of effort was produced, which has made an enduring contribution to improved
working relationships.

Impact

Now that three years have elapsed, we can assess the
operational consequences resulting from use of the Interface
Conflict-Solving Model. The mechanisms designed into the flow
chart that allowed for plant engineering and yet enabled central
engineering to oversee it have proved successful in use and have
undergone further refinement. Of greater importance, however,
is that the removal of this source of friction has opened up a
new basis of cooperation that was unforeseen. Illustrations include extending the budget cycle, cross-plant standardization,
and reduced reliance on outside engineering consultants and
contractors. All of these contributed substantially to a reduction of expense.

The key to the breakthrough during the Interface Conflict-Solving Modeling that made these changes possible came
when one group sought to demonstrate how the model produced by the other group might be made to work. Both groups
had to think through possibilities rather than to reject them
out of hand. This style of rejection, characteristic of central
engineering, is explained by that group being "in the saddle"
and therefore closed to an examination of options other than
those currently in force. Working through possibilities opened
to examination a strategy of future collaboration that relieved
the tensions in the relationship, permitted a wider use of resources, and significantly reduced expenses associated with engineering.

Dynamics of Change

Neither Edwards, vice-president of engineering, nor Phillips, vice-president of power generation, participated in an
active manner, and other members did not encourage them to

do so. It is important to understand what their limited presence contributed. It was not from disinterest that they observed and listened rather than tried to influence outcomes. They constituted a level of executive management that would be key to authorizing changes that might result from the activity but they were not sufficiently close to the problem itself to be able to contribute substantially to its detailed analysis. The operational level of administration of both departments was carried out through the assistants—Nelson in engineering and Lincoln in power generation. The presence of both vice-presidents permitted them to learn more about the details and to think through the logic inherent in the recommended solution to the problem. Thus they were in an excellent position to give their approval to the solutions that were developed, which they quickly did.

In a number of other cases, we have seen the beginning of a breakthrough as the groups escape the status quo by formulating optimal or soundest solutions. (This did not occur in the Consolidated Utilities interface.) The engineering group might be described as frozen to its position and literally unable to see the viability of any alternative to it. Reinforcing this frozen condition was the conviction shared among them that any change meant "giving up territory and loss of control." In operational terms they interpreted this to mean the watering down of engineering standards as well as creating increased exposure to the risks of violating federal, state, and local regulations.

Nowhere in its deliberations did the plant management group reject the idea of dividing operations from engineering. What they rejected was the character of the division that existed over the long term and that remained in place. For them this division prevented their engineering competence from being utilized under conditions where they in fact could contribute. This reduced their own sense of wholeness and pride and professionalism. The division was particularly costly in terms of the profitability of the company. For the engineering group, the breakthrough came not by reshaping the definition of the division but by investigating how an engineering product check might flow through the system in a flexible manner that would permit

their engineering resources to be used effectively while maintaining the professional standards essential for needed uniformi-
ties and code compliance.

The dramatic moment occurred after the plant management had presented this formulation only to meet a wall of resistance to it among the central engineering group, who summarily rejected examining its possibilities. The breakthrough
was made possible because the critical next step was diagnosed:
calling on central engineering to take the plant management
model and walk an engineering project through it to see how it
would work. This turning point challenged central engineering
to demonstrate their understanding of the model by using it.
In our view, this Interface Conflict-Solving session was successful because, as modified, it dealt with two important considerations of change that are sometimes present. One is that people
reject possibilities without understanding them. A second consideration is that a trial run based on a model can only be taken
when rejection of it has been suspended.

One of the sources of resistance to change among the central engineering group was the notion that any "give" on their
part meant loss. The trial run proved the opposite. It resulted in
a gain, which came about through two new insights. One was
that local engineering could be done at the plant level against
suitable standards. This relieved a source of chronic antagonism
between engineering and the plants and made it unnecessary for
central engineering to assign expensive manpower to relatively
minor and unimportant work. The other gain came from the insight that plant management can now put into the flow chart
small projects that had previously been carried out under conditions of subterfuge, resulting in an overall elevation of standards for all engineering work.

CHAPTER 6

இ௦௨௦௨௦௨௦௨௦௨௦௨௦௨௦௨௦௨௦௨௦௨௦௨௦௨௦௨

Resolving
Union–Management
Disputes

Union and management groups provide perhaps the most vivid
example of win-lose interface conflict. Since each group is
equally powerful in terms of influencing outcomes, neither can
impose its will on the other through the exercise of organization or legal authority. Even though unions and managements
are mutually dependent on one another to achieve their own
objectives, the relationship frequently is characterized by bitter-
ness, hostility, and mutual antagonism rather than essential cooperation. Often both jealously protect their own vested interests even when larger interests are at stake. Like true enemies,
either group may be willing to place itself in peril to deprive the
other of a "victory."

The following case describes the use of the Interface
Conflict-Solving Model in resolving tensions between union and
the management where a history of mutual distrust and destructiveness had characterized the relationship for some years. It is a

An article abridged from this chapter appeared as: Robert R. Blake
and Jane S. Mouton, "Developing a Positive Union–Management Relationship," *Personnel Administrator* 28, no. 6 (1983): 23-140.

particularly good illustration of how developing a model of the soundest possible relationship serves to initiate a positive motivation for change.

Hillside, a large modern plant serving the paper products industry, exemplifies the negative effects of an unresolved management-union conflict at the interface. The plant had suffered two major debilitating strikes in its recent history. Management's primary interest as this study began was to gain concessions in the interest of cost containment from the union while avoiding a third strike.

Jeff O'Hare, plant manager at Hillside, summarized the problem. "As far as I'm concerned, we've got one last chance to find a way to work with the union. At this time we're on a collision course headed toward a contract expiration date only five months away. We've got nothing to lose—if we can't get a positive, productive relationship established by then, we'll have to take them head on. I'm not sure how we'd survive another shutdown, but I'm sure that when and if we start up again, this plant won't be operated by the same people who operate it now."

Getting Started

Against the backdrop of mutual antagonism, Hal Floyd, corporate employee relations manager, proposed a four-day, union-management Interface Conflict-Solving session to plant manager O'Hare. Floyd had read an article describing situations similar to Hillside's where the Interface Conflict-Solving Model had been used successfully to shift from industrial warfare to industrial statesmanship.

O'Hare was skeptical that the deep antagonisms between union and management could be solved, but reluctantly agreed to take part. "But my motivation is not 100 percent pure. I'd rather try it than have you come back at me after a strike and say that we might have avoided it," O'Hare said.

With O'Hare's reluctant approval, Floyd explored the possibility of an interface activity with Rick Keenan, the president of the local union, then with the international union's representative, Bruce Boyd. Their reaction reflected the same pessimism and doubt expressed by O'Hare, but they agreed to attend on the premise that things at Hillside were so bad that it probably couldn't hurt. Furthermore, Boyd wanted to maintain his reputation for willingness to confront management face to face and to avoid the possible accusation that he was unwilling to respond to a gesture of cooperation from management.

Floyd contacted us and secured our agreement to serve as Hillside's interface design experts for the proposed effort. Floyd played a significant leadership role in the preparation stage by securing the commitment from corporate headquarters to engage in the interface design in advance of approaching the union. The headquarters group had to give its approval so that the plant management would be free to engage in problem-solving activities that were not likely to be reversed after the fact by persons higher in the organization. Later Floyd participated as part of the Hillside management group. His major contribution was his evident enthusiasm and genuine interest in reaching a valid, "right" solution to the union–management controversy, but his attendance also reflected the degree of positive support from headquarters.

Convening the Adversaries

The Interface Conflict-Solving session was scheduled for the week before Christmas at a conference center in a northern city. It seemed that the cold, inclement weather provided a suitable climate, given the frigid initial attitudes of union and management toward one another.

Participants, shown in Figure 5, include the six members of management and six union officials who attended the meeting. All of the management members are in the top group, except for Mike Barret, who was a front-line foreman and former union president. He enjoyed the respect of both management and the union and was included because he had been known in the past to challenge management's interpretations of events when their information about what goes on at the lowest levels of the organization had been scant.

Figure 5. Hillside Management and Union Participants.

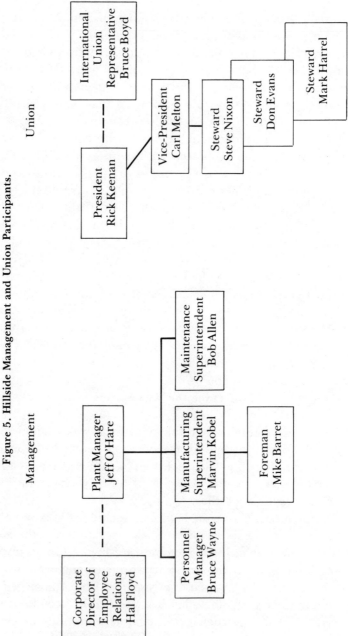

Management

Union

Blake began the session by reviewing the interface development activities to introduce four primary goals that could be realized if the session was successful: (1) establishing the basis for a problem-solving relationship between the two groups, (2) developing concrete plans for moving away from the historical adversarial relationship toward one of mutual trust, respect, and collaboration, (3) creating task forces to solve identified problems, and (4) planning follow-up and reevaluation at specified intervals to stabilize the developing relationship.

"These objectives," Blake explained, "are accomplished through a planned conflict-resolution strategy based on practical industrial experience." He continued with a brief outline of the relationship-building steps: "As a first step, each of your groups meet separately to prepare descriptions of a sound union-management relationship for Hillside. As each of you identifies key elements of sound interaction, these are recorded on newsprint for later comparisons in a joint session. Similarities and differences in your separate sound relationship descriptions are then identified and explored together. The next step is creation of a single, consolidated model to which both management and the union can be committed. Once agreement has been obtained on a sound *model* for a problem-solving relationship, the *actual* relationship will be examined by each of you for all of the important elements."

"Reviewing the history that led up to the present conditions will help determine what brought about the actual tensions and conflicts," added Jane Mouton. "Separate descriptions of existing conditions are compared and discussed in a joint effort to achieve common understanding of the problems at the interface. Finally, you will be able to identify steps that can move your relationship away from the counterproductive situation that has led to two strikes and continued tensions and toward the progressive, productive model. When that point has been reached, you'll have the opportunity to formulate a specific plan of action, assign responsibilities for follow-up, and schedule review and reevaluation activities. This is the 'big' map, but we will not stay with it in a rigid manner. If there's a turn of events that would lead us in new and possibly valuable directions, we will take advantage of that and move along new lines toward progress. Any questions?''

To break through the frigid, silent atmosphere, Blake gained the attention of participants by asking, "What would a sound relationship between the union and the company be like?"

"Cooperation," offered Bob Allen (management).

"Mutual trust and recognition," Rick Keenan (union) suggested.

"Common sense," Carl Melton (union) replied.

"And what is the actual union–management relationship here today?" Blake queried.

"No trust, total lack of cooperation," was Allen's observation.

"Stalag 18," said Mark Harrell (union).

"A guard-prisoner relationship," another participant said.

"Is it understood that what we say won't be held against us?" Keenan asked.

"If we're going to have open, candid discussion of the kind that can change things," Blake responded, "we must get a free flow of valid information. This point was discussed in our original discussions with management. They have made a commitment that there'll be no retaliation for any ideas or opinions expressed here. If you're willing to accept that at face value, we can proceed on that premise.

"Our contribution is in managing the process that permits groups to choose between continuing an unsatisfactory, destructive relationship based on fear and suspicion and developing a problem-solving relationship based on mutual trust and respect. We're not here to 'fix' the union or management," he emphasized, "but to help both sides in the controversy lay the foundation for change if change is what you want."

Visualizing the Soundest Relationship

Following this orientation the two groups worked independently. Blake and Mouton, as the two design administrators, sometimes monitored each group separately and sometimes together, but they did not divide up with one monitoring one group and one the other. In this way they were able to double-check one another's perceptions and interpretations of what was going on and to discuss whether interventions would be appropriate and, if so, when.

Management's View

Management's exploration of a sound relationship with the union began with O'Hare questioning the union president's motivations: "I wonder what Keenan meant by 'recognition'?"

"Special treatment for the president is my guess," Barret (foreman) replied. "We all know they want to run the plant."

"You're right," Kobel (manufacturing superintendent) agreed forcefully. "They're always pushing—those guys are never satisfied. No matter what we do, they always want more."

"Give 'em an inch and they'll take a mile," Allen (maintenance superintendent) said. "I've seen it over and over. If they get their way, they'll squeeze this plant dry, even dryer than it already is."

"I can't respect Keenan or his tactics," Barret noted. "Maybe we'd be better off with somebody else as president. He's a political animal. He doesn't care about the plant or the people; he just wants to move up the international ladder."

Management decided that Keenan wielded considerable influence over the membership. If he personally favored a management proposal, it was presented in a straightforward, positive way. If he wanted a proposal rejected, he would twist it to emphasize negative implications and work to see it defeated.

"I think he's so manipulative that some of our proposals don't even reach the members," Wayne (personnel manager) remarked.

This discussion continued with management's suggestion that the union was responsible for a loss of support from "good" people. Management felt that dependable, reliable workers suffered through the union's unwillingness to get their members to work overtime. Management did point a finger at itself, however, in identifying inadequate first-line supervision as an additional factor in declining management support among workers. Frustration and resentment often arose because inexperienced supervisors would reprimand an entire group rather than confront an individual rule violator.

"Management makes the rules around here," said Barret, "but supervisors don't enforce them. We either ignore rule violations or come down so hard on them that they turn the people off. We need some kind of system to make sure our supervisors follow up without alienating the work force."

After this period of ventilation, Blake encouraged management to remember and concentrate on the objective of the session, identifying the elements for the soundest relationship, which they did.

Union's View

The flow of discussion in the union meeting was similar in that members quickly agreed on the ingredients of a sound relationship. By the end of the allotted time, as is typical when the focus is on a sound relationship model, the union perspective did not differ substantially from that expressed by management.

Table 8. Critical Elements in a Sound Relationship.

Management's View	Union's View
1. Mutual trust and mutual respect for one another	1. Trust: standing behind your work
2. Honesty in our dealings with one another	2. Openness: speaking freely without fear of reprisal
3. Effective communication within and between our two groups	3. Communication: listening to both sides with an open mind
4. Problem solving in order to resolve real issues between us	4. Problem solving: living by the spirit of the contract in day-to-day dealings
5. Consistency in contract interpretation	5. Consistency: applying the contract uniformly in every section of the plant
	6. Good supervision in terms of work and contract administration
	7. Timely resolution of grievances

As both groups walked toward the general session room, Melton whispered to Keenan, "We'll see this kind of relationship with those buzzards when hell freezes over." Keenan nodded agreement with the apparent truth in Melton's scathing remark.

Can Agreement Be Reached?

When management and union convened to share their separately developed models to obtain agreement on the soundest relationship, designated spokespersons, not the formal leaders, made their presentations to the groups. Blake had explained that in this way ideas are more likely to be received as a group product and not as a reflection of the leader's own thinking.

After the spokespersons had presented the groups' descriptions of elements in the soundest relationship, it was apparent that the lists were similar, but not identical. Blake explained, "The next step is to place the items in order of priority from the most important down to those that are of less significance, but still important enough to be included." Reading from the instructions, he said, "The groups together now jointly consider the elements presented by each to reach agreement on the most important elements in the relationship, in order of importance, and then to agree on a single list of elements to be considered on an element-by-element basis later in the activities. Spokespersons continue to represent each group and to discuss with each other, in the presence of both groups, what the single list is to contain.

"In choosing the most important elements, it is often useful to agree in advance on a list of criteria for importance, such as the following:

- Strong influence on the nature of the relationship.
- Applicable to all or most group members.
- Capable of being influenced through joint action of participants.
- Represents an area of specific problems within the past year.

"The consolidated list of elements can then be recorded on flip chart paper. Elements which have not been included in the consolidated list, because it has been agreed that they had lower importance or were not equally applicable to both groups, should be labeled and recorded on a 'save list' for possible later consideration."

Blake then encouraged the groups' spokespersons to question one another for clarification after the presentation of each soundest model, but there was little interchange; at this time, achieving a sound relationship seemed so remote that neither the union nor management viewed it as a realistic alternative.

The spokespersons for the two groups got started sorting out and matching the elements so that similarities became self-evident. Because the two lists were close to begin with, this step was accomplished without the need for additional discussions within each group; the joint list, in the main, reflected the seven points from the union's view.

A View of Real Life

Having completed the joint description of a sound relationship, union and management were anxious to explore the current situation. Preoccupied with details of recent conflict and perceived injustices, each side wanted to describe actual conditions, the real battleground.

Management's View

Lively discussions characterized management's considerations of the actual relationship. Their list of actual conditions more or less paralleled the sound view, but contained several tension points regarding power and authority. From their perspective, the union intended to usurp authority and responsibility that rightfully belonged to the company. This core perception explained to management's satisfaction the prevailing distrust and disrespect that they felt about the union. Poor communication and severely reduced problem solving caused management to be as tough as they felt was necessary in interpreting the contract in a manner that made the company profitable. Therefore, management's self-justifications were premised on their concern for the economy and efficient operation of the plant. Their list of actual circumstances follows.

1. Adversary relationship in terms of we-they.
2. Cooperation means consenting to union demands.
3. Mistrust on both sides.
4. Union wants co-management.
5. Union does not give its members true picture of management's position.
6. Low credibility of union president.
7. Lack of cooperation in promotion of efficiency and economy.
8. Use of outsiders to resolve internal issues.
9. Management team has low credibility with union members.
10. Management is seen by the union as inflexible.
11. Management is enforcing existing rules and agreement interpretations as it sees necessary to increase efficiency of work practices.

Union's View

Predictably, the union held different opinions. Through their own eyes, they only sought what had been earned through contract bargaining. The union didn't want to run the plant, but they certainly wanted people in the plant to be treated with dignity and respect. As the people's voice and their elected representatives, union officers expected a degree of consideration—not contempt. The union's description of the actual relationship included the eight items listed here.

1. Hopelessness; a shutdown is necessary to bring them to their senses. We're ready for the showdown.
2. Cooperation is one-sided—do what the company says.
3. Hopelessness extends to all workers.
4. Dignity is lost in a guard–prisoner relationship.
5. Management only cares for production; people be damned.

6. Management seeks to destroy people's loyalty to union and
    its officers.
7. Union can't get its foot in the door to solve problems.
8. Management blames past regimes for problems—they see no
    deficiencies in themselves.

Joint Presentation

In the joint meeting that followed, each group presented
its description of the actual relationship to the other. Both
management and union seemed stunned at the depth of the
cleavage between them. Management looked particularly shaken
by the union's conviction that progress was impossible given
prevailing attitudes and behavior. With the plant's future clearly
on the line, along with their careers, management simply could
not reconcile itself to giving up hope. Separate meetings were
scheduled next to allow time for each group to digest the implications of the other's input.

Can a Strike Be Averted?

Management began its comparison and analysis of the actual descriptions of the relationship. A sense of the depth of
their disturbance is revealed in management's discussion of the
second item, where their perception of the actual relationship
is, "Cooperation means consenting to union demands," whereas
the union's perception is, "Cooperation is one-sided; do what
the company says."

"How could two groups work in the same plant grappling
with the same kind of problems and see each other so diametri-
cally opposite?" asked O'Hare. "What do they mean, 'Cooperation is one-sided; do what the company says'? In the past ten
years, we've given away more valuable clauses in the name of
cooperation and, while we haven't gotten it, we've lost more
management prerogatives than other plants in our area of competition."

"As far as I can see," said Kobel (manufacturing superintendent), "when we say 'given away,' literally that is what it has
been. We have given away paragraph after paragraph and have

gotten nothing in return. Productivity changes have been at a standstill."

"You can say that again," piped up Allen, the maintenance superintendent. "I'm so tied up with job description rigidities that some people have to sit on their fannies waiting for other people to work in situations where if one could add a helping hand to the other, they could get the job done in half the time. We keep falling further behind. And they say, 'Cooperation means doing what the company says.' "

"I propose," said Wayne (personnel manager), "that we just flatly disagree with it. We can't agree and maintain any self-respect."

"Hold it, fellas," said Barret (foreman). "What's been going on in the past few weeks? Let's examine these situations one at a time and see how they might have come to such a statement. What have you heard them say in meetings you've been having with them?"

"Well," said Wayne, "they think we're trying to erode the contract by putting unreasonable interpretations on various clauses and then challenging them to file grievances. They file a grievance, we rule against it. We say, 'arbitrate.' I've heard them say this is a 'search and destroy' technique."

As they continued to talk, discussion kept returning to the first item on the union's list, the "hopelessness" comment.

"Does Kennan really speak for the membership when he says a strike is inevitable," O'Hare asked, "or is he just trying to shake us up?"

"It doesn't matter," Floyd responded. "If he wants a strike he can convince the people."

"Has anyone talked to the plant nurse?" he asked. "She's usually the best listening post for hearing things."

"And," added Barret, "they know it. Sometimes they feed her items just to annoy management when she reports. I think it's a tit-for-tat standoff. When you 'use' her, they do, too."

"What are you hearing," questioned O'Hare, "when you talk to people outside of the plant? Is there talk in the community about a strike? Are spouses unhappy?"

"As far as I can tell, Keenan has the strike vote in his

pocket," came Wayne's retort. "He can easily get them riled up. If he doesn't have complete support now, he will have by the time May comes around. He and his cronies are persuasive enough to convince the rest of the people that a strike will ultimately be to their advantage. I've overheard their discussions on the floor. Make no mistake, he's a strong leader."

"Maybe we'd better look at ourselves more objectively before pointing any more fingers at them," O'Hare suggested. "How have you seen me relating to Keenan and the others in the past?" he asked.

"I see you coming across as strong and hard nosed," Allen replied.

"I think you're open, forthright, and honest to the point of being naive," Floyd observed. "You've always had a good reputation as a production and people man. Lately though, I've seen you change to a posture of using force; no alternatives, pure force."

Wayne added, "I've seen you as open, honest, and fair; you listen well and take good advice. I have noticed a definite shift though toward a tough attitude."

"I haven't seen much of a change since you've been here," Barret observed. "It seems to me you've always been very direct and aggressive."

Kobel spoke last. "I don't have much to add," he said. "Basically, I agree with what you've said. O'Hare is fair, but firm—to the point of being stubborn, I guess."

Having heard the others, O'Hare summed up his own feelings. "You're right," he said. "I think I'm so determined to turn this thing around that I've become somewhat unreasonable. It's been much easier to blame our problems on my predecessors or cast aspersions on Keenan and his cohorts. I hadn't realized my own attitude had been so visible. I thought I'd kept a pretty open mind, but if my biases were obvious to you, they were probably obvious to the union, too."

"I'm one of the most outspoken tough guys," Barret volunteered. "I may even be antagonistic at times."

"Basically you're our resident 'labor lawyer'—a technical person who advocates management rights," O'Hare commented.

"I'm tough because that's what's needed here. I'm proud of my image," said Wayne. "I've never seen a situation as bad as the one here at Hillside."

"You've never changed since I've known you," O'Hare noted.

"Right," the others agreed. "Wayne has always had anti-union tendencies and has to work hard to keep his feelings under control."

"You've pictured me as a hard-nosed guy right down the line; promanagement and antiunion," Wayne responded, "but I do care about this plant, and I care about the people. I won't be a barrier to our progress with the union. I want to be part of the solution, not just part of the problem."

Attention then shifted to Allen, Floyd, and Kobel, with each person's basic orientation toward the union considered in turn. All shared the same basic attitudes and opinions about the union and its members, but each recognized how destructive their actions had been. Only Barret stood out as a member of management who could see the problem from both perspectives. He never failed to speak as a conscience for a sound relationship when the opportunity arose.

Management was now firmly convinced that a strike was a realistic possibility. In view of the potential individual and organizational costs, management became committed to a search for genuine understanding and avoidance of further polarization. Their earlier talk of a strike threat had been more hypothetical than real, but the specter of an imminent shutdown provided the impetus for an objective self-critique.

While management grappled with its own contribution to the current conflict, the union collected evidence of management's refusal to deal with them constructively. They admitted that after the relationship had deteriorated, they had responded to management in ways that increased the win-lose attitude between them. However, the union continued to feel that it could only respond to management's initiatives.

"It's no use trying to help," Melton (vice-president) concluded. "Management sees only what they want to, and they want to see *us* as responsible for all of their problems and failures. What they never seem to realize is that Hillside is an assignment. Two, three, or four years and they're gone. For us, it's a lifetime."

"They think we're an obstacle to their success. We know they're an obstacle to our happiness. Do we want a plant that is not a profit maker? Of course not. Nothing could be dumber, because it could seal their fates as slaves, assigned to overtime shifts in an arbitrary way that hides management's inability to stimulate people to be on the job rather than to be absentees. You can go the last mile to help them, but to go beyond it destroys our own self-respect," added Keenan (president).

"That's true," said Harrel (steward). "But we can either continue to escalate or help to defuse the relationship."

"I'm eager to do anything to move in a more positive direction," said Evans (steward). "This constant hassle is killing my stomach."

Once each group had the opportunity to formulate a response to the other's assessment of their actual relationship, they again met in the joint session room to share their reactions.

Testing Reality

The union initiated this session with their reaction to management's actual description. Melton (vice-president) served as spokesperson.

"We're astonished that you think we see this relationship as a game of win or lose," Melton began. "We're not keeping score, we're just trying to resolve a number of outstanding issues."

"Is there a we-they situation?" asked Kobel (manufacturing superintendent), who was acting as spokesperson for the management group.

"Mr. O'Hare, we used to think, especially when you first came in as plant manager, that there was mutual respect and mutual interest in being heard, but what we had hoped for never happened. Every time we approach management, you react negatively. We don't demand anything, but you seem to resent our even making suggestions or proposals," Melton responded.

"Are we both feeling threatened then?" Kobel probed.

"That's the way it seems to us," Melton replied, "on both sides. When I'm threatened, I react. During the past six to eight months, management has tried to bypass us and go directly to the people. Take overtime for example. You keep telling people every situation is an 'emergency' just because you've got the word 'emergency' in one of the clauses. It's only when you can't get them to work overtime for you that you come to us."

"That's our job," Allen (maintenance superintendent) burst out defensively. "We're responsible for getting the work out, and we need people to do it."

Turning to Allen, Kobel asked, "Do you want me to be the spokesman or not?" This reestablished the pattern of communication between spokesmen that had been in force.

"And we don't tell them what to do or what not to do," Melton continued. "We only provide information. You think we want to run the plant, so you won't even give us the time of day. You're right when you say management has no credibility —you can't expect to get respect from others when you dehumanize and depersonalize them in every possible way. We're prisoners. We can't escape because we need the work, and we can't feel self-respect when we are not respected."

O'Hare whispered to Kobel, "Ask if that is why they said 'Stalag 18'?"

His stage whisper was heard and Melton quickly responded, "Yes sir, Mr. O'Hare, that is correct."

As the session continued, the self-examining reversal in management's attitude became evident. They became less intent on defending their own positions and more interested in obtaining genuine understanding of the union's perspective.

Kobel led management's reaction to the union's characterization of actual conditions. He raised a number of questions about each of the different union points: "When we read your list, we are disconcerted and shocked. Why do you feel the situation is hopeless? If you brought us to our senses, what would be our change in behavior? If cooperation were two sided, what do you think it would look like? What specific things are we doing to make people feel hopeless and that they have no dignity?"

He continued, "We have to be concerned for production —that's our job, but what past and current actions lead you to conclude that our concern is with production only? We're not perfect, but we're not responsible for every problem in this plant. We inherited a good number of them and we need your help to solve them, but we just can't let you have as much say as you seem to want."

"We think you're being defensive and dishonest with us," was the union's reaction to Kobel's comments. Melton continued, "Our feeling of hopelessness is based on constraints in our present system. Once we're locked into a contract, our only relief is the grievance procedure. We feel hopeless because you force us to arbitration and that incurs expense for our members. We just can't afford to pursue every grievance. But the other side of hopelessness is the incredible resources we have to give, but you deny us the opportunity to contribute. We want this plant to be successful. If anything, more than you. After a couple of years here, you can walk and say to your executives, 'Given that bad situation, we did a great job and we think the plant will pull out of it' as you take your next advancement. We say, 'We are here forever and we think it's your responsibility to be guardians of our future, which can only be sound for us when it is sound for the corporation.'

"You know I'm an elder in a local church. I have just given you the sermon I would have given you were you my parish." Pointing to the other union officers, he said, "I hope the stewards bear with me in this.

"On the issue of cooperation, it all comes down to assisting management in daily situations that arise in the operation of the plant. Considering the contractual agreement and individual rights, we feel we were beginning to be successful in this until the last several months." He paused, apparently waiting for management to respond.

"From your interpretation, when should we call on the union?" asked Kobel.

"You should let us know about contract problems that

require our assistance and for input we can offer before you act. Sometimes you go off half cocked. When we think so, we can tell you," Melton replied. "The company's role is to assist the union to assist the company, keeping in mind the employees' best interests at the same time. We feel this has been violated. In addition, we want it made clear that we do communicate your messages to our people. If people are confused, it's because of your letters to the homes, your inconsistency, especially with respect to overtime. The rules are applied differently at different times. We also feel there is a loss of dignity in such things as un-warranted suspension, warning letters, threats, work assign-ments—prisoners is the only name for it—and the attitudes of some supervisors who say, 'Do as you're told, not what you know is right.' "

After this exchange, there were no other questions be-tween the two groups. Each returned to its own separate session for further deliberation on the issues and problems raised in the general session.

The union reviewed the work and came to its conclusions rather quickly. Without a shift in management's posture, they could see little hope for the future. Yet they desired to respond in a positive way to any constructive steps on management's part. They identified several examples of how withheld informa-tion in the past had served to only aggravate the hostility on the part of management and spotted ways in which steps could be taken to restore a problem-solving posture were management to lead the way.

Management Explores Alternatives

Management began discussing the implications of the union's lack of trust in it. Management took the lack of trust as a bad sign. Allen ended the discussion of trust by saying, "It's clear that any improvement that's going to come about will probably have to come from us."

"But how do we change?" Barret asked. "How do we exercise leadership to get out of this adversary relationship? How do we escape from our history?"

At this point, Blake entered the conversation, concentrat-

ing on the dynamics involved in interface relationships. Adverse
consequences of we-they, win-lose attitudes were discussed.

"When win-lose competition is present between groups,"
Blake explained, "interactions are characterized by mutual suspicion and distrust. The groups tend to develop negative views
of one another, just as union and management have done here.
Thinking becomes distorted and subjective interpretations replace objective evidence. It becomes impossible to agree,
because these feelings and attitudes blind each group to their
own common interests and to points of similarity in their opinions and convictions. You're attuned to differences. Within
your own group, fierce loyalties arise as you band together to
fight your foe. The group's position becomes every individual's
position—to think differently from the group is traitorous.
Under these conditions, change is a virtual impossibility."

"Well then," O'Hare began, "where do we go from here?"

"What kind of relationship do we want?" Floyd asked.
"What can we do to shift away from win-lose?"

"Look at what we've done in the past few months,"
Allen remarked. "We created the image that we're only out for
production—that we care nothing for people. They say we've
destroyed the incentive for people to have any input at all."

"What if we try to change now," O'Hare posed, "and the
union says 'No thanks, we feel safer with win-lose'?"

Mouton recounted the differences between slow-moving
evolutionary change based on modifying traditions, precedents,
and past practices by bits and pieces in comparison with systematic, planned change. "Take conflict for example," she explained. "It looks as though you've been trying to deal with
the union through conventional power plays and suppression of
differences instead of relying on a problem-solving approach."

"What do you mean, 'problem-solving'?" asked Wayne.
"They have been the *problem*."

"If you want to change, you'll want to say to yourselves,
'We're not dealing with *our* problems successfully—we need to
resolve our conflicts in a more effective way. To be effective,
our attitudes and behavior toward the union must be different
in the future from what they've been in the past.' You'll have to

face yourselves and recognize that a hard, never-say-die norm is guiding your actions. Since almost all of you seem to share negative attitudes and values about the union, the one-sided 'we're right, they're wrong' view is a condition of management's acceptance of one another. Anyone who suggests looking at both sides of an issue risks being labeled a traitor or soft or weak. If you want to change, it's necessary that you all change together, and establish a new norm of shared cooperation."

"I suppose we've failed to recognize that our plant and the union are made up of people who need involvement, respect, and open communication to be productive. I think we've had the right idea in terms of increasing individual commitment and contributions, but we've sure gone about it the wrong way," O'Hare reflected.

"Are you telling us to soften up?" Wayne asked.

"Maybe there's some kind of middle ground for us—something not too hard, but not too soft either?" O'Hare added.

Mouton responded quickly, "By middle ground, do you mean a position halfway between hard and soft, or do you mean a sound position that doesn't compromise, but integrates production and people concerns? Are you looking for an easy way out of your current dilemma by accommodation, or are you committed to establishing a problem-solving relationship based on a true spirit of cooperation and teamwork?"

O'Hare responded, "We want to do what's best, not just what's easy. We're willing to invest the time and effort necessary to achieve the sound relationship we've agreed on."

"That's an important first step toward progress," Mouton said. "It certainly isn't easy to turn around years of antagonism, frustration, and disappointment, and your recognition of the hard work involved is a positive sign."

"Be assured that you have corporate support," Floyd responded.

"What about the rest of you?" O'Hare asked.

"What other option do we have?" Kobel responded, as the others nodded affirmatively.

"What should we do now?" asked Allen.

"What do you want to communicate to the union?" Mouton queried.

"Aren't we convinced that we've painted ourselves into a corner . . . that we've been wrong in the past and that we want to change for the better?" O'Hare answered.

"Okay, then, let's prepare a summary of our quandary and present it to the union," Floyd suggested.

For its written summary, management listed five descriptive statements of their current thoughts and feelings.

1. We recognize that we have a deep win-lose orientation toward the union.
2. We want to change!
3. Barriers to overcome: Convince the union we want to change; convince ourselves we have the patience, skill, and convictions to change.
4. We're responsible to bring the rest of management on board.
5. We recognize the risk but want to resist the temptation of reverting to win-lose when it gets tough.

Convergence of Convictions

O'Hare opened the final joint session by introducing the management self-study description. Because of the deep and widespread shift in values represented by the conclusions to be presented, O'Hare, the leader of the management group, became the spokesperson to further emphasize the sincerity and true changes that were reflected in their self-study.

"I guess we were concerned and put out with you in the beginning. There was a lot of blaming and finger pointing until we began to really look at ourselves." After his presentation of the self-descriptive items, O'Hare asked for the union's reaction.

"Speaking spontaneously for the union," Boyd (international union representative) replied, "we're really pleased to see that you're willing to take these steps. Both of us stand to benefit. Let us go back and talk a moment among ourselves. This comes as a total surprise against the way things have been building up."

On the way to their own session room, Harrel (steward) commented to Blake, "We might have hoped for such a reversal, but never really believed it was possible." After a brief intermission, the groups reconvened with Melton's initial remarks, which summarized the conclusions reached from their separate sessions.

"Our reaction to the management self-description is that it is a giant step from what we see to have been management's attitudes for many months past. We recognize that it must have been hard to initiate such a drastic change. We cannot indicate strongly enough the welcomeness of that kind of shift.

"As far as we're concerned, it would be our sincere attempt to cooperate in any way to assist in bringing about the change demonstrated here. We realize that we have acted in provocative ways also in the past. We recognize that both parties will not be saying the same thing all the time. We hope to be able to maintain a constructive attitude. We believe the key to doing so is to remember the basics of this change effort."

The tensions underlying the relationship had been broken. Both groups saw the real possibility of pursuing a shared goal, each contributing from the standpoint of what is in the best interest of the plant. This positive attitude led to a desire to get to the specifics and to develop a list of outstanding issues between them that could be jointly worked on in the near future. The following items were quickly written down and agreed to.

1. Contracting out—amount of lead time, specifying work activities of contractors.
2. Overtime—call-ins, sleep time, control of excess overtime.
3. Grievance procedures and complaints—fact finding with respect to concrete cases, resolving problems before they become grievances.
4. Setting up an implementation meeting to discuss the specific way in which these issues would be addressed by a joint committee of union and management members.

Each of these issues was assigned to a task force pair for further detailed planning. One pair, O'Hare and Keenan, was asked to look at the seventy-seven grievances that had been filed. Keenan commented, "I'm sure we have filed a number of grievances more for their annoyance value than for the merit of the issues involved."

O'Hare quickly responded, "And we have dilly-dallied in answering them and have opted for 'no' whenever we've had a legalistic possibility of doing so."

"Maybe we could appoint a joint task force to clear up the situation, identify the real issues, answer those that management can respond to in a clear way, and withdraw those that have annoyance value only."

"Can we get together tonight to start on this?" asked O'Hare.

"You bet," Keenan replied, "there's no time like the present."

Another counterpart grouping was composed of two union representatives—one from production and one from maintenance—and two management representatives. They were asked to "identify and recommend steps for increasing the consistency of contract interpretation." The third task force was commissioned to reexamine safety, training, and so on, and the fourth took responsibility for overall planning and follow-up activities.

Communication Within the Plant

Management realized its real work had only begun. O'Hare pondered the dilemma.

"We're on board, but what about middle management and all of the front-line supervisors? We've been pressuring them to toe the line and they will see our attitudes as capitulation."

"You're right," agreed Allen, "but there's nothing we can do about it. Each of us can report to our people, but their attitudes are entrenched. They'll hear another pendulum swing. We're just going to have to plow through and convince them by our actions that we've gone from hard, not to soft, but rather that we're heading for sound."

"Once they see us really trying to solve problems, they'll realize we're marching to a different drummer, but it's a sounder beat," said Kobel.

"It may be all to the good to say that people learn by example, but they also learn by using their heads and thinking things through," suggested Floyd. "Why can't we take a page out of the same book and design some way that gives them the kind of experience of background and understanding we've developed?"

The group then proceeded to design a plantwide approach to setting norms and standards for dealing with the union that would involve the entire management. Two one-day conferences included the approximately sixty members of management. The purpose was for everyone to get the chance to answer a key question, "How can better relations between union and management be achieved?"

The thirty participants in each conference carried out discussions in three diagonal-slice groups—in which participants represented different departments and levels of the organization but without any vertical boss-subordinate reporting relationship present in the same group. O'Hare, the plant manager, Kobel, the manufacturing superintendent, and Wayne, the personnel chief, led the discussions, but their goal was to promote a true exploration of feelings rather than to guide the discussion toward predetermined conclusions. Clarification of thinking and differentiation of ideas began to appear.

Group after group came to recognize the one-sidedness of their historical viewpoint as well as the dead-end pessimism they connoted. Time and time again some member eventually became impatient with the bitter feelings others expressed and asked them to explain why they felt as they did.

Constructive concepts began to surface as deeply submerged attitudes and feelings were identified, expressed, explored, and shared. The groups realized that genuine improvement in union-management relations can only be initiated when their own subjective attitudes blocking problem solving are set aside and replaced with a new orientation.

The leaders interrupted the group sessions after such attitudes had been explored sufficiently to reveal the implication of the activity. They collaborated in conducting a joint session in which they walked through the main features of the

Interface Conflict-Solving Model as it had developed with the union. Many questions were posed and a number of expressions of reservations and doubt echoed concern about management's sincerity.

O'Hare dealt with most of these comments, primarily from the standpoint of inviting participants to examine the consequences of driving forward as they had in the past or of plotting a new direction. As he explained, management fully expected to retain its initiatives, but to exercise them consistently with the contract; union's reactions did not have to be seen as red flags blocking movement, but as yellows, indicating cautions the union wanted examined.

Although no single generalization was reached by all groups, the following statement summarizes what developed: "Regardless of what the union officers are, personality-wise, and what their history has been, the only way for bringing about a resolution of conflict is through treating them as officers, according them the dignity and respect that people who have been duly elected should receive. Our role is to search with them for whatever conditions of cooperation and collaboration are possible and to make progress within that framework."

A plantwide norm of warfare with the union was replaced by a new norm for building a problem-solving relationship. The union officer group met formally with the membership to review the activities and commitments, and thereafter officers continued to work informally to strengthen the relationship. Then it was possible for the management as a whole and the bargaining committee to solve many problems that had become chronic standoffs.

Impact

Five-and-a-half years have elapsed since the Interface Conflict-Solving intervention reported here was completed. In exploring the aftermath of the Hillside interface development session, the consultants spoke with key Hillside managers. One of those managers is Rob Larkin, the assistant plant manager who "held the fort" while other members of the management team participated in the change effort.

"How has Hillside changed since the union–management session?" Bob Blake asked Larkin during a follow-up discussion.

"When the session was held," said Larkin, "Hillside was eleventh in economic performance of Carlton-Harris plants; today Hillside is number one. As a result of the session," he continued, "ten task forces were appointed to grapple with and solve identified problems or groups of problems. Each task force worked on the assigned problems, then brought proposed solutions to O'Hare. He'd consider the recommendations and either approve or modify them, or provide a full and satisfactory explanation for why he could not. This put the union and management on a good basis. This is what has led to the lasting improvements at Hillside. There have been no strikes during this time, and our relationship with the union is the best in terms of problem solving of any of the plants."

Dynamics of Change

Although the model calls for beginning with an explanation of what an ideal relationship between the two groups would be, many times it is not practical to expect participants to start at this point. Each group is likely to start by exploring its own hostile feeings and tensions toward the other. Since the hostilities and tensions expressed are not heard by the other group, this ventilation does not come across as an attack; it is little more than blowing off steam. The design administrator does not intervene to stop this ventilation, unless group members persist and fail to orient themselves to the purpose of the session.

Exchanges *between* groups are public, thus keeping everyone informed simultaneously. The importance of this would be difficult to overemphasize. Because of the public character of communication that is created, all members of each group undergo a shared process of change. Short of treachery, there is no way for one group to mislead or deceive the other group. The changes agreed to are likely to replace the status quo with new concepts for working arrangements.

This should be contrasted with change when the effort is to bring it about on a one-after-one basis, when the second person doesn't know why the first one's point of view has altered. Not knowing the rationale, the second person is likely to interpret it based on a sense of distrust, feeling the first person "sold out" and is a "traitor to the cause" or a weakling. When the second person changes, the third person's suspicions are likely to be aroused and so on down the chain. Another adverse result can be pointed out. The first person does not receive the support of the second, the second does not receive the support of the third, and so on, with the result that the processes of change are retarded, not accelerated.

The design administrators were somewhat more active in the Hillside situation than ordinarily would be the case. It is instructive to understand the reasons for this. This company had no deliberate plan for management or organizational development. As a consequence, the management had not participated in the kinds of human resources development seminars that center on management by objectives, group dynamics, or conflict resolution. The same applied to the union, which had had a minimum of training outside of bargaining and negotiation sessions. A generalization flows from this. The less organizational development that has taken place within a company, the more desirable it is to rely on external consultants to conduct sessions such as those in the Interface Conflict-Solving Model and follow-up.

The impact of the Interface Conflict-Solving Model at Hillside started from the discussions that permitted participants to lift their thinking above the status quo and to envision a model of the possible. By doing so, the actual relationship is seen in a different light and the possibility is present of creating a new relationship rather than trying to reduce the negative aspects of the present one. Since protagonists themselves are responsible for the content of the activities, they come to feel responsible for the change brought about by their own exercise of initiative. This further creates the likelihood of success.

The next trigger to change came when one manager said to the others, in effect, "Here's the way they see it. . . . Let's not explain to them why they are wrong, let's try to identify what we do that leads them toward their perceptions." This step toward self-examination led to the breakthrough point when O'Hare further personalized the interface conflict by saying, "What is it that I do? . . ."

A significant aspect of the change process involved management's coming to terms with itself by reviewing each of its member's attitudes toward unionization (while providing an opportunity for the union to reexamine its own attitudes toward management). Once this was done, management could shift as a group and see that the union was not an enemy, but a potential ally. The negative features it had observed in the union's conduct were a consequence of the initiative that management itself had exercised; that is, the hard attitudes produced in the union created the very resistances that management itself deplored. Management had come to see the union as the "problem" when, in fact, management itself was the "problem." By seeing themselves as responsible, management was able to specify, in terms of its own actions, what could be done to modify ineffective behavior and thus change the relationship.

The major turning point in the relationship occurred when O'Hare was finally able to say to the union, "We recognize we have a deep win-lose orientation toward the union. We want to change." This open declaration of the need for mutual support provided the necessary foundation for the rebuilding of trust.

CHAPTER 7

᠙᠙᠙᠙᠙᠙᠙᠙᠙᠙᠙᠙᠙᠙᠙᠙᠙᠙᠙

Achieving Integration Among Corporate and Field Goals

This chapter describes how the Interface Conflict-Solving Model was used to strengthen the interrelationships between a headquarters and several of its subsidiaries operating in various parts of the world. It shows that integration between headquarters and its various field locations is enhanced when every field location can trust that whatever actions it takes on behalf of the corporation's success will be matched by other subsidiaries conducting themselves according to the same norm.

Tim Pendleton, an outside consultant employed by us, had been working with the human resources department of Comtradco on a variety of assignments. One of them included an interface modeling project between components within the human resources department and their counterparts in field locations. The second design administrator was Hal Levinson, a vice-president of human resources at Comtradco. Levinson had been in the Interface Conflict-Solving Modeling activities just mentioned, which had placed him in an excellent position to understudy how to conduct the process with Pendleton at that time.

The study is an example of a three-way intergroup. The

172

headquarters' group is a family in the sense that they have direct reporting relationships with one another. The second group is composed of the heads of the major domestic locations in Chicago, Kansas City, Houston, and other large cities. These heads are on an equivalent plane in the organizational chart, but they have no reporting relationship with one another. The third group is composed of the heads of numerous field locations around the world. They, too, have a reporting relationship to headquarters, but they do not report to one another. With the foreign and domestic groups working separately, the standards and norms of conduct that governed the operations in one location were significantly divergent from those governing conduct in other locations; this difference enabled participants to discover and resolve some of the issues that are involved in commitment to uniform standards of conduct among them.

The turning point is of particular interest because it illustrates how the formulation of an ideal model aided participants from different international locations to see and agree on how a cooperative relationship among them could both further their self-interests and simultaneously improve their contributions to corporate achievement.

Any complex organization with local P/L (profit/loss) accountability is likely to encounter the problem that prevented Comtradco from increasing its corporate P/L. A subordinate organization may act against corporate interests when it decides a problem in terms favorable to local profit and loss. The problem is exaggerated when the headquarters rewards a subordinate component based on P/L, even while denying that it is influencing its own judgments. As a result, a major dilemma facing executives today involves securing commitment to a global corporate strategy from operating managers in all parts of the world. As organizations expand beyond national boundaries, a healthy interface between headquarters and field locations is critical for mutually supportive efforts in pursuit of corporate goals. Neither centralization nor decentralization offers an optimally effective approach to needed cooperation and collaboration if these run counter to the exercise of sound judgment or the advancement of or protection of vested interests.

When an organization has worldwide interests, centralization is perhaps impossible and certainly impractical. Managers in the field need flexibility and adaptability to respond to changing political, social, and economic conditions. Headquarters is typically at a disadvantage in terms of detailed information or current perspectives on global developments. Field managers are in positions to have the maximum amount of pertinent data. Since they are also responsible for implementation, headquarters' intervention into the decision-making process may be regarded as interfering, or even inappropriate.

Decentralization is not an entirely attractive alternative. Effective utilization of available corporate resources demands some degree of centralized decision making, budgeting, accounting, supervision, and development of senior personnel. Achieving corporate objectives requires concerted effort in a deliberate direction according to an agreed-on master plan. Every separate field location is a component of the large corporate puzzle and must interlock with others for the entire picture to be complete.

Since both centralization and decentralization offer problematic answers to how best to manage a global organization, many executives search for a third alternative, some middle ground that perhaps provides an acceptable, if not fully sound, approach. In some organizations the pendulum swings back and forth between the two extremes. When either is practiced for awhile and becomes untenable, the other appears more acceptable, is adopted, and the cycle repeats itself.

The intervention reported here illustrates *integration,* an effective way to coordinate geographically dispersed operations, enhance commitment to a global strategy, and ensure cooperative effort in their achievement. Integration is not a compromise between centralization and decentralization. Instead, integration describes a process of participation and involvement applied between the corporate level and divisional components in a way that brings motivation and attitudes into congruence with the requisite problem-solving structure for maximizing gain. The same process occurs in smaller organizations at the department or division level.

Integration can occur when headquarters and field locations jointly outline a corporate strategy in global terms and design a structure for implementing it on a continuing basis. With this model providing guidance and direction, interdependent action replaces independence and dependence or imposition and resistance. Then separate entities can clearly understand their contribution to corporate results and expect and receive headquarters' encouragement as well as agreed-upon support. Neither side holds the upper hand, because the headquarters-field relationship is based on trust and respect rather than power and authority or abdication.

The Need for Change

Comtradco was established early in this century to conduct business in natural fibers—primarily cotton and wool, but also jute, flax, and raw silk. Although its origins were in production, a major portion of its business is now in commodities futures trading. Julian Lombard, chief executive officer, has little patience with performance that falls short of expectations or results that fail to meet objectives. Lombard is accustomed to success and measures diligence and dedication primarily in terms of profit. A powerful force in Comtradco, Lombard initiated the interface intervention recounted here.

Leadership from the Top

Lombard summoned the senior vice-president for Worldtex, Joel Myerson, to discuss the division's most recent results. The balance sheet in front of Lombard reflected the same distressing slow growth pattern he'd been seeing for months. Frustrated and disappointed, Lombard was looking for answers to critical questions of competence, commitment, and return on investment.

"Some time ago," Lombard began, "we gave you the worldwide textiles group to pull together. Your recommendations and expertise in the trading area shaped the division. . . . You created the current structure, essentially centralizing many of the functions. You said it would work. Three years have passed and even now we're barely breaking even on this part of the business."

"I know our results aren't what they should be," replied Myerson, "but what more can I do? We're working hard, but we don't seem to be getting anywhere.

"Our people in the field aren't used to headquarters' guidance yet," he continued, "and while procedures are in place, sometimes they find ways to get around them."

"I understand that," said Lombard, "but how long can we wait? Policies, guidelines, and procedures are there to be followed. I just learned of a case where two of our domestic locations were bidding against each other for the same order. Do we have so little competition outside that we have to manufacture it internally? We ended up paying 15 percent above market. No wonder you're not making any money! What kind of coordination and direction by headquarters does this indicate? Furthermore, when I'm out in the field, many of those managers say the New York desk people are incompetent. Are they? I want to know what's really going on. What are you doing about these problems?" Lombard questioned.

"Look," sighed Myerson, "I thought things would work out in time, but they haven't. Maybe we should try something else . . . change the structure again."

"No! We've tried all that countless times before—you know it won't help. Something dramatic and constructive has to be done now," replied Lombard. "I'm not going to let these problems continue. That's a promise. I want you to think through this whole situation and be prepared to give me a recommendation for corrective action by next Monday. I suggest you talk with Levinson. He stays close to what's going on in all parts of the company and he might be a good sounding board. Maybe he'll be able to suggest an approach we haven't tried before, like making an example or two of what results from deliberate noncompliance. Since we elevated him to vice-president of human resources, I think he has exerted a strong and positive influence."

Support from the Staff

Myerson invited Levinson to join him and Lombard to discuss the problem and gain his perspective and suggestions for next steps. "My neck's on the line," Myerson admitted, "but I really don't know what I can do or what you can do. Lombard says you might have some ideas . . . or just a fresh look at the situation. I'll take whatever help I can get."

"From what you've said in meetings and to me from time to time, as well as what Lombard has said or has been quoted as saying, I think I'm pretty much up to date on the major problems," Levinson replied. "In a nutshell, you've tried to put a new structure in place and implement a revised set of procedures, but the old attitude and behavior patterns haven't changed. Profits are down and Worldtex still isn't meeting its objectives. Corporate P/L is too often sacrificed in the interests of local P/L. Each location is still operating as a decentralized, autonomous entity without regard for others around the world. That's my diagnosis."

"Right on target," said Lombard. "What's the treatment?"

"Well, let me tell you my story," Levinson continued. "When I came I had a somewhat similar situation, except it was related to our personnel policies around the world. The practices in the various operating segments had grown up independently in different countries. My first charge was to bring these procedures together into a set of policies that could more or less be applied uniformly around the world. This was particularly important as we moved people from one location to another. The national differences, antagonisms, egos, and vested interests were strong."

"What did you do?" asked Lombard.

"I worked with an organization development firm, with Tim Pendleton in particular, who helped us through a strategy for changing organizational *cultures* by assembling the various principals to first diagnose their organizational practices, which were inefficient and out of date, and then learn how to shift them by working together to set corporate objectives and design a program to achieve them."

"Do you think that same approach could help us?"

"I have a summary of the one we did in my files that describes the approach and provides a rationale for what takes place pretty well; I think it might be worthwhile for you to take a look," replied Levinson.

"Get the materials to me, if you will. If I decide I'll ask you to contact your consultant and we can review the situation face to face. Okay?"

Perspective from Outside

Five days later, Tim Pendleton (consultant), sitting in the boardroom with Lombard, Myerson, and Levinson, recalled the urgency in Hal Levinson's voice the week before. He had phoned Pendleton, described the problem, and asked if they could have a more in-depth discussion of the problem and the potential of the Interface Conflict-Solving Model for dealing with it.

"As Hal probably told you last week," Lombard began, "Joel's new organization just hasn't jelled. His situation is so unique I thought it would be wise to see whether these ideas and strategies might apply to Worldtex. . . . Based on what you and Levinson did last year, he thinks so."

"What can we expect if we decide to do it?" asked Myerson. "My files are bulging with studies full of recommendations and prescriptions. The last thing we need is another study that promises so much and delivers so little."

"This approach is somewhat different," Levinson replied. "It doesn't create reams of paper or try to tell management what should be done. The interface process aids in creating a model for change. It provides a methodology to increase the participants' awareness of the need for change."

Pendleton added, "It helps participants understand that corporate history is the real enemy, then it assists in creating a climate that supports a shift away from the unproductive practices of the past and toward the kinds of attitudes and behaviors that increase the likelihood that your goals will be met."

"Will we have to slowly evolve into what we want to become?" Lombard asked. "Myerson needs to show improvement right away."

"Culture is much too powerful to be changed easily." Pendleton answered. "Lasting results require consistent effort and ongoing follow-up, but you can make a beginning in just a few days."

Once responsibility shifted to someone else, Lombard excused himself.

"What do we do to get started?" Myerson asked. "I need to make progress fast."

"I'd like Hal Levinson and myself to have discussions with some of your staff in representative U.S. locations and with several of the overseas managers," replied Pendleton. "He knows the ropes from his own experience and together we can diagnose and verify the basic problems from these interviews. Then, I'd suggest scheduling a meeting with all your key managers who are involved in the problem."

"From all over the world? Review it for me again. What would we be doing?" queried Myerson.

"Basically, taking some simple, progressive steps toward positive change," said Pendleton. "First, agreement is reached among all the principals on the soundest basis for operating a worldwide trading company in a profitable and sound manner. Normally, this can be achieved fairly readily, as thinking in ideal terms and from the perspective of the problem's internal logic facilitates arriving at an optimal solution. Next, the actual situation is described. Agreement here is not easy, but less difficult than you might think, because descriptions can be based on specific instances and examples. Participants explore the situation's history, actively focusing on how and why relationships, practices, procedures, and so on, have developed in certain ways and not in others. Achieving understanding and agreement in this area is critical to lasting cultural change. Finally, action plans are developed to overcome history and bridge the gap between the soundest and actual situations."

"With people from so many places involved, can we realistically expect to get all of them together on anything?" Myerson asked. "I've been here a long time, and I'm not even sure we could agree that black is black or white's white, and the tensions between headquarters and the fields will be a major impediment to any progress."

"Finding objective solutions to a problem knows no nationality, and the organizational components involved do not constitute a barrier. Differences in attitudes and values can never be completely resolved, but they do not have to impede problem solving," Pendleton noted. "Although there are differences in national sociology, there are no real differences in underlying human psychology and value systems. The same behavioral theories apply the world over. The multinational nature of your organization isn't an insurmountable barrier in gaining shared commitment to a global strategy."

"Is it really a good idea to be so open about things like this?" questioned Myerson. "Won't it just result in arguments, accusations, resentment, and hostility and reopen old wounds? At the best, what will we get besides good intentions, which may never materialize? We've had that already."

"The integration plan earns the commitment of everyone who participates in creating it and motivation generated through the integration process translates good intentions into sound actions. There'll be disagreements, as there are now, but they can be resolved through openness and candor that permits differences to be confronted. Follow-up is then needed and *wanted*, but this is a strong beginning," said Pendleton.

"Well, look," said Myerson, "I don't want to be a damper or a wet blanket, but what are the risks in this kind of thing? That's what I want to know."

"The risks are of two types. Let me deal with each," Pendleton continued. "The first is no progress will be made. That in itself is not a genuine risk, but the *attitudes* associated with failure to make progress is the risk. Continuation into the future of the same problem can result in people becoming disheartened, discouraged, and feeling defeated. They may be even less ready in the future to make another attempt at a solution than they are at the present, and I take it there isn't even all that much enthusiasm right now. This is not to be minimized because the experience of failure can have the demoralizing effects I have described.

"The second potential risk is to the futures of individuals. In this kind of confrontation session, competencies become more apparent than they may be in one-to-one dealings, but the same goes for incompetence. Incompetence, too, is subject to public scrutiny, and the person who suffers from publicly unveiled incompetence is in a weaker position in the future than he or she may have been in the past. This use of the term is almost a misuse, however, because organizations do not exist to protect incompetence. They exist to use resources to the fullest. If a person's competence is above some significant minimum, then administrative actions related to replacement are rarely considered. If competence is below that threshold, it probably is in the best interest of that person in the long term to find employment within his or her area of competence. It certainly is in the interest of the organization that it employ people who have the competence to solve problems that keep the organization viable and growing and that can give security to the many."

"There is an associated risk here," Levinson added. "It's not related to competence but to integrity. There always is the possibility that individuals will have been dealing in an underhanded manner. We know that organizations are correctly characterized as political institutions as well as systems of accomplishment. If people have been dealt with in an underhanded or unfair way, or if practices of deception are tolerated, these qualities also are likely to come into public view. When they do, it can be unfortunate for the person whose behavior is exposed, but again, this is a risk that is by no means an unfair risk. Deception and Machiavellian ways of operating are destructive of the system in the first place, and bringing these into the light reduces the risks to organizational health that are associated with them."

"The gain to the organization is that managerial actions can be taken that reduce the likelihood of its recurrence. This means a more open and authentic organization that is characterized by greater integrity. These are values that make for effective organizational problem solving rather than reduce it. That's my assessment of the risks involved," Pendleton said in conclusion.

Myerson remarked, "If that constitutes an assessment of the risks involved, the only one of any concern to me is the consequences associated with failure to be successful. I understand that and I appreciate your putting it in perspective, but it gives us another dilemma. Either we don't try for fear of failure, or we try and run the risk of failure. Which is better? Is it better to live with the status quo, which is less than satisfactory, or to risk an attempt to improve it and to fail?" Having asked the question, Myerson continued, "When I analyze the situation this way, I, for one, am ready for us to make a positive decision.

"It seems like the best alternative we've got," he continued. "I'd like to give it a try, but I'd still like to do one more test before reaching a decision. I'd like to know more about it from someone who's experienced it firsthand."

"You might call Charlie Goodwin, the president of Nonelco in New York, or Roger Elliot. Roger heads up Paterno, their largest American subsidiary. Either of them can give you a firsthand view of the process that got underway a few years ago and is still unfolding," suggested Pendleton.

"Okay," said Myerson. "After I check with Elliot and if it all seems ready to go, I'll get in touch with you and get to work on setting up the interviews. Levinson can take the lead in setting up the details of the meeting. I assume you two are going to work on it together. Is that right?"

Diagnosing the Situation

After the decision to go ahead had been made, interviews were conducted with Worldtex division managers from headquarters, regional operating locations, and a sample of international operations. Based on these discussions, Levinson and Pendleton discovered the core issues firsthand and became aware of tensions that surrounded them. Excerpts from these interviews give their flavor.

The View from Headquarters

Division headquarters is manned in the usual way with technical and staff groups giving background support. The key players are four "desk heads" roughly comparable with the more common corporate structures and a shipping director: Rodgers, cotton; Figueroa, wool; Swann, jute; Rod Ames, flax, silk, and exotics; and Cally, traffic and shipping.

Pendleton and Levinson conducted a group interview with these five key people. They were thirty-five to fifty-five years old, and only John Rodgers had not had field experience in the United States or Europe.

"Our biggest problem is that roles and responsibilities are unclear," explained Mark Swann.

"As I see it, we're intermediaries between operating locations and a market information clearing house," said Ames. "There are different markets, but all of them are interdependent, since they are interconnected in one way or another. This means that some centralization is needed to get the locations to play the same game by the same rules, or our size and diversity can work against us. Without order and predictability, it's a situation of prima donnas, each performing like a ballerina, each performing according to her own score."

"We don't have a crystal ball," Swann added, "so we usually just provide information and advice. Managers 'out there' generally make their own decisions."

Pendleton asked, "Would I be correct in understanding what you are saying if I summarized it this way: 'a number of strong components but without effective headquarters' direction and coordination'?"

"That's it. We try to give directions but they are not accepted and we seek to coordinate, but we have difficulties there, too," said Swann.

"We're also responsible for approving some contracts," said Maury Figueroa. "We put together all the information and prepare the paperwork because we have a broader perspective than any local office. You'd think the traders would appreciate the help, but they seem to think they could do better without us."

"Basically, we're running so hard that we lose track of where we are," said Jim Cally. "Each of us makes high-pressure decisions based on the situation and the person involved, not according to an intelligent, systematic master plan. Many of our efforts are shortsighted. They put out the latest fire, but don't prevent new ones."

"I want to get back to the issues of direction and coordination because that's where our problems seem to lie. What the others have said is true," agreed Swann. "As a result, we seem to operate on personalities, not policies. We're still looking for a direction. We'd have a rebellion if we put out stringent policy and guidelines; the field would see them as straightjackets. These are men of responsibility and pride. We can't afford to dictate to them, but we don't want to go back to the free-for-all of the 1970s either. We need some middle ground," he concluded.

"In trying to pull this whole thing together," said Cally, "Myerson sometimes supports the idea of crystal-clear policies enforced by a strong headquarters. Other times, it's hands off. Sometimes we're like parole officers and other times we're strictly advisers. I think the field's even more confused by our inconsistency than we are."

"Our efforts to enforce established procedures are interpreted as centralized control, not direction and coordination," Figueroa added. "We need to clarify roles if we're ever going to go anywhere, but after all this time, I think we've come to tolerate and cope with ambiguity. As a matter of fact, I think the issue is not one of tolerating ambiguity, but actively promoting it in the name of local option, decentralized decision making, and all of the rest of it, which is justified under the traders' banner of 'wheel and deal.' "

"Maybe this meeting that's planned will help us get a better handle on things. At least we'll know better where we really stand," Ames remarked.

"What we've painted," said Rodgers, "is a pretty grim picture. If I were to summarize it, I'd say our comments add up to describing a headquarters that is not in control and a field that is out of control. It's a frightening situation. When you come right down to it, we are controlled by a world environment rather than being able to take actions that move us forward in a world environment. I think we've described the symptoms; personally, I don't feel that we're gotten down to explanations for why this situation is as it is. Having said that, don't ask me. I'm as baffled as anybody else."

Comments from U.S. Locations

The next visit was to several of Comtradco's offices in the United States, talking individually with Harris (Chicago), Thomas (Kansas City), Simpson (Houston), and Lewis (Portland)—the people who head the regional locations. Their comments, summarized below, focus primarily on headquarters' past performance.

> *Harris:* I'm not sure they know what they're doing on the headquarters' desks. In fact, they don't even seem to know what they're supposed to do. The desk heads have had to cope with high turnover and their new people really haven't caught on yet. If a desk head is away—sick or on vacation —their staff is helpless.

> *Thomas:* I know they're trying to be helpful, but more often than not they just slow us down. I work well with some headquarters' people, but most aren't responsive at all or they steer you the wrong way. I don't have time to put up with that nonsense, just because procedure says I should. They complain I don't follow the rules, but my business and bonuses have held up well enough so far. I'm judged on my own P/L, and so long as that's the case, I'll do whatever I think is in my own best interest.

> *Simpson:* Sometimes they help us put things together for a big contract. It's good to know their thinking on the markets even though I don't always agree. But in day-to-day operations they're less often a boon and more often a barrier. We almost lost my biggest contract of the year last month because it took so long to follow all the procedures. We've learned to work around them because it's so cumbersome to work with them.

> *Lewis:* It's mostly a matter of individual personalities and abilities. Some in headquarters are

okay, but I have a huge problem with John Rodgers on the cotton desk. He's given me bad information, then tried to deny it, or blamed some new staff person. I pay as little attention to him as possible. Another problem with headquarters involves the big contracts they're responsible for. When everything works well and Myerson and Lombard are pleased, headquarters takes all the credit. If a deal starts to go sour, they suddenly lose interest and leave us to pick up the pieces. "Get into trouble together, get out of it alone" is the motto around here.

Perspective from Abroad

Two managers from abroad, Felipe Mitjana (Spain) and Enzo Barrani (Italy), provided a view of Comtradco's international locations. The discussion took place in Mitjana's Madrid office. The head man from Singapore was interviewed while he was visiting headquarters.

"I'm happy enough with the way we work with headquarters overall," Mitjana began. "Most of these people try hard, and the ones who've been around awhile are knowledgeable. Much of our trouble centers on two or three who are either incompetent or have so narrow an outlook that it has the same effect. I think they look at everything from a U.S. angle and don't understand our markets here in Europe. We have somewhat more flexibility than the U.S. locations do. We're far enough away to be pretty well left alone. This has always been a decentralized operation so we can take advantage of fast changes at the local level without long delays in getting approvals from afar."

"That's the point," said Enzo Barrani, the Italian trader. "They sit in headquarters, close to all that goes on in their own country, but all they know about Italy is pasta and Sophia Loren. They're so myopic, they think Rome is only a city in upstate New York. I don't want them breathing down my neck, but I would appreciate some support once in awhile."

"Frankly," Mitjana suggested, "I think we could eliminate the headquarters desks altogether and get on just as well—maybe even better—without having to check with them for everything. I seem to spend as much time explaining to them what I need to do as it takes me to do it. I need more legitimate autonomy. Their so-called coordination sure isn't helping my bottom line."

"I've been in this organization for fifteen years, and the international locations are still treated like stepchildren," said Barrani. "I like the company overall or I'd go elsewhere. It's more than just nationality, it's a matter of consistency and objectivity, as well as knowledge and ability."

Mitjana agreed: "They know intellectually that things can't be done in all locations exactly as they're done in the home market, but they labor over every exception, so that it's preferable to inform them after the fact of what you've done —not to ask them beforehand. There *are* good reasons for some variations, but they filter everything through that big American lens and don't want to see something different. If consistency is the hobgoblin of small minds, the New York gang has got to be a bunch of pinheads. They worship it as an intrinsic value rather than a framework from which deviations that move the company forward are encouraged. What they regard as consistency we see as rigidity."

"Let me give you an example," Barrani interrupted. "Hans Mueller from Geneva has worked two years to open some new markets for us in Iraq and Sudan. It takes a lot of time and flexibility, and the U.S. headquarters desk is uncomfortable with anything that's 'different.' They want the kind of quick simple business that they've always had. Next month's meeting will be a good chance for them to get to know us," concluded Barrani. "I'm not sure we can honestly expect much more from it. Companies like ours seem committed to maintaining the status quo. It's a matter of evolution. We'd even make Darwin impatient."

Releasing the Hold of History

Twenty-four managers from the Worldtex division of Comtradco, Hal Levinson, and Tim Pendleton met within six weeks of Julian Lombard's pronouncement to Myerson that "something drastic must be done." Participating managers were organized into three groups: headquarters (including Myerson), U.S. regional locations, and international locations.

At the first joint session, each group was seated at its own table in the large central conference room. Levinson and Pendleton introduced the meeting and quickly called attention to the importance of the three groups reaching agreement on the soundest model for operating the world trade division. The model would provide a framework for organizing divisional resources so that all parts of the operation would fit together.

"In our interviews with you, the question of how centralized or decentralized you ideally would be emerged as a critical issue," Pendleton began. "We propose this issue to serve as a point of departure and suggest that an ideal position for integrating this organization be developed around it. A sound beginning is to list all the *elements* that are essential to the interface between headquarters and the field locations, if the business is to be conducted in the soundest manner. Then, for each element, describe the optimal basis for interaction."

"How idealistic can we be?" asked Jim Cally from the headquarters table.

"The first step is to develop a model of excellence," Hal Levinson responded, "without regard for the past. If you could make the relationship a perfect one from your standpoint, what would it be like? If it sounds general or abstract, try to make it concrete with examples and illustrations. Later on we'll add further specifics so that everyone knows what the generalizations are intended to mean in operational terms."

Designing an Optimal Model for Headquarters–Field Integration

Following several hours of discussion in separate rooms, the groups reconvened to share the three models of the soundest relationship between headquarters and operating locations. A spokesperson for the U.S. locations began by presenting charts describing the model they had produced. International and then headquarters followed with explanations of the elements in their soundest relationship models. Spokespersons rep-

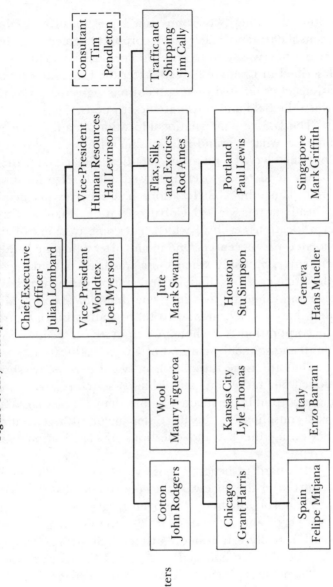

Figure 6. Key Participants in Comtradco.

resenting the other two groups asked questions for clarification. To consolidate and reach final corporate agreement, the four-point method was used to arrive at conclusions. (This procedure is described in Chapter Three.) After the U.S. and international locations consolidated their perceptions, agreement was reached between the field and corporate descriptions.

The U.S. and international locations had the same general feeling for what a sound relationship with headquarters would be, but they were by no means identical. The U.S. locations felt that they tend to be oversupervised and foreign locations felt ignored. Thus the U.S. locations had a better perspective on how headquarters viewed global operations than was true for foreign locations, each of which had come to think of itself as an isolated profit center. One might offer a helping hand to another center, but only when there was little or nothing to lose. As the broader issues of global integration came into view, both foreign and domestic locations saw that a local action might be needed that was detrimental to that location but advantageous to the corporation as a whole. A corporate perspective was preferable to and sounder than that of a regional location.

Thus the issue turned not on what perspective should be employed but rather on establishing a sound reward system for taking a corporate perspective rather than a local one. After the list was consolidated, the next step involved a general session for reviewing the list and questions of clarification regarding next steps.

"It's hard to believe," observed Myerson (Worldtex vice-president) after the review of the consolidated list, "we've come up with the sort of things I've been trying to get us to grapple with for years, and we've done it ourselves as a team effort."

"I'm really astonished," offered Cally from headquarters. "We've already accomplished more than I thought we would."

"Same here," agreed Lewis from Portland. "Our group is especially surprised to see how much importance we all place on mutual trust and respect. Our group feels it's really a pivotal issue, and the degree of emphasis we've placed on it must show how much we need to work on it. Frankly, we never expected headquarters to say that they'd trust each of us to do a good job."

Table 9. Ideal Formulations.

Element	Headquarters' View	Field's View	Composite Perspective
1. Corporate orientation	Each location recognizes and contributes to corporate priorities and places corporate interests above local interests.	Headquarters evaluates field performance from a corporate rather than strictly local perspective. Field contributions to corporate profit are recognized and rewarded.	Headquarters operates with competence and knowledge, providing a location with sufficient resources and attention as required by unique needs. Contribution to corporate profitability is the basis for rewarding location performance.
2. Mutual trust and respect	Headquarters is given appropriate respect by field locations and is trusted to do a good job. Equal consideration is given to domestic and international markets so that accusations of U.S. bias are unfounded.	Locations are recognized as true experts in the business, and our opinions and recommendations are weighed carefully before decisions that affect us are made.	Headquarters and field recognize one another's roles and responsibilities, appreciate one another's competence and abilities, respect one another as committed, competent professionals, and trust one another to do a good job.
3. Global perspective	Headquarters assumes major responsibility for all decisions which affect market penetration, both foreign and domestic.	Locations are encouraged to exercise initiative and independence in developing new foreign or domestic markets where the potential for profitable operations exist.	Headquarters and locations work cooperatively, pooling their best resources in a collaborative effort to identify and develop promising geographical areas or commodity markets.

(continued on next page)

Table 9. Ideal Formulations, Cont'd.

Element	Headquarters' View	Field's View	Composite Perspective
4. Strategic orientation	Headquarters establishes long- and short-range strategies based on broader corporate perspective and greater understanding of world markets. Locations comply with headquarters' guidelines.	Strategic corporate plans reflect the thinking of those most intimately familiar with market needs and requirements—the location managers. Our input is solicited prior to planning cycle and we have approval/disapproval authority over product.	Long-range corporate goals, shorter-term objectives, and strategic plans are the product of teamwide effort and involvement. Locations and headquarters staff are committed to agreed-on strategies and tactics and are willing to forego smaller short-term profits for greater long-term advantages.
5. Conflict resolution	Headquarters has the final say when conflicts arise between locations or between locations and headquarters. Locations are expected to comply. Locations should not assume that headquarters is always wrong.	Conflicts should be resolved at the lowest possible level. Locations should not be subject to arbitration from headquarters, but should work things out for themselves. Headquarters should not assume they are always right.	Time and distance do not limit our ability to recognize and face up to conflicts. Differences are confronted and resolved through mutual understanding and agreement.

"We have the same reaction to headquarters' sound statement about domestic and international markets," said Felipe Mitjana (Spain). "We're still somewhat skeptical, but international is very encouraged that headquarters recognizes and is concerned about eliminating the U.S. bias."

After spirited discussion of the meanings and implications of the various elements, Barrani (Italy) brought the discussion toward a conclusion, "I subscribe to what you have up there. Give us the answers to those questions and we'll leave two days early and get back to making money."

Harris (Chicago) added, "Those elements are about as big and basic as the paragraphs in the American Constitution."

"It probably is difficult to achieve," said Thomas (Kansas City), "but let's not try to add to it, because if we do, pretty soon we'll have a twenty-first amendment, a twenty-second amendment, and then a thousand interpretative rulings on what is intended by those five. We have the spirit of what's trying to be accomplished. That's what's important. If we understand one another's intentions, we're halfway home. I'd like to ask that we accept it as it is now written and move forward. Could we?"

Levinson reentered the discussion by asking, "Are there further questions? If not, let's take the model as produced to represent a tentative statement and see how well we can work with it. It's a sound basis for making progress in strengthening the development of direction and coordination throughout the system."

"Traders buying in to the concept of a corporate orientation is like a dream come true," quipped Myerson. "If there wasn't so much to be done before the sound model can become an actuality, I'd suggest we all go home."

"We're just getting our Fiat out of first gear," Barrani concluded. "Now that there's a model that we all agree represents excellence in our relationship, we can look at what we really do by comparison. Our sound model represents a challenge to which we're all committed. I'm anxious to move forward."

Exploring Actual Conditions

For the next activity, the groups were asked to describe actual conditions for the first element, "corporate orientation." As part of this task, they identified historical events that might explain current conditions.

Corporate Orientation Versus Emphasis on Local P/L

Following separate discussions, each group presented its perceptions of actual circumstances surrounding corporate orientation through spokespersons. Discussion centered on the appropriate importance to place on local P/L in evaluating performance and determining bonuses.

"The corporation's best interest is certainly what we emphasize, at least in principle," said Barrani, "but let's admit that the system doesn't reward or reinforce that principle. Headquarters wants and recognizes an entrepreneurial, competitive attitude, and that's the way it's always been. I'm responsible for the Italian P/L and my bonus every year is based on what I can produce."

"That might have been true before," Cally, spokesperson for the headquarters group admitted, "but not any longer. Our priority is overall company results—and has been since the world trade division was formed. Emphasis on local P/Ls is a vestige of the past."

Lewis, representing the U.S. locations, objected strongly. "Maybe you'd like to think things have changed, but the evidence says otherwise. Just last month Myerson was really upset with me for my big profit drop last quarter. I acted in the corporate interest and transferred an order to Los Angeles for a better delivery schedule, and all I got for being such a nice guy was a hard time."

"And what about Griffith's predecessor in Singapore?" added Barrani. "Everyone knows about how he served this company well for many years, but yet when his local P/L went down close to break-even two years ago, he got shafted. Even though he'd made substantial contributions to the overall profit

Table 10. Actual Formulations for Corporate Orientation.

Element	Headquarters' View	Field's View	Composite Perspective
1. Corporate orientation	Some headquarters policy and procedures are inconsistent with corporate orientation. Criteria for bonus payments reflect greater emphasis on local profit and loss than on corporate contributions.	Field staff are not committed to corporate profit. Priority is placed on maximizing local profit at all costs. Compensation system inconsistent with corporate interests.	Policy and procedures for performance appraisal and compensation are inconsistent with corporate rather than local priorities. Headquarters and field are at cross purposes because of problems with these systems.

picture, you all were disappointed with his individual results and he received no bonus that year. Now he's no longer with us. No matter what you'd like to think, out in the field we all know that looking out for number one is infinitely preferable to looking out for the corporation."

"It's not that we're disloyal," said Lewis (Portland). "We all know how important corporate profit is to the health of our individual operations. We're just asking that the reward system encourage a corporate orientation rather than discourage it."

"And when headquarters evaluates a trader's performance," reminded Barrani, "we'd appreciate your being consistent with what you say about corporate versus local interests. In other words, practice what you preach. In the field what we see is a headquarters that operates by a double standard. When a P/L is unfavorable, we catch hell for that. When we resist entering into a contract that will make the other guy look good and us bad, we catch hell for that. See what we're saying? You can't hold us responsible on a P/L level and ask us to sacrifice business in the corporate interest at the same time. Play it one way or play it the other way, but you can't play it both ways. As long as you headquarters types are not prepared to act according to a single set of criteria, this confusion, lack of coordination, and contradiction will continue. To capture it all in one word, 'chaos' will prevail. Another way of saying that is 'cutthroat' competition between commodity traders rather than coherent cooperation."

"Barrani," said Myerson, "you may have trouble spelling, but you sure can alliterate."

"Okay," responded Cally. "I can't argue with the weight of evidence you've presented. Historically, I have to say we've been inconsistent, but we're committed to making whatever policy and procedural changes are needed to ensure that things are different in the future."

"Right," added Myerson. "Now that we've surfaced old resentments and frustrations, maybe we can focus not on how things have been, but how they might be. We'll all ultimately benefit from the changes you've requested and we endorse. In order to solve this double standard, we need to create a strong reward system consistent with supporting corporate P/L."

Trust and Respect

Trust and respect was the second element considered. The trading groups agreed that many of headquarters' policies and procedures were unnecessary, given the high degree of competence and professionalism demonstrated at both the U.S. and international locations. Headquarters countered that the traders did not appreciate or value headquarters' expertise and their efforts to encourage traders to get the best deals when considered from a corporate point of view. They felt that their attempts to be helpful were often interpreted as interference.

In addition, much of the discussion circled around the trust and respect problem until it reached individual persons and their contributions or lack thereof. One example of candor emerged during the trust and respect exchange when the U.S. traders pointed to specific instances where Figueroa had shown personal bias in determining the fair market price at which goods would be sold from one region to another.

Another example involved Rodgers and the traders' perception that he refused to take responsibility by covering up his mistakes, often placing blame on another staff member or on the locations. Rodgers twisted on his chair when Myerson asked for specific instances. The U.S. traders cited several in which Rodgers failed to do his job properly, then refused to admit it.

Barrani made a similar generalization from international's perspective, stating, "There is also one major exception to the trust and respect we hold for headquarters staff, but we don't believe that a meeting like this provides a proper forum for discussing individuals. We're all agreed on this," he said, looking to other members of his group for support.

"But it doesn't help to say you don't have trust if you don't provide facts," said Myerson angrily.

"We just don't think it's right to point fingers in public," Barrani replied. Several members of his group nodded to confirm their agreement. "We'll take care of it in our own way, privately and quietly. That's the only gentlemanly thing to do."

The room fell silent. One could suddenly hear the sound of fresh air circulating and muffled sounds from the hallway. After a lengthy silence, Pendleton remarked, "It seems we have an example here from which we can learn something about openness and candor. The key point is whether or not international's approach is consistent with honesty and forthrightness. Is it truly 'gentlemanly' or helpful to suppress or sublimate conflict? Does reluctance to confront these issues reflect trust and respect or doubt and suspicion?"

"Each group will choose a course of action it feels is appropriate," added Levinson, "but the choice has consequences in terms of others' reactions. Openness elicits greater openness, repression results in greater withholding. The best way to ensure that others will be honest and forthright is to set the example. Withholding troublesome information encourages others to be less than candid in return. Relationships suffer, to say nothing of the costliness of failed decisions to the corporation."

The subject of trust and respect was concluded in the first few minutes of the next morning's general session. John Rodgers stood up the moment the room had quieted.

"You probably already know that international was talking about me last night. Their complaints were essentially the same as those that the U.S. group spoke about. It involves the accusation about my covering up mistakes and shifting the responsibility for them to others. I'm committed to seeing that this doesn't happen again, and if I backslide, please let *me* know so I can make immediate corrections."

Everyone listened thoughtfully, as though somewhat skeptical yet hopeful that public acknowledgment and Rodgers's evident "change of heart" and invitation to challenge any relapses would move him in the direction of solving a basic problem.

Global Perspective Versus Location Perspective

Once this level of trust and respect was present, discussion of the global strategy surfaced and several issues and problems could then be publicly analyzed and resolved in a way that brought forward the full complexity and subtlety of issues necessary for finding creative solutions.

Generally, headquarters admitted its need to work more closely with the international locations and to rely more heavily on traders' firsthand knowledge of regional, political, and economic conditions. Examples were cited wherein headquarters had erroneously assumed an "expert" orientation and, without the latest information and operating from its own remote location, had provided faulty advice. Conversely, either feeling they would not be listened to or out of apathy, locations acknowledged that they had failed to keep headquarters well informed of important national developments. Improved communication was clearly needed for traders to have access to important information and for headquarters to make intelligent, informed recommendations, particularly as they related to cooperation in the corporate interests among locations.

Specifically, pros and cons of developing a market with China were reviewed. Griffith (Singapore) explained the enormity of the potential. "For some of our basic fibers," he said, "the ultimate potential could be more than 10 percent of our current worldwide sales. We can also develop a huge quality source of supply, particularly in silk and other exotics, but we'll have to make a substantial investment and offer at least a 5 percent discount. Locating and securing supply sources will require frequent contacts and visits, and I think we should get started there before our competitors. Singapore provides us a window into China and it's a key listening post for all of southeast Asia. If it's in the corporate interest, I would be willing to take initiative to do so, but I would need headquarters' support in terms of a whole new way of looking at the Asian business."

"That sounds right to me," agreed Myerson, "and it reflects the global corporate perspective we need. If your local P/L falls off while you concentrate on this key piece of business, others need to take up the slack. Headquarters needs to adapt to facilitate this and other corporate-oriented initiatives. The days of just counting the cash register at the end of every month have got to stop. We're building for the future."

"But look at what you've just said, Joel," exclaimed Griffith. "You've just spoken the double standard again. In one breath you say local P/L and in the next 'building for the future.' This is our problem. You want it both ways. You want to judge us on cash register earnings and then you want us to take actions that impact adversely on short-term profits. The only solution that I can imagine for this kind of thing is that we move in the direction of an MBO [management by objectives] orientation. Joel, you and I can do an in-depth study for the prospects of southeast Asia and southern China, and we can also look at swap-out opportunities that arise for the Singapore office when we have contracts for Australia, Indonesia, and Thailand. I tell you my best estimate of profit and loss for whatever length of time reasonable stability can be assumed in the context of developing the China trade, and so on. You provide your inputs of what you expect of me based on the possible swing deals that headquarters may be able to create with Singapore as one of the principals.

"Once we hash that all out," Griffith continued, "that becomes my MBO contract with Comtradco, and I would expect you to judge my performance in the light of its terms corrected for unforeseeable eventualities like the border clashes between Vietnam and Thailand and the uneasiness between Vietnam and China. Then you'd be judging me against a jointly developed plan, Joel, not against some numbers at the bottom of a page and not against some subjective judgment of the adverse effect on corporate P/L from trying to penetrate the China trade. If we could do this, and all of the other major traders as well, it would give you deeper insights into our operating problems and opportunities and us greater confidence in headquarters' contracts and deals."

"Well, it sounds to me as though it would stop this swing between local P/L and corporate interests," responded Myerson. "What do others of you think?"

"And that would mean that from now on no more complaints about the Iraqi venture I've been out on a limb on," exulted Mueller. "Nobody else would touch that business because of the fighting, and it's taken a huge amount of work. Even though headquarters thought the effort was unjustified, it looks now as though it's paying off. If the whole place doesn't blow up, we'll be number one for years in a market that neither we nor our competitors have been able to penetrate before." He looked intently at Rodgers who grinned and raised a thumb.

"Sudan is another good example," Myerson noted. "They, too, have unique requirements like special terms, different delivery guarantees, extended payment schedules, and so on. I suppose progress there requires additional departures from standardized ways of doing business."

"I'm really beginning to understand," said Rodgers. "The trouble is that these out-of-the-ordinary efforts take so much time and seem unnecessarily complicated. Now that I know the background I can see that conventional approaches wouldn't work. I'll be giving this kind of activity more attention in the future. It can really make the difference for us if we're successful in these areas."

The discussion of the actual issues continued, centering on the fundamental issues already identified: corporate orientation versus location perspective as the basis for business decisions, the impact of performance appraisal, incentive compensation programs, undertaking new market development and absorbing the expense locally, and the distortions of performance related to uncontrollable factors such as border closings and unavailability of transportation. Table 11 summarizes these concerns.

After completing the consolidation of the actual description, Myerson summarized his conclusions and perspective on the next steps. "We've always needed this clarity and agreement, but I thought it was still years away. Now I see that many of the barriers were here at home—in the headquarters group, generally, and in my own leadership, specifically. I think our first step should be to identify specific actions we need to take for headquarters to improve its operation and exercise real strategic leadership and for the locations to strengthen and modify their efforts, and thirdly, specific things we need to do together to get our relationship straightened out. I'll take personal responsibility for investigating how to bring a reward system into place that recognizes the contribution to corporate P/L that locations contribute. I will have recommendations to

Table 11. Actual Formulations for Remaining Elements.

Element	Headquarters' View	Field's View	Composite Perspective
2. Mutual trust and respect	Generally, locations do not give us credit for doing a good job, but point fingers in our direction every time something goes wrong. They hold us responsible for problems we do not create and cannot control.	Headquarters staff think they know everything, but they all make mistakes from time to time. We spend more time to time justifying ourselves to them at times than we do getting our jobs done. Excessive regulations, policies, and procedures are all evidence of their lack of trust.	Lack of clarity surrounding appropriate headquarters' role contributes to misunderstanding and lack of trust. Strict adherence to standard operating procedures interferes with needed flexibility. Expertise and experience in the field not always afforded due consideration or attention.
3. Global perspective	Headquarters cannot keep current on political and economic activity throughout the world. Things change too rapidly and we do not have adequate staff to keep up with daily developments. Our guidance is not always appropriate.	Locations are dependent on headquarters for guidance and direction, but they lack sufficient knowledge and expertise. We do not always inform headquarters of what we hear and learn from our travels and contacts.	Poor communication and coordination between headquarters and field hampers development of global perspective. Headquarters is more aware of domestic than of foreign markets. Headquarters must rely on locations for information and interpretations of world events.
4. Strategic orientation	Short-term objectives are given greater time and energy than long-term goals and plans. Headquarters is reluctant to subsidize market development activities until they become profitable.	Locations do not get involved in strategic planning. Headquarters is too busy putting out fires to plan properly. No one is giving strategic planning the attention it merits, much to our detriment.	Strategic planning is done, if at all, on an elementary and informal basis. Too much time is spent on activities which will have little if any long-range impact. Our emphasis is narrow and shortsighted for the most part.
5. Conflict resolution	Differences are either ignored, smoothed over, or degenerate into win-lose confrontations over who's right or wrong. As a last resort, headquarters claims ultimate authority to hand down binding resolutions.	People are discouraged from saying what they really think so that potential conflicts are avoided. Boat rocking is frowned upon, especially by headquarters brass who expect us to comply with their authoritative dictates.	Conflict is avoided because there are no constructive systems in place for dealing with it. Differences of opinion are viewed as negative and threatening. People are encouraged to go along and get along.

present to you within the next two months. This will give us time to set plans in motion and to iron out the bugs in what needs to be done based on the work we'll finish here."

Planning for Change

When the session was opened for consideration of specific steps, groups were restructured to include proportionate representation from headquarters, the U.S. locations, and the international locations. This reinforced the need for collaboration among those present.

Four groups responded to the following task question for this activity: "What specific steps can be taken on the authority of those present, by whom, by when, to achieve what specific results?" Every group discussed the "trust and respect" element and one of the other four elements. The newly structured groups formulated specific plans then presented and critiqued them in a general session. Activities, timetables, and assignments of responsibility were clearly established and specific follow-up steps were outlined.

"To wrap the session up," said Myerson, "I'm not here to pronounce a benediction, but I would like to place what we have accomplished in perspective. Our division has not done well for the past three years. I suspect it is reasonably widely known among you that Julian Lombard has been concerned that the actions we have taken haven't brought about the turnaround that's needed for long-term health. He was dubious about this meeting, but he asked me to probe possibilities with Hal Levinson. Hal put us on the track that we've been through.

"I can now tell you with confidence that I am prepared to go to Lombard and report that in my view—and, speaking for what I've heard others say, for your view too—we now have the framework for lifting ourselves by the bootstraps. We have a commitment to take actions to bring about what we want to occur. These have been intense days. I realize that many of you have come long distances. This meeting is another interruption of your family lives. There's no way to correct for this, but there is one way of acknowledging it. I want to express my personal appreciation for the efforts made here."

"Speaking for the group," said Barrani, "you have our support for talking to Julian Lombard as you have said you will. I now suggest that we break for the bar."

Three years later, steady progress has been made toward improved organizational integration. With an exception or two, the corporate orientation has been factored into local decisions and the reward structure changed so that the incentive compensation is based on corporate contribution. An equitably administered compensation program has reinforced reliance on the corporate orientation in local decision making.

Dynamics of Change

Comtradco's shift away from individualized, vested interests to a global, corporate orientation illustrates the dynamics of change described in Chapters One and Three. By analyzing the intervention in these terms, change is clearly seen as a dynamic process, not an isolated event of dealing with individuals, one after another.

Influence of History

A negative history was at the core of conflict in this headquarters-field relationship. Initially, historical perceptions and misperceptions continued to block progress and impede change. As history was explored, analyzed, and positively dealt with during the development session, change became a viable possibility and eventual reality.

Headquarters had developed a view of the field as unappreciative, disrespectful, sometimes devious, and often uncooperative. Examples of perceived resistance to headquarters' attempts to provide guidance and direction (headquarters' perception) or to exercise control (field's perception) reinforced this opinion. In headquarters, the field was seen as a group of free-wheeling entrepreneurs, willing to sacrifice the corporation to achieve its own objectives. Members of the headquarters group began the interface development session convinced that nothing short of a miracle could generate field commitment to the greater corporate good.

Both field groups held similarly negative perceptions of headquarters as incompetent, inconsistent, too bureaucratic, and overly controlling. Their arsenal of complaints was loaded with historical instances of perceived injustices and inequities. As their initial comments and behavior illustrate, the field obviously held little hope for constructive attitudinal and behavioral change.

Since history was shielding cooperative, collaborative alternatives from view, strategies for coping with poor interface relationships failed to surface and conflict was masked. Headquarters managed as best it could by dealing with each location on an individual basis rather than as part of an integrated whole. To avoid open conflict, managers learned what individual locations would or would not tolerate and adapted their behavior accordingly.

Likewise, the field learned which headquarters people to trust and which to avoid. The field became expert in evading established procedures, short-circuiting requirements, and circumventing channels. The rule was to get by and to accept mediocre relationships and results as unchangeable, if not inevitable.

Modeling Excellence

With the model of a sound relationship embraced as a standard of excellence, the groups no longer accepted poor interface relationships, but strived instead to optimize their interaction and results.

Commitment to a superordinate goal, that is, implementing a corporate orientation, and the kind of motivation required to achieve it, is an integral component of this intervention's success. The turning point occurred when both headquarters and field came to recognize how strongly they believed in the same things—trust, respect, a sound corporate strategy, and a global business perspective. Once a basis for agreement became self-evident, the goal of corporate profitability received broad endorsement. How to's were readily resolved in the climate of mutual trust and respect, which developed when these groups realized they ultimately wanted and needed the same things.

Beyond the specific accomplishments that flowed from this conference, the stage was set for a much longer-range and sounder approach to organizational success by linking such organizational development goals as mutual trust and respect and corporate orientation to a reward system tied to corporate profitability rather than incentives dependent on local performance.

Shared Objectivity

Shared objectivity was achieved by the thorough probing of history, which produced agreement on what had been and what needed to be changed. Progress was made when each group could recognize its past actions that had led to problems and its unwitting role in preventing their solution. Myerson's comment, "Now I see that many of the barriers were here at home—in the headquarters group, generally, and in my own leadership, specifically," represents the level of perceptual objectivity achieved.

Membership Norm Shifting

No individual member was forced to risk negative sanctions by changing from a group-held position in isolation. Group members had the opportunity to think through and evaluate alternative behavior patterns and new attitudes collectively, so that change could occur in the entire group simultaneously. As they became aware of the unsatisfactory norms controlling their behavior, headquarters and field reached consensual decisions to forsake the past and pursue a sounder future.

Group discussions of problems included exposing and dealing with specific past transgressions, presenting opposing viewpoints candidly, and facing personally ineffective and inappropriate behavior. The field's reactions to Rodgers's perceived incompetence demonstrated the potentially positive effects of candor and confrontation. Rodgers's acknowledgment of responsibility generated a sympathetic feeling toward him although he had violated norms of integrity and resulted in others extending credibility to him for his readiness to be forthright. This is a fundamental in rebuilding trust.

The Comtradco interface was a vertical relationship among the headquarters and the other two groups; headquarters' power over the other two put it in a position to mandate a solution on the basis of coercion, if nothing else. As the study demonstrates, headquarters was able to suspend reliance on power and authority for dealing with the problem while the field locations were able to deal with the higher-level organization in an open way, devoid of politics. The field locations also embraced a corporate orientation once it became clear that each of the field representatives was prepared to commit to one another a mutual obligation to act according to the same standards of decision making. This mutual obligation was the basis for shared confidence that equitable treatment by headquarters would be based on overall contribution rather than only on looking good in the local context.

CHAPTER **8**

ᘓᘐᘓᘐᘓᘐᘓᘐᘓᘐᘓᘐᘓᘐᘓᘐᘓᘐᘓᘐᘓᘐᘓᘐᘓᘐᘓ

Overcoming Conflicts Between Parent and Subsidiary Organizations

The use of the Interface Conflict-Solving Model in a vertical relationship is introduced in this chapter. The case study here details its use for seeking a resolution to a standoff between a headquarters and its most significant American subsidiary. A widespread notion exists that the exercise of influence downward through an organization is a far more practical possibility than the exercise of upward influence. By and large, this is a correct perception of what takes place in real-life organizations. However, there are many outstanding examples of exceptions in which subordinate units actively resist influences exercised on them from above. When this happens, the options available to the higher level are substantially narrowed. They can either live with and accommodate the resistance or seek to solve it by replacing those responsible for it. Accommodation is an unacceptable alternative to many, and replacement of an entire

An article abridged from this chapter appeared as: Robert R. Blake and Jane S. Mouton, "Out of the Past: How to Use Your Organization's History to Shape a Better Future," *Training and Development Journal* 37, no. 11 (1983): 58-65.

layer of executive personnel at a lower level is not only costly but also is unrealistic in many cases.

Two features of this application should be mentioned. One is that we, the authors of this book, served as design administrators in this application of the model. We did so because the top corporate executives in the headquarters were a part of the problem and therefore could not be regarded as neutral; in this context, the neutrality of design administrators was seen to be of critical significance to the participants from the subsidiary. From their standpoint, anything other than a neutral support for the design would have been regarded as an unacceptable pressure from headquarters and, for all practical purposes, would have resulted in the subsidiary's participation being nominal in character.

A second feature illustrated in this application of the design involves implementation discussions carried out in a functional way by counterparts from both sides of the cleavage, that is, the two presidents met together to explore implementations that only they could commit themselves to; the same happened between marketing personnel, the human resources function, and so on. This variation is of importance because it demonstrates that some implementation decisions involve a specialist's analysis and therefore cannot be widely shared. Other decisions, such as those that involve the two presidents and what they might be able to implement as a pair, are primarily subject to their own assessment only.

Nonelco is a large multinational corporation headquartered in New York. Paterno, in the Sun Belt, is its most important domestic subsidiary. Conflict at the interface revolved around the subsidiary's resistance to headquarters' guidance and direction. In the past few years, Nonelco has become increasingly frustrated with Paterno's apparent foot dragging whenever headquarters tried to tell Paterno what to do.

Exploring the Issues with Outsiders

Nonelco's president, Charles Goodwin, described the problem and his thinking to Blake and Mouton. "I wonder what's

left to do after years of trying everything to bring Paterno into
the corporate mainstream, and they're still operating on the
outskirts. Looking at the choices left, the only solid one is asking Roger Elliot to resign . . . and I'm not sure I'm willing to
pay that price."

"How do you see Elliot?" inquired Mouton.

"As Paterno's president, Elliot is respected by his organization. His commitment and competence are evident, as is his
strong sense of personal loyalty to Paterno. If I ask him to resign," Goodwin reasoned, "I not only risk destroying the man,
but the short-term profitability of Paterno as well. It's also an
admission that we at Nonelco are not creative enough to solve
this without power and politics."

"Do others in Nonelco share your views?" asked Blake.

"Yes, my people have the same feelings and biases. Maybe we need to take a fresh, objective look," said Goodwin. "The
problem between our two organizations is obviously not policies or structures; it's relationships and people. We haven't done
the best job of getting a good fit between technical and financial aspects and we've made even slower progress on the human
side. I'd like your suggestions as to how this impasse might be
resolved. Do you remember enough about the Paterno acquisition years ago, or should we begin by reviewing the details?"
Goodwin asked.

"I think we're familiar with the background and mechanics of your assuming control," Blake answered.

"Let's concentrate on how the relationship between
headquarters and Paterno has been developing since then," suggested Mouton.

"Well," Goodwin began, "it's been tough from the start.
Our organizations have completely different histories and cultural patterns. We're internationally oriented; they're national
in scope, but heavily influenced by their Southwest origins.
We rotate managers through various functions and into different countries and political environments, so our executives are
highly sophisticated and cosmopolitan generalists who have a
global as well as a multifunctional orientation. Paterno's key
people are specialists, and their perspective on international

issues is pretty limited. Company leadership has traditionally been provided by engineers who have strong technical backgrounds. Mind you, no subsidiary in our system has stronger people who justifiably pride themselves on their technical competence. In some unique way they have not seen themselves as students of management in the professional sense and have not kept themselves as fully aware of changes in managerial thinking that have been emerging over the years as we have in Nonelco.

"We've been trying for years now, and it's hard to believe, but we still don't have a good handle on their operation," Goodwin continued. "Our recommendations for improvements and changes to some of their costly and ineffective practices are usually dismissed with a cursory 'that's okay for headquarters to say, but it really wouldn't work here.' Our efforts to help them become a vital, contributing part of our organization have failed to result in much progress. They apparently feel some deep antagonism toward us, and we're feeling resentment and hostility toward them in return.

"But I need results!" Goodwin emphasized. "If Elliot can't manage his people and get them to play by the rules, I'll have to replace him. It would be my last resort, but I'm willing to take drastic action. These issues have to be resolved!"

"A new president might be able to establish and maintain better patterns of interface cooperation and collaboration," replied Blake. "However, often he or she fails to consider the strength of traditions and practices as well as inevitably negative group reactions to individuals who disregard or violate their long-established norms. Much of what took place in the past is inadvertently transferred into the future as new leaders seek acceptance and approval by learning group expectations and fitting in with them."

"A new group member," Mouton added, "largely depends on others' versions of what's going on or explanations of what happened in the past. In learning about history, the new member is, perhaps unwittingly, influenced by the biases and prejudices of others. As the new leader or member responds to the cues provided by peers, superiors, and subordinates, the old attitudes, values, and behaviors that the new leader might have changed are sometimes adopted instead as desirable and appropriate. In a few weeks, he might join them and see things their way and enjoy their support rather than keep seeing things your way and then try to whip them into line."

"Do you think it would work," Goodwin posed, "to confront Elliot directly? What if I just tell him to cut out all the bickering, one-upmanship, and game playing? I can spell out the need for better cooperation and collaboration then set some definite expectations. Since it's likely to be a hot session, I might arrange for you to sit in as a referee or umpire, or to get it back on course if it gets diverted. You might serve as a facilitator to keep the discussion moving."

"If change were so easily accomplished," Blake replied, "interface conflict would soon disappear. Is this a conflict just between you and Elliot or does it involve policy makers at headquarters, too?"

"Oh," said Goodwin, "we at headquarters all feel this way and I expect the Paterno people live in Elliot's shadow. I suspect it's not just me and him, but us and them. Is this not a correct reading of my colleagues? You've been in and out of the company over a number of years and heard informal conversations among them regarding Paterno—am I not reading them accurately?"

"There are variations on it, but many have the same basic theme. There is no question but that there is a prevailing shared view among your executives about the Paterno situation. Therefore, I'd question the soundness of such a three-way discussion," answered Blake. "If the problem involves the key people on both sides, then the solution should involve them in finding creative ways to resolve it."

"From our experience," Mouton added, "mandated cooperation seldom has the impact expected of it. Compliance with historical standards and precedents is reinforced and rewarded while mandated change all too often is treated as a deviation from 'normal' and is either ignored or resisted."

"Okay then," Goodwin conceded, "what will work? Could you two spend some time with Elliot and others in Paterno and see if you can understand their views of the interface problem?"

"We can go to Paterno," said Mouton, "and search for explanations that make sense for these ongoing problems in the relationship. After we've explored the issues more thoroughly, we can suggest an approach for resolving the tensions and establishing a basis for ongoing integration between the two organizations."

"You don't know Elliot, and he's reluctant to have you in. I suggested several times that he might want to contact you for improving and strengthening his top team, but he's taken no action. I don't know why this is unless it's because he knows you've been associated with headquarters in the past. But our need," Goodwin reiterated, "is to establish some foundation for understanding and cooperation, but at this point I'm not sure that's possible. So I'm willing to take the initiative on this and set it up."

"I'd be interested in how you plan to introduce our visit to Paterno," said Blake.

"I'll call him today and make the necessary arrangements. Rather than suggesting that he have you in, I will ask him for his approval, and I think I'm unprepared to take 'no' for an answer," Goodwin responded. "Let me mention though, they'll probably resent you. No matter what I say, your visit may not be favorably interpreted, so you need to be aware that arrangements for you to visit there may entail my overcoming their protest that we're telling them what to do. This can put you behind the eight-ball, but I know of nothing else. If push comes to shove, it's this or termination."

"I hope it doesn't come to that, but if it does, then the challenge is on us to work through to resolve the resentment if we can," replied Blake. "If we can't, I expect not a whole lot will have been sacrificed in the attempt."

Diagnosing the Problem

Arrangements were made for Blake and Mouton to spend the time necessary for getting to know the Paterno organization. After a typical exchange of formalities for a first meeting, Roger Elliot became guarded and serious. "I want you to know," he addressed them, "you are unwelcome guests. We resent having you imposed upon us and we doubt there's much you can help us with. However, we are gracious people, and we'll cooperate as you carry out your assignment. How do you intend to work? Study our problems and then give a report to Goodwin?"

"No," said Mouton. "We are not his representatives in any sense like that. Even though you haven't asked for it and have indeed indicated that you don't want it, our responsibilities on this assignment are to you. We would regard it as inappropriate to discuss anything we learned about Paterno with Goodwin unless you asked us to do so or approved of our doing so."

"Why is that?" asked Elliot. "He's paying you. Aren't you obligated to him?"

"Our obligation to him is to try to do a good job," replied Mouton, "not to investigate for him or recommend to him what we think he should do. If we were to do so, it would weaken the connection between you and him, and from what we understand at the moment, that linkage is not strong. If it were strong, I suspect we would not be here. But in our view, problems at this point must represent far deeper and more pervasive problems than the working practices between you as two executives."

"I don't feel that's the case, but perhaps we'll have a chance to explore it more later. Indeed, I'd like you to have a chance to see things from my point of view," replied Elliot. "But let's solve the housekeeping matters so that you can get settled in. I've arranged for you to have an office in the personnel department while you're here, so I'll introduce you to Tom Adams, our personnel vice-president. He'll take care of those details of your stay."

"I'd like to talk about that further," said Blake. "We'd prefer not to be officed with personnel."

"Why?" asked Elliot.

"By proximity we'd take on their character and reputation," Blake explained. "Successfully completing this assignment requires that the organization regard us as experts in applying behavioral science theory to dilemmas of organizational life, not as extensions of the personnel department. There's no implication regarding their reputation. It's just that there are so many stereotypes about consultants that we'd just as soon avoid taking on *this* stereotype."

"Where do you want to be?" queried Elliot.

"It's probably best for us to be located near you and your key staff," Mouton suggested. "That will provide us the access we need to make the most productive use of our time."

"Okay, there's an empty office we can set you up in," Elliot noted, "and I'll have my secretary provide you with a list of appointments. I'll arrange for her to offer whatever secretarial support you need."

"Thank you; that will help a lot. If you don't mind, we'd prefer to make our own interviewing arrangements," Mouton said. "We'll call the people we'd like to talk with directly, introduce ourselves, describe what we want to do, and manage our own schedule, if that's okay."

"It's more informal if we meet with people in their own offices," Blake observed, "and we prefer a degree of informality."

"Looking ahead, we'd like to spend some time with you, possibly Friday afternoon two weeks hence, to review whatever we feel merits discussion at that time," added Mouton.

"I suppose so," Elliot responded, "but I doubt you'll learn much we don't already know."

For the next several days, interviews were conducted with Paterno's key executives beginning with Elliot and including Carey, executive vice-president; Mason, vice-president of administration; Sloan, vice-president of marketing; Adams, vice-president of personnel; and Price, vice-president of manufacturing. In addition, Blake and Mouton attended various executive committee meetings and interviewed other executives and a diagonal slice of their organizations in different locations.

From these brief but intensive discussions, Blake and Mouton gained a clearer picture of what seemed to be blocking effective cooperation. A typical conversation with Elliot reveals the underlying dynamics.

"Since Goodwin arranged for us to be here, it's evident he sees some problems in your relationship with headquarters," Blake observed.

"It seems there are always minor irritations between a

headquarters and subsidiaries," Elliot remarked, "but I don't think we have any major problems with Nonelco. They're a progressive, forward-thinking organization, and even though they don't understand us or our history, we've done our best to accommodate them. Almost none of the issues has been concerned with our technical performance. Every one I can recall over the past years has involved our productivity levels, our pay scales, and our promotion practices, union matters—that kind of thing."

"What people problems have there been?" Mouton inquired.

"Oh, nothing serious, really," said Elliot. "They say we're overstaffed by comparison with other subsidiaries, but I think the comparisons are unjustified and invalid. They just look at the numbers, not at what people are actually doing. They even asked me to transfer some of my best people to assignments in the corporation or in other subsidiaries, but with an exception or two I've convinced them otherwise. I can't release my key people and still meet their expectations and our own standards of excellence.

"I don't see what else could be bothering them," Elliot continued confidently. "We're their biggest money producer and we've never failed to make a sizable contribution to the corporate coffers," he said with pride.

"How open have you been to their overtures and initiatives to become involved in Paterno's operations? For example, to what degree have you used their extensive technical resources?" questioned Mouton.

"Look, we've given them everything they've asked us for," Elliot replied impatiently. "As for using their resources . . . I really don't see the need. Our technical prowess is unmatched, and we're doing quite well on our own. Indeed, it's our technical organization they have wanted us to release people from in order to buttress their weaker organizations. Frankly, I'm sure everyone here will tell you more or less the same thing."

When opportunity permitted, Blake and Mouton compared their observations and conclusions. From their perspective, Paterno's reluctance to accept the reality of their subordinate position was a primary barrier to developing an effective relationship with Nonelco. Alternatives suggested by Nonelco for increasing Paterno's effectiveness and establishing a productive, positive relationship with them were thought to be essentially hidden from Elliot and his staff by virtue of their history of fierce independence, pride, and self-reliance. For all practical purposes, they appeared to be operating with blinders on, essentially unaware of the depth of Nonelco's dissatisfaction and reasons for it. This perspective reported by Nonelco needed to be verified in the interviews with Paterno.

After three days of discussions and interviews, Blake and Mouton recognized that opinions of Paterno's people were monolithic in presenting a solid front of pride without even a hint of problems. The kinds of questions Blake and Mouton routinely asked to bring forth doubts and reservations about the quality of the relationship between headquarters and the subsidiary had produced essentially nothing. From what they heard, Blake and Mouton surmised that this organization had disciplined itself to embrace positive attitudes and a can-do spirit—attitudes and emotions that work against self-criticism. The net result was that accomplishments were emphasized to the exclusion of acknowledging weakness, even extending to the tendency to discourage new ideas except in technical areas. Under these conditions, tensions with headquarters were unrecognized, rationalized, and underplayed as inevitable or as resulting from feelings of jealousy.

"The way I see for opening up this relationship," Mouton said to Blake as they reviewed their learning to date, "is through an interface development session. The members in each group are in agreement as to a shared perception of the other. The problem is not owned by Elliot or by Goodwin. If Goodwin and Elliot were to come together and have a meeting of minds, it's a good bet that the one who changed would be seen as a traitor to his group—the one who capitulated by giving away his own convictions. It's almost a situation where no one can afford to change unless they all share together in revising their attitudes. Goodwin might be seen as a hero to his group if he got Elliot to change, but Elliot would surely be seen as a traitor in the eyes of the others at Paterno."

"I agree," Blake replied. "Paterno's group has been unable to accept headquarters' concerns on a one-to-one basis when these have been expressed. Also, they are unaware of how hopeless Nonelco is beginning to feel. The interface design has sufficient strength to throw these problems into bold relief, to create conditions that can break through the deafness that is blocking effective communication, but how do you think we might go about getting the two groups together?"

"Direct confrontation may create the needed awareness by Elliot," said Mouton. "Also, Nonelco needs to face their own attitudes of withdrawal and turning away from Paterno in frustration."

"Paterno doesn't recognize how they're seen from a headquarters standpoint. Elliot's feeling of righteousness have deafened him to Goodwin's words; as a result, he has no sense of Goodwin's frustration. Based on our conversations with him, Goodwin seems committed to drastic action," Blake added. "This is a costly step and might not really help all that much since there is such a wall of uniformity in attitudes among the entire top group."

"Let's double-check this with Elliot first thing in the morning to see how much of his understanding of Goodwin's position is the same as ours," Mouton suggested.

Gaining Commitment

Blake and Mouton met with Elliot the next morning. "The most important thing we've learned," began Blake, "is that neither you nor your key people seem to recognize the depth of the cleavage between yourselves and Nonelco. We're here because Goodwin feels there are serious problems, but this sense of concern is not mutual. How do you explain the discrepancy?"

"You're the experts, maybe you can explain it!" Elliot said provocatively. "If they've got a problem with us, it's *their* problem. Within reason we've done everything they've asked, we've been successful, and we're cooperative up to the point where we experience intrusion. Maybe they're resentful because we manage to do so well without them!"

"The depth of the concern indicates real issues. For whatever reason, it looks to us that you've failed to recognize them," said Mouton.

"Something else we think it's important to consider," Blake added, "is that Nonelco's problems with you, right or wrong, are ultimately your problems, too."

Elliot sat quietly, considering these points carefully. Finally, cautiously, he concluded, "There may be something in what you've said. Maybe those problems I dismissed as minor aren't so minor after all. Anyway, I think it's important that we clear it up, and I'm willing to explore it. What do you suggest?"

Blake and Mouton then presented the approach they had discussed between themselves the previous evening. They also explained the primary objectives of the Interface Conflict-Solving Model that might be used if Nonelco concurred: to identify underlying causes of the apparent interface conflict, formulate concrete actions for its resolution, and establish a basis for collaboration that brings into alignment headquarters' attitudes of distrust and suspicion with the subsidiary's attitudes of confidence and well-being.

"It might be helpful," said Blake, "if we describe the kind of activities that take place." He proceeded to give a broad outline of the activities involved. "If you are open to participating in this approach, we'd like to go back and relate our discussions to the executives at headquarters. If the cleavage between Nonelco and Paterno is, from their perspective, essentially as we've described it to you, we'd like to get your two groups together as soon as possible," Blake summarized.

"Okay," Elliot concluded. "I don't think there are gaps of that magnitude, but the points you've made do have a true ring against rumblings I've heard from time to time. I'm not sure it's really necessary. I certainly don't want my staff to feel I have bowed to headquarters, and in fairness I don't want to say you have placed us under pressure in any way. Let me discuss this proposal in the morning staff meeting. If we do it, I want everyone to be behind it 100 percent."

On returning to Nonelco, Blake and Mouton met with the

executive staff to recount their discussions and conclusions and
the agreements reached with Elliot who, along with his staff,
had decided that it was important to take a next step to try to
improve the relationship.

Goodwin gave immediate support to the diagnosis and to
suggestions for the next steps. Others gave their support, as if to
say, "This may break the logjam."

"What you've described," said Goodwin, "provides an accurate picture of what we see, though I think the problems may
be even more serious. I'm encouraged that Elliot is open to
examining the problems between us in depth. Progress may now
be possible."

"We'll get back with Elliot and set a date for the meetings," Mouton volunteered.

"The sooner the better as far as we're concerned," Goodwin concluded.

Setting the Stage for Change

The Interface Conflict-Solving Model session was scheduled at a location where participants (see Figure 7) could concentrate full attention on grappling with the issues at hand.

After preliminary remarks, Blake introduced the process
and described the activities. "It's clear," he began, "that at least
from Nonelco's point of view a cleavage exists at the interface
between Nonelco and Paterno. Entrapment in history frequently blocks progress toward a mutually beneficial integration.
Until history has been examined and evaluated, and specific
plans implemented to reduce its influence, the past will continue to hamper how you deal with one another in the present
and future."

"Before constructive change can be implemented," Mouton noted, "it's important to examine both organizations for
traditions, precedents, and past practices that may be ineffective and problematic. You may find that established ways of
doing things are leading in different and unsound directions,
and therefore become more aware of the need for change and
generate sufficient motivation to bring it about."

Figure 7. Key Participants in the Interface Development Session.

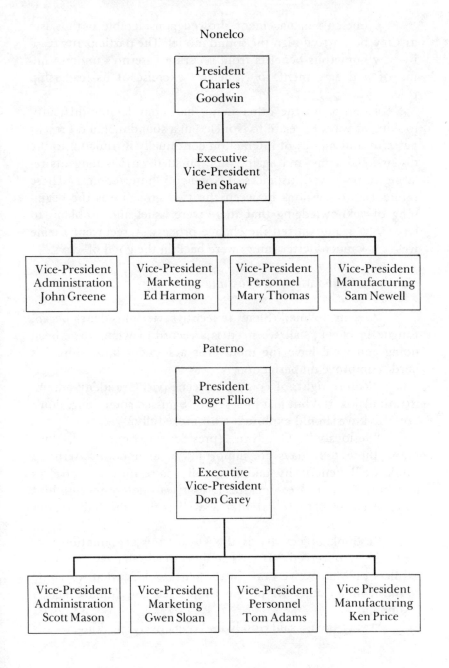

Describing a Sound Relationship

Nonelco's management showed considerable enthusiasm as they began to design the sound model. The participants readily saw numerous benefits from securing Paterno's understanding of and agreement to Nonelco's exercise of its leadership role.

Paterno, on the other hand, had considerable difficulty looking at ways to relate to Nonelco in a sound manner. Present patterns and modes of interaction continually intruded into the discussions. Time and again, they pursued various tangents relating to perceived instances of Nonelco's "interference." These references to tensions between the two groups was the beginning of acknowledging that there were issues and problems to be resolved and started the change process. A recurrent theme was "how much better things were back in the good ol' days."

Nonelco's Sound Model Discussion

"Seems to me," Shaw (executive vice-president) began, tongue in cheek, "all we need is a record of what we've been doing and we'll have the model for a sound relationship. It's hard to improve on perfection."

"You're right, of course," Greene (vice-president, administration) joked, "but just in case we've missed something, don't you think we should explore it a bit more fully?"

"Seriously," Goodwin (president) commented, "we know these four days are important to us and to Paterno. I think we'll benefit by taking a really close look at ourselves and how we ourselves operate. Let's try to determine the best way for us to relate to Paterno—as well as the other subsidiaries for that matter."

"I think objectivity is the key to this examination process," Shaw observed. "If we can get outside ourselves and, regardless of what we've done in the past, look at what would be sound from an objective perspective, it seems we'd have a good beginning."

"Okay then," said Goodwin, "objectively speaking, what's

the best possible relationship between a headquarters and subsidiary in our business, particularly between Nonelco and Paterno?"

"I've always liked the analogy of a wheel," Newell (vice-president, manufacturing) offered, "with us as the hub and each of the subsidiaries representing a spoke. Neither of us can operate as well without the other."

"That's a good point," said Harmon (vice-president, marketing), "but taking it one more step, all the spokes have to be the same length. There has to be a certain degree of uniformity."

"Right," Shaw nodded. "I don't want to take this analogy too far, but if we look at four wheels as representing our interests in four major world markets, all of them have to be moving in the same direction and turning together. This would give us the fully integrated company we want."

"What we're saying then," Goodwin reflected, "is not that we want to control our subsidiaries, in the classical sense of a centralized operation, but that we do need the ability to influence them. We want them to have input into the corporate direction and a sense of commitment to it, then to operate in a self-responsible, efficient, and effective manner . . . maximum delegation within an integrated framework."

"And," Thomas added, "we want to create a give-and-take expectation. In personnel, for example, my hardware and software for planning and forecasting are sufficient to handle Paterno's needs, but they've resisted entering their human resources information into our data base. Their records of personnel transactions are only semiautomated, and in spite of their size they have virtually no planning or forecasting capability. It's hard for me to make sense out of why they won't join up when our MIS could be so helpful to them."

"We could certainly help in the area of marketing," said Harmon. "Their key marketing people have grown up in that business, but have little firsthand knowledge of other functions. Their attitude is, 'once a marketer, always a marketer.' As specialists, they are less likely to see options beyond their functional experience. They all share the same attitudes and stereotypes and act accordingly. That's what leads us to say 'parochial.'

We think our way of personnel rotation through major functional areas provides a firmer foundation for achieving a broad background. Once a marketer, then a manufacturer, then on into personnel, and sometimes up into general management."

"I know these observations have merit," Shaw interrupted, "but aren't we straying from what we're here to do? Let's get back to what's sound and try not to get hung up on the actual."

"If we convert them to sound statements," Goodwin suggested, "we can incorporate them into our sound model description."

"I think my point involves leadership and direction," Harmon stated. "Ideally, Paterno would adapt their strategic plans to our overall directions and follow our lead while at the same time contributing to the shaping of our direction."

"That relates to the wheel analogy," said Shaw, "so leadership seems to be a key element of our relationship."

This snapshot view of Nonelco's discussion of a sound model, along with additional elements summarized in Table 12, depicts the character and nature of their interaction as well as the content of their discussions.

Paterno's Soundest Model Discussion

"Well, we've already faced the fact that we're subject to their policies and procedures," Carey (executive vice-president) stated. "I wonder what else they want from us?"

"I don't know, I can't read them," said Elliot (president). "They say we're an independent, autonomous arm of the corporation, but what they preach and what they practice are two different things."

"Maybe they resent us because we're so different from their other subsidiaries," Carey suggested. "For example, I've heard that the willows in Green Park bend when the New York wind blows."

"Well, no one can accuse us of being weeping willows," Elliot remarked. "If Goodwin expects us to bow and scrape to stay on New York's good side, it's no wonder he's disappointed."

"You all know how I feel," commented Adams (vice-president, personnel). "I think we've been doing a good job, but I guess if they thought so, we wouldn't be here."

"Harmon's a perfect example of their interference with our operation," said Sloan (vice-president, marketing). "I've spent twenty-two years coming up through our marketing department. I know this company inside out, yet Harmon seems to have a problem with the way I do things."

"Look here," Mason (vice-president, administration) stated in exasperation. "We're griping and complaining about 'them' when we should be focusing on what we'd like to see in a sound relationship with Nonelco. If we don't like what they're doing now, let's describe what we think they should be doing."

"But I'm really baffled by what they're trying to tell us," replied Price (vice-president, manufacturing). "Our abilities are apparently being questioned, and I can't understand why."

"Neither can I," agreed Carey. "I guess that's what really ticks me off . . . the implication that we don't know what we're doing."

"We've never failed to turn a sizable profit while I've been in charge," Elliot noted. "It seems to me that they should trust us. We've proven how capable we are by our results."

"I think you've put your finger on the real problem. If they trusted us, they wouldn't always be probing in a way that suggests that they're suspicious of us!" exclaimed Carey.

"Maybe trust is an issue then," Mason said. "Can we list 'trust' as an element that would be present in a sound relationship?"

"Put up trust and respect," Adams recommended. "If I can get Thomas to respect me, maybe she'll pull back on those far-out ideas of hers. I've told her their MIS isn't needed here . . . but she doesn't believe me."

These comments and perceptions demonstrate Paterno's point of view of Nonelco's supervision. Key elements contained in the remainder of Paterno's discussions are reflected in Table 12. At this point in the session, Paterno's executives clearly felt that their management prerogatives were threatened by Nonelco's compulsion to invade their legitimate privacy, that the

Table 12. Descriptions of a Sound Relationship.

Key Element	Nonelco's Perspective	Paterno's Perspective	Consolidated Model
1. Leadership/ authority	Subsidiaries operate as integrated components, developing their directions in collaboration and within the framework of corporate strategy.	Subject to policy guidelines, we conduct our own affairs, developing along lines dictated by our resources and our particular competencies.	Subsidiaries operate as integrated components developing their directions in collaboration and within a framework of corporate strategy, each concentrating its efforts along lines dictated by their resources, particular competencies, and so on.
2. Trust/respect	Mutual trust and respect based on candor and openness and reflected in effective collaboration and cooperation.	Appreciation for one another's uniqueness along with recognition of mutual competencies.	Trust and respect for one another are consistently demonstrated through open and candid communication leading to understanding, collaboration, and cooperation. Positions, people, and proposals are accepted at face value.
3. Staffing	Staffing is lean and is supported by use of temporary services, contracting out, and so on, as necessary.	Staffing should allow for self-sufficiency, without reliance on outside or temporary resources unless required for emergencies.	Staffing should be lean, but sufficient to allow uninterrupted operation in crisis situations; other internal and external resources, considered from a corporatewide perspective, supplement available staff.

4. Integration	Personnel should be interchanged between headquarters and subsidiaries and vice versa as necessary to strengthen integration to provide future leadership promoted from within.	Subsidiary capable of managing itself with its own people who remain with it for their careers.	Personnel should be interchanged between headquarters and subsidiaries and vice versa as necessary.
5. Personnel practices	Subsidiary personnel practices are developed along headquarters' guidelines for performance appraisal, rotation, and management development. Systems for forecasting, career and succession planning, and so on, are implemented as components of effective human resources.	Personnel practices follow from management philosophy. Complex systems are not needed for personnel development. Concern for people is demonstrated in every aspect of our operation, with on-the-job training and coaching relied upon for development.	Subsidiary develops personnel practices congruent with headquarters' guidelines.
6. Compensation	Pay, promotion, and benefits in a subsidiary are based upon individual ability and contributions to both company and corporate objectives. Competitive scales are maintained.	Pay, promotion, and benefits are maintained at a level comparable with the highest of our three top competitors.	Pay, promotion, and benefits should be viewed and evaluated in the broader context of corporate strategy.

necessary delegation a subsidiary needed to move on its own initiative was under threat, and that Nonelco was pursuing a program toward recentralization of control. This apparent challenge to their autonomy is one way of understanding Paterno's resistance to Nonelco—a resistance evident in the attitudes and underlying thinking characteristic of Paterno executives.

Consolidated Model for Soundest Relationship

After the presentation of Nonelco's separately developed model to Paterno, and vice versa, the two groups separated for several minutes to discuss it in whispered terms.

Mouton spoke, "The next step is to consolidate these into one model for a sound relationship to which both groups can commit themselves. Let me suggest a way of moving." She wrote on a flip chart as she described the procedure. "One approach for doing so involves using a four-point scale as you examine each element of the other team's report. Any one of the following four points may apply to any part of the model:

4—'We disagree with the statement for the following reasons.'
3—'We wish to ask the following questions for further clarification.'
2—'We agree with the statement as rewritten in the following way.'
1—'We agree with the statement as written.'

"Then ask a member of your group to explain to the other group why your numbers are as they are. We will reconvene as a general session to exchange these findings. This portion of the project is finished when as many 2's, 3's, and 4's as possible have become 1's on both reports. When the two reports are characterized by 1's, this reflects mutual agreement, and the two can be made into one."

"Before studying the models on this four-point basis," Blake suggested, "it might be useful for each group to spend some time thinking through what you've already heard about yourselves from the other group. When you've sorted through this, it may help in understanding what the other group intended to convey in their model."

"Sounds good," said Goodwin. "We'd welcome anything that'll get us moving in a positive direction."

"Let's clarify this a minute before we split up," Newell said. "Do we put a 1, 2, 3, or 4 by a statement as a whole, or is it better to break it into separate points and assign a number to each part?"

"It is better," Mouton answered, "to put a number by the whole segment when you agree with it entirely. If there are parts with which you agree, then give them a 1. If there are parts you can't agree with, then score each part as either a 2, 3, or 4."

"Okay. Thanks," said Newell, as everyone got up to go to the team rooms.

After the groups broke, Blake and Mouton talked about the situation. "As I read it," Blake reflected, "a fundamental difference between Nonelco and Paterno is that Nonelco is really in the process of moving toward a professional management while Paterno retains a good number of characteristics of a paternalistic organization—overmanning, specialization of management functions, and personnel practices that haven't been thought through at a deep level. At the least, I should think they would look for opportunities to release people to higher-level assignments rather than resisting promoting them into headquarters assignments as a loss of indispensable talent."

"I agree," said Mouton. "It seems like the barrier to integration is really a clash of two concepts of corporate culture and responsibility, but Nonelco is certainly not without blemish. They 'tell' the subsidiary what to do, and up to now they've had a very limited developmental perspective on how to help bring desired results about. We've repeatedly heard them engage in 'themism,' that is, 'The problems are all in the subsidiary; we are pure.' We know that in the guise of nominal supervision they have sent people into the subsidiary for surveillance rather than for guidance purposes. This kind of a scam is certainly not easy to condone even though it reflects frustrations at the headquarters with its inability to get desired changes made. Nonelco has a lot of work to do, too."

Blake continued, "Paterno may be able to provide some insights for Nonelco to think about. The clash of value systems probably has to be confronted. I believe that the first step is contingent upon Paterno's gaining insight into its managerial philosophy and coming to see that its value system is based on its own history and regionalism and that it is out of step with sound organizational practices. Then Nonelco may be ready to listen to what might be helpful for them to learn about themselves. If these sessions help to begin the integration, it may prove useful later to reconvene to help Nonelco work on their own problems."

"Yes, but that would only work," interrupted Mouton, "after Paterno has earned the respect of Nonelco by facing the antiquities buried in their own operations."

"If there is a Paterno breakthrough," Blake said, "this certainly should have a motivating effect on Nonelco by opening it to more objective self-examination."

"In listening to the two discussions," commented Mouton, "it is apparent that Paterno is trying to diminish the differences by downplaying them, and Nonelco is trying to increase the differences by emphasizing or exaggerating them. Neither one is being terribly objective now; that's why this 4, 3, 2, 1 business is so essential to pinpointing real differences so they can be resolved and identifying agreements so they can be built on."

"I'm glad that we asked them to approach the consolidation problem in this manner," said Blake, as they approached the team rooms.

In the Paterno room, Elliot observed, "It doesn't appear that the differences between our models are very significant. I'm sure we can iron out discrepancies and proceed to a discussion of actual conditions."

At about the same moment in the Nonelco team, Goodwin said, "There clearly are similarities in our ideas about what a good relationship between us would look like, but there are also some critical disparities we're going to have to work out with them."

"But they're really minor, don't you think?" Newell asked.

"Hardly," Goodwin answered. "Let's take the staffing and personnel issues, for example. Our view of a sound approach in a high-tech industry like ours is a core of highly trained, highly competent people in essential positions, each producing at, say, 90 percent of capacity at least 90 percent of the time. There's no padding in our model and no room for anyone who's just along for the ride to retirement. Contrast that with their ideal formulation," Goodwin challenged, "and I think there's a big difference."

In the other room, Carey (executive vice-president) was countering points Elliot had made earlier. "Around here we have to be prepared for emergencies and all kinds of contingencies," said Carey. "Maybe we do tend to staff up, but it's good planning to be prepared for whatever happens. We like to keep sufficient personnel to respond to crises and take advantage of opportunities without spreading ourselves too thin."

"As for production," defended Adams, "our people resent pressure. We've developed a reputation for taking good care of them. We're understanding and appreciative, and I don't think that's necessarily the same as unproductive and inefficient."

This back-and-forth discussion was typical in each group as members were trying to minimize the difference or justify the soundness of what they had said in comparison with the other team.

"So, Thomas," Goodwin said, "I think we should put a 4 on their statement regarding staffing, item 3 down from the top, and get it out into the open that we have different ideals for how their company should be managed."

"As for myself," added Harmon, "I think I could put a 1 beside their statement of trust and respect. What do the rest of you think?"

"I'd like to get the words *candor* and *openness* into the final consolidation," said Newell.

"At a deeper level we're in agreement on a 1 rating. I'd

like to put a 2 on it and add at the word level, not at the level
of convictions, these two words to make it feel more sound and
more complete. But I don't think they'll get anywhere if they
continue to see us as interlopers, interfering where we don't be-
long," said Shaw. "Our interest in their operation is legitimate
business practice, not just nosiness, and that would be present
I think if we had the kind of trust and respect that our statement—theirs for that matter—describes."

Completing the Soundest Model

Blake was near the coffee pot as team members took a
break after the general session. Goodwin and Elliot joined
him.

"Well, what do you think of our progress?" Elliot asked
Blake. "Are we moving slowly, or is this about what we might
expect?"

"Well," pondered Blake, "I'm sure it's not possible to put
a standard time schedule on this kind of thing. The real measure
is depth of thinking and clarity of shared understanding."

"Oh, I think we're getting that," said Goodwin. "I was
really struck by the number of 1's and how readily the 2's were
converted into 1's by a simple rephrasing. There are a couple of
4's that undoubtedly will give us trouble before getting them
converted into 1's, but I feel we're developing an overall mutual
understanding that'll get us there.

"It was fascinating to watch the two representatives up
there at the newsprint chart talking with one another as though
none of the rest of us were present and finding agreements that
we obviously are all together on," Goodwin continued. "At
least that's what happened as far as the first three items are concerned. Later we had more difficulty, and each of our representatives had to come and consult with us frequently."

"I think you're right, Charlie," responded Elliot, "but the
striking thing to me is that while you and I have discussed many
of these, I must admit that they mean different things now
than they did in our previous discussions. That disturbs me. In
fact, it may explain why we are here. I'm looking forward to

getting to the actual model and seeing where we stand when it comes right to it."

"Thanks, Roger," replied Goodwin. "I'm pleased that you agreed to participate in these sessions. I can already see that our situation will be a good deal different than it has been in the past."

"And I think better," added Elliot, as he smiled. Leaving to enter the next general session, he patted Charlie on the shoulder as he walked away to take the next step toward completion of the consolidated ideal.

Table 12 summarizes the results from each group's separate deliberations and their consolidated effort. As the table indicates, two of the items, "integration" and "personnel practices," were vastly different in terms of the sound relationship from each group's point of view. The consolidated model for these two items was left for further work. The general description reflects mainly headquarters' perspective, which was characterized by a different concept of management than Paterno could envisage. Thus, Blake and Mouton decided to have the groups proceed with the actual descriptions and to complete these two items later in the session. Looking ahead to the counterpart discussions, we see that these items were discussed in detail after a breakthrough had occurred in the relationship and a satisfactory resolution was achieved.

Making Progress

After the consolidated ideal descriptions had been completed, Nonelco and Paterno agreed to discuss the "leadership" and "trust and respect" elements first. Many of the concrete issues relating to the other elements emerged during the course of these two interchanges.

Nonelco's Discussion of the Actual Relationship

"I'd have to say that Paterno has primarily a paternalistic leadership orientation," Greene (vice-president, administration) began.

"What do you mean by that?" asked Newell (vice-president, manufacturing).

"I mean they see themselves as parents to their organization and protectors of the family against outside influences such as we are," answered Greene. "As in a family, members are expected to exchange dedication and compliance for security within a climate of approval."

"That's why there are so many 'lifers' among top management," remarked Thomas (vice-president, personnel). "Promotions are generally the reward for loyalty and for steady, dependable performance. This creates a real dilemma in terms of competency. I think the Peter Principle tends to be more evident in companies with a paternalistic orientation."

"It may also be one reason why they seem to reach consensus so easily," observed Goodwin (president). "It isn't polite to disagree with the boss. Beyond that, it can be interpreted as disrespect. Peace and harmony are maintained through apparent agreement."

"That's one of my primary sources of frustration with them," said Shaw, as if to himself. "I can remember so many incidents of talking to several of them at one time, and they're all nodding together as if they were many bodies with one head. Just once, I'd like to see that someone has nerve enough to express a minority opinion. As a start for our view of the relationship, I'd say, 'A nominal relationship—our influence is reduced because Paterno doesn't respond.' "

"Maybe we'd find the same thing throughout their organization," reasoned Harmon (vice-president, marketing). "That could explain why we think it's so hard to get any kind of change into their system. Change generates differences, and they seem to find differences disturbing to their sense of unity."

"That may be right," Goodwin agreed, "but another difficulty that I've felt in trying to change Paterno is their multilayered hierarchy. All those layers impede effectiveness. It takes so much time for them to switch directions, to accommodate new developments or advanced technology, to say nothing of the burden of expense that this creates."

"It could be they need those layers to take care of the

people they're reluctant to terminate," said Thomas. "At least it fits with their system of promotion as a reward, not so much for competence and contribution but for compliance and devotion."

"That squares with my thinking," Shaw added.

"What about the trust and respect issue? That's a big part of the situation facing us now," Thomas suggested.

"It's clear they don't trust us," said Newell.

"And after the last few years," Greene queried, "how could we possibly trust them? We've felt they've blunted practically every effort we've made to bring them around."

"Someway," reasoned Goodwin, "they have to trust that we are not out to get them, do them in, or to force our will on them in a unilateral way. They have to know that we are prepared to respect them and value their judgment and that we want future actions based on mutuality of conviction. Buckling under won't do it."

"Possibly we haven't communicated that message because we don't really feel it," Newell observed. "What we've shown is that, even though we say we appreciate their knowledge and experience, we still think we know how to run things better."

"You may be right," agreed Shaw. "I wonder if we haven't sometimes insisted on change just for change's sake or to prove to them who's boss. Maybe our growing frustration has led us to pull rank more and more frequently and they buck. Just because they do things differently than we'd do them doesn't necessarily mean they're not done as well."

"When you put it that way, Ben," said Goodwin, "I guess I can see where some of their resentment may be justified. After all, they're not solely at fault for all the relationship problems. We have to shoulder some of that responsibility ourselves. Perhaps we came on stronger than we needed to or were aware of in response to what we interpret as resistance and resentment. Perhaps they've been influenced not only by what we've said but also by how we've gone about it."

"Let's capture some more of these thoughts for our written description of the actual relationship," offered Harmon.

"I think we can add to the first item, 'Our relationship is

unsatisfactory for achieving our needed degree of integration,' "
said Shaw. "That captures the basic problem. Indeed, we have
not had much more than a closed 'nonrelationship.' In a way,
we keep describing what we think goes on in Paterno as a reflection of discrepancies between what we would like to see and
have been unable to influence and what we actually see in their
management."

"We've had no reason to tell them what our attitudes are
because we have probably made the assumption that they *knew*
how we feel about them," said Newell.

"I'm sure you're right," agreed Greene. "If we asked them
to do things our way, I presumed that they'd understand we
didn't like what they were doing."

"Yes, but we really didn't try to communicate our thinking based on analysis and reasoning. It was more a case of telling them what to do," responded Newell. "I do think we need
to examine our own behavior more closely in terms of how we
could have done things differently in the past so we can correct it in the future."

By studying themselves more closely, Nonelco came to recognize and identify the real differences between themselves and
Paterno and to see many of their own mistakes and their unwitting contribution to the ongoing conflict. (See Table 13.)

Paterno's Actual Description

"I hate to admit it," Elliot (president) began seriously,
"and I'm not entirely sure, but it looks as if we may have been
our own worst enemies in this situation."

"Unless we'd all like to start looking for new jobs elsewhere," said Carey (executive vice-president), "I think we need
to take a close, hard look at ourselves and our contribution to
our relationship problems."

"It won't be easy," Mason (vice-president, administration) noted, "but let's be as candid and objective as we can. If
we aren't honest with ourselves, we'll end up doing more harm
than good."

"I find this very painful," remarked Adams (vice-president,

Table 13. Descriptions of Actual Relationship.

Element	Nonelco's Perspective	Paterno's Perspective	Consolidated View
1. Relationship	A nominal relationship—our influence is reduced because Paterno does not respond. Unsatisfactory for achieving our needed degree of integration.	We have sought to protect ourselves by keeping them out. The result is excessive polarization on a number of problems, that is, staffing, compensation, personnel practices.	Tensions between us have reduced our relationship to one of proper formality with occasional efforts by headquarters to seize initiatives, but with a consistent Paterno response at resisting these attempts.
2. Leadership	A professionally managed headquarters seeking to provide appropriate directions pulls rank with a paternalistic, hierarchical organization that resists change. Paterno sees and resents headquarters' influence as unjustified intrusion and interference.	Rooted in a history of paternalism. Have not been open to headquarters' initiatives. New ideas are typically rejected. Positions have become firm before being tested in light of corporate strategy.	Professionalism-paternalism conflict has resulted in too little give and take, polarization of positions, and win-lose controversies. Paterno has not been deeply enough involved in establishing corporate strategies and lacks commitment to them. Paterno has not sufficiently recognized Nonelco's interests in its operations as legitimate.
3. Trust/respect	Mutual suspicion and distrust has led to lack of respect on both sides for opinions and expertise of the other.	Motivations and intentions are continuously questioned by both sides. Actions interpreted in context of fear and misunderstanding. Neither of us has earned the respect of the other.	Interaction is characterized by fear and suspicion on both sides. Neither of us is fully respected by the other. Actions are contrived rather than genuine.
4. Staffing	Overstaffed.	Somewhat overstaffed.	The staffing problem can be resolved through attrition, transfers, and promotions.

(continued on next page)

Table 13. Descriptions of Actual Relationship, Cont'd.

Element	Nonelco's Perspective	Paterno's Perspective	Consolidated View
5. Integration	Even though we have solicited nominations of their best people for headquarters' assignments, with rare exceptions they have resisted; hordes its people.	We offer career employment and protect our people from kidnapping.	Paterno has not given sufficient consideration to how it can contribute to corporate strength through an interchange of talent. Opportunities to develop generalists are not utilized through advancement to headquarters' assignments. Efforts to place headquarters and other subsidiary personnel at Paterno have sometimes been interpreted as Trojan horse maneuvers on Nonelco's part.
6. Personnel practices	Personnel practices rooted in paternalism. Emerging management practices, which we have sought to communicate to enhance efficiency, productivity, motivation, and so on, are neither accepted nor understood by Paterno.	Though resented by Nonelco, our practices are appropriate to a loyal organization composed of "permanent" employees.	Paterno's approach to human resources needs greater depth and sophistication. Emerging management practices should be studied and implemented.
7. Compensation	Pay, promotion, and benefits have been used as the reward system. Compensation is more closely tied to tenure than to performance. Efforts to "be good to their people" have put Paterno's compensation levels out of line with the competition and domestic corporate locations.	Pay well enough to ensure access to the best people. People who stay are rewarded for demonstrated loyalty. We value tenure, sometimes even above merit.	Subsidiary affords seniority and friendship more influence than merit in pay and promotion decisions. Benefits are too high relative to total corporation.

personnel). We've always prided ourselves on the excellence of our company, our commitment to keeping people whole, and our loyalty to them. Now we're told that we're overstaffed, inefficient."

"Look at our bottom line," said Price (vice-president, manufacturing). "How can what they say about us be accurate in light of our results?"

"But we're faced with the reality of a contradiction between how we see ourselves and how they see us," Sloan (vice-president, marketing) observed. "How can we explain it?" she asked.

"How about starting with me?" Elliot volunteered. "I've spent my life trying to set a good example, but apparently I haven't been very successful. I'm afraid they see me as negative . . . uncooperative . . . and as bucking their efforts to straighten us out."

"That may go for all of us," Carey seconded. "We may have all been trying to hold on to the past, afraid to change, threatened by events we feel we cannot control."

"Can we continue then by describing ourselves as conservative?" Price asked.

"I think that's a safe bet," Adams responded. "We've shown steady and good growth over the years—nothing really outstanding, but we've been very predictable."

"Do you think we've lost potential opportunities for growth and development by being *too* conservative?" ventured Mason.

"The way the economy's been over the past decade, I don't think you can be too conservative," Elliot countered. "By my definition, what we've done is manage responsibly. After all, we owe it to our people to stay solvent and keep the doors open while contributing a damn nice penny to the corporate coffers."

"That's the way I see it," said Carey. "Think of all the people who depend on this company—our employees, their families, customers, suppliers, stockholders, the community— how can we risk the lives and futures of all those people?"

"Spoken like a true paternalist. Well, you can call that attitude conservative," Mason retorted, "but I wonder if we're confusing conservatism with paternalism."

"I've never had a problem with seeing this organization as a family," said Elliot. "If that causes me to have parent feelings, what's wrong with that? Why else is our turnover so low? Why are our people so loyal?" he continued. "It's because they recognize how well they're treated. Other companies give lip service to the idea that people are their most important resource—we say our people are a top priority and we show it every day."

"And why is our production substantially lower than comparable organizations while our costs are significantly higher?" Sloan challenged.

"Are you and Mason disagreeing with the rest of us, then?" Adams chided.

"You might say we are," Mason retorted. "It's about time somebody played the devil's advocate. I'm tired of this superficial show of agreement for the sake of loyalty. For the moment, I want to speak my mind without concern for consequences."

"That goes for me, too," Sloan rejoined. "There've been thousands of times over the years when I've gone along for the sake of unity and harmony—both valued because they allow us to put up a united front. I think we've suffered by putting a higher value on deference than on convictions. I wonder if we should reexamine our priorities related to Blake's little lecture on loyalty and logic in the last session. That struck me as being close to the heart of our problem."

"In fact," Mason added, "I think this company will be a lot better off with vocal dissenters to challenge the rest of us to speak our minds."

"But not one of you has admitted these feelings before," Elliot said thoughtfully. "Have you kept your doubts and reservations hidden? Nodded and smiled in the interests of pseudo-agreement? If so, what does that say about me as a leader? Does it say that my closest people are afraid of me . . . afraid of being seen as disloyal if they disagree?"

"Look," remarked Carey, "we've probably done the same thing with our own people. It's a part of our history, our culture. I'm not sure how we can break the tradition of putting loyalty above logic. It's become a way of life with us."

"I'm not sure either," said Elliot, visibly shaken, "but I know we have to try and turn ourselves around. When I think how we may have dampened people's initiative, to say nothing of creativity."

"Now maybe we're coming closer to understanding what Nonelco's seen in us all along," said Mason. "Some of their complaints and criticisms have probably been more justified than we've cared to admit. Can we check ourselves out in this new light?"

"I think we should," Carey offered. "It feels good to be able to speak more freely, without being constrained by fear and doubt."

"We are getting ready to establish a new beginning," Elliot mused. "It'll take time to win Nonelco's trust and respect, but we've already made a start. I think this new insight and perspective will place us on a sound footing. How can we put some of these thoughts into our written description?"

"If we look at the actual relationship between us and Nonelco then," suggested Mason, "we have protected ourselves by keeping them out."

"Let's get that up on the newsprint," Sloan said.

"Okay," replied Mason, going to the chart pad. "What else can we say that pictures how we have resisted working openly with them?"

The interchange that took place in this discussion among the Paterno team represented the high point of the drama in this session of interface conflict resolution. This was one of those rare moments that sometimes happens when the insight attained and the release of feelings that occurs from the candid discussion permits the development of high levels of commitment. It demonstrates that the turnabout shift in Paterno management was not a concession to headquarters' pressures but a forward movement based on convictions and rooted in understanding and in an enlarged view of management values and perspectives. The relationship between the two organizations was further strengthened by the counterpart discussions that took place later in the sessions. The next remark by Elliot, which relates to his altered point of view, indicates a genuine transformation in his thinking and convictions regarding the future leadership of Paterno and its relationship to Nonelco. He said, "From my perspective, it's been a win-lose battle all the way and we've won more than we've lost up to now. But, in the end, this may be a case of winning the battles but . . . ."

Closing the Gap

When the groups reconvened in a general session, a sense of enthusiasm and commitment began to emerge as each reviewed the progress already realized, and it was apparent that the magnitude of the changes that would be required was no obstacle to getting started at implementation.

At the coffee break, Blake and Mouton discussed the next step. "Working through these two descriptions and bringing the 4's, 3's, and 2's to a 1-level of agreement turned out to be much easier than I expected. What's your explanation of it, Jane?" queried Blake.

"I think it's Elliot's attitude," offered Mouton. "Whatever else, he's totally honest. He's dedicated his life to developing Paterno as a fine corporate citizen. In his view of what corporate citizenship entails, he has done a masterful job. I couldn't admire him more than when he turned to his own group and said, 'Am I the problem?' That was like pulling a cork out of champagne. After that, everything else began to fall into place."

"I personally think," Blake suggested, "that we'll see him exercising the same dedication toward creating a dynamic organization that he did in the past when his strong efforts resulted in a paternalistic one."

"I feel that, too," said Mouton, "but all that remains to be seen. What do you think we ought to do next?"

"It would be natural to ask people to convene in counterpart subgroups, where each subgroup could explore, in private, the implications of the shift model for what they need to do in the future. Then we can ask the counterpart subgroups to reveal their conclusions in a general session," suggested Blake.

The counterpart groups were given the following task description by Mouton. "There are undoubtedly many changes that will accelerate shifts within your own job descriptions. These are actions you are free to undertake directly or to authorize others to take under your initiative. You may or may not want to reach decisions at this time; nonetheless, it will be useful to explore possible steps and to test each other for reactions and implications. A second step is to decide what aspects of your private discussion you'd like to report in the general session."

"We'd like to propose that the two presidents get together for a private discussion, the two marketing people, the personnel people, manufacturing, and so on," said Blake.

The Two Presidents

"I want to apologize, Roger," said Charles Goodwin, "for not having moved more rapidly toward trying to bring the problem you and I have had to a head. My lack of initiative caused us to move farther and farther apart. All I can say is that I am glad that we have now reached common ground."

"Thank you," Roger Elliot replied, "but apologies are inappropriate, I think. In many respects, you made the effort to bring such a meeting of minds about. I take responsibility for having resisted what to me and us seemed to involve intrusion."

A moment of silence followed, then Elliot said, "What is needed is some way for you and me to spend a more extended period together. What has been in conflict here is two philosophies of management, and these philosophies will not be cleared up in a session such as we have had. They can be identified, but there is a great difference between identifying the issues and finding all of the ramifications as they appear and reappear in decision after decision."

"I agree," said Goodwin, "and I wonder if we could consider something like the following? I have a program of travel that will take me to many of the subsidiaries this spring. I wonder if we could arrange for you and me to take this trip together? It would be appropriate for me to invite you to attend the review sessions that I will be having. This would give you a chance to learn more in detail how I think by the way I deal with the many, many problems we face around the world. It would give me an opportunity to have a sounding board from a different orientation than my own, helping me from the standpoint of reviewing problems and making decisions."

"I'd like that," responded Elliot, "and I think it's feasible. Is this an invitation?"

"It is," said Goodwin.

"Okay, then, it's a deal. I need to review being away for that length of time and see who will substitute for me, who will act in my place," said Elliot.

"There's another possibility here," added Goodwin, "in terms of trying to make double-fast progress. Could we ask Ben Shaw to take a temporary assignment as the acting president of Paterno?"

"That would be a very neat way for Shaw to learn about our operation on more of a firsthand basis. No major decisions are programmed in that period, so he would not be at a disadvantage for dealing in an intimate way with problems that have some long-term history or other," Elliot responded.

"How would Don Carey react to that?" queried Goodwin. "Ordinarily, he would step up and this might come as something of a put-down. What do you think?"

"I don't think we need to worry about that," said Elliot. "Don is a level-headed guy and he'd grasp what we're seeking. He'd support it in every way."

"Then let's ask Don and Ben to join us soon to discuss this possibility," Goodwin suggested. "But right now, I need a little time to run this by the chairman and the board committee concerned with senior management moves. Although there's nothing permanent involved here, I think it would be in the best interests of all to keep them informed."

The decision by Goodwin and Elliot of taking the review trip was confirmed when Shaw and Carey joined the presidents. They explored the implications of asking Ben Shaw to take over as the acting president for Elliot during his absence. No decision was reached, because it seemed desirable to sleep on it to ensure that other implications unforeseen in this quick discussion did not appear.

Personnel Counterparts

Tom Adams started the discussion, saying, "Mary, I feel that you pushed too damn hard on this MIS thing. We know human resources management can and should be buttressed by a much more refined information system than we now have. We feel what you have been asking us to do would centralize records so much that we would be creating conditions that would bring an end to the autonomy we think is fundamental. The kind of local decision making essential for ensuring that the right person gets put into the right job, and that the right development program be established for the right people, and so on, is the kind of thing that might get sacrificed."

"But, Tom, that's not the problem. No computer can make these final judgments. That has to be a management function," Mary Thomas retorted.

"Yes, Mary, I realize that," said Adams. "The real issue is who makes those final judgments—whether they're made by people who know the total situation or whether they're made by headquarters people who tend to rely excessively on statistical analysis rather than exercising the subtleties of human judgment and comprehension of the total situation and the implications of all other alternatives that are available."

"Well, I appreciate what you are attempting to say," Thomas replied. "I don't know that there's any solution to it except trust and confidence. That's the trust and confidence that leads to a spirit of collaboration. It promotes our readiness to keep as much personnel decision making in the hands of subsidiaries as is feasible and yet have a master file of human resources available to us from all the subsidiaries. Then we can consult the computer for the range and depth of talent throughout the total organization. When unusual opportunities arise, for example, we can offer our local jobs to our people rather than going to the open market. It's an obvious advantage to our own people when unusual opportunities can be offered them."

"I understand that," said Adams, "and, furthermore, I agree with it. But I still wonder if we don't need to review and get an agreed understanding on these kinds of implications. I'd like to before we get ourselves entangled in a series of decisions that might cause difficulties when you and I move on and others take over. For example, I know my people will resist this integration of information, particularly in a headquarters computer. I want to review the pros and cons, the advantages and disadvantages, the gains and losses they all will have in their minds. Then we can get together and examine what issues are real and what imaginary, and what actions can be taken and what actions should be delayed in our efforts to phase in a better integration."

"That is more than acceptable to me. As I've said before, my goal is to ensure that we have the best system possible for mobilizing the human resources of the entire system. I'm prepared to explore with you, and others from Paterno for that matter, whatever needs to be discussed before we make any decisions."

"Okay," said Adams. "Let's leave it at that."

As Blake and Mouton completed their tour of the various counterpart subgroups, they saw that a major breakthrough had been achieved. Openness and candor prevailed in each discussion, and thoughtful consideration was being given to how best to approach some major problems that must be faced next. It appeared that perhaps a five-year objective could eventually result from these sessions, that much of what had been discussed (and more) should be completed within that time. For Paterno, this meant a turnaround of basic management attitudes to a new and more modern orientation that puts a higher degree of focus on contribution, merit, creativity, and initiative than on duty, loyalty, and obedience as mechanisms of control and problem solving.

The Interface Conflict-Solving Model broke the barriers that had previously blocked progress and change. Nonelco and Paterno joined forces as interdependent components of an interacting system with strenuous efforts devoted to increasing the rate of Paterno's own development. High mutual expectations for progress and improvement were translated into meaningful and lasting results.

Dynamics of Change

The dynamics underlying the change in relationship involved three distinctive considerations. The first of these was the reliance on outsiders to probe the attitudes among the senior executives of Paterno and then to confront Elliot with the contradiction they experienced between what they knew about Paterno from a Nonelco perspective and what they learned about Paterno from within. Acceptance of that discrepancy was resisted by Elliot at one level, yet it made sense at another level by providing a basis for understanding the undercurrents previously heard but not given the attention they merited.

Obtaining Elliot's approval for reviewing these same discrepancies with Nonelco executives was the second important consideration. This step of progress respected Elliot's position as the Paterno president. Had he said, "No," this line of communication would have been closed, at least until further evidence could be brought to Elliot in the effort to reopen the issue.

The discussions within Paterno created the turning point when Elliot was confronted with his paternalistic leadership by his own people, who had acquiesced to it. This confrontation enabled the Paterno group to examine fundamental assumptions embedded within its own traditions, precedents, and past practices, and enabled them to see ultimate possibilities for change.

The next step forward was in the acknowledgment of these deeper ideological differences with Nonelco personnel. By doing so, an avenue to the collaborative acceleration of change was opened up. The consolidation of gain is apparent in Goodwin's proposal and Elliot's acceptance of joining together for an extended foreign trip to review subsidiaries, which would give them ample opportunity to get to know one another better while examining issues of organizational leadership. This step forward was strengthened when Shaw agreed to be the acting president of Paterno; this role provided him a window for the deeper study of organizational practices in Paterno.

These several steps led to the opening up of communication between the two groups and made realistic the building of a solid relationship, which resulted in dramatic shifts in Paterno's operation.

Impact

The two conspicuous areas of changes were in personnel practices and profitability. Promotion practices were changed to favor merit over seniority. As a result, those promoted are three years younger on the average, the length of service for those promoted has been reduced by nearly three years, and the promotion rate to higher positions outside the plant is up by 31 percent.

Significant increases in productivity and profits came about with an overall labor reduction of over 500 employees out of 8,000. At the same time, reductions in controllable costs such as wages, maintenance materials, utilities, and fixed overhead over which management had decision-making control led to a profit contribution amounting to millions of dollars. Most impressively, a productivity index per employee rose by almost 30 percent without the aid of substantial investment in plant and equipment.

CHAPTER 9

ᏇᏇᏇᏇᏇᏇᏇᏇᏇᏇᏇᏇᏇ

Making Mergers Work

One of those organizational changes fraught with difficulty involves bringing two previously independent yet often competing organizations into a single entity via merger or acquisition. In a study of ten mergers evaluated throughout a decade, an estimated 80 percent of such contributors failed to meet the projections made in the feasibility studies.[1] This level of outright failure suggests that the dynamics of bringing two into one need to be far better understood than they are at the present time.

The study reported here illustrates how the Interface Conflict-Solving Model has been employed to maximize the likelihood of success when two independent organizations are being merged into one. In this example, Transway, an American company, acquired Intertrans Ltd. of the United Kingdom. Early in the merger, it was anticipated that differences stemming from the national cultures of the two organizations might be a source of conflict between them. On deeper examination, the outstanding differences calling for analysis were related to business practices characteristic of each organization and subject to resolution in these terms.

The model used here is equally applicable to internal mergers—for example, when two departments, sales and customer services, are brought together to reduce excessive labor

---

[1] Arthur M. Louis, "The Bottom Line on Ten Big Mergers," *Fortune* 105, no. 9 (May 3, 1982): 84–89.

or duplication of efforts. Often each department has characteristic ways of operating that may not be compatible with the
other. Then the Interface Conflict-Solving Model can be used to
help reduce tensions and achieve the expected profitability
gains.

Transway is a large, multinational manufacturing corporation headquartered in Chicago. One of its major divisions, Sero,
is an important supplier of chemical products used in industrial,
medical/dental, pharmaceutical, and commercial applications,
primarily in American markets. On a more limited scale, Sero is
involved in similar activities in Europe.

Intertrans Ltd. produced essentially the same products,
with its market concentration in Europe, but some market
penetration in America. For some years, Transway had held a
50 percent interest in Intertrans, while Damon Ltd., one of Europe's largest textile companies, retained the remaining 50 percent. Transway, never directly involved in Intertrans's management, had begun to compete with it in both Europe and America.
Transway was content with this arrangement until a declining
European market threatened Intertrans's continued profitability and heightened competition with Sero. Faced with a potential loss of Intertrans's profit contribution and the specter of
intensified market overlap, Transway offered to purchase Damon's interest and assume complete control of Intertrans's
operation. Transway and Damon negotiated terms for the trans-
action. The Sero plant, which reported to the Transway vice-
president, John Reston, was similar to the Intertrans operation.
Because increased profitability could be projected from merging
the two operations, the implementation was headed by Reston;
he began to formulate the strategy to consummate the merger
by contacting an organization development (OD) firm that his
headquarters' top team had been working with for some time.
He then met with the OD consultant, Paul Williams, and with
Greg Morton (plant manager, Sero) and Tim Casper (personnel).

"Williams," Reston began, "now that the Intertrans trans-
action has been completed, we are about ready to merge Intertrans with Sero to integrate the chemicals operation. I know
from some of the interface work we've done that the human

dynamics involved here are likely to be at least as important as the financial and other aspects in making a go of it, so Morton, Casper, and I wondered if you could help get us started on the right foot."

"Yes," Williams responded, "we've developed an approach to the merger problem that focuses on behavioral dynamics that exist at the interface as the takeover organization begins to make decisions about the company that is being taken over. Dealing with these in a sound fashion aids in getting to the operational issues in a problem-solving way. It's similar to the activity you participated in last year with the marketing and sales teams where we were able to work out some of the tensions that were causing problems. It should lay the groundwork for a smooth integration using all available human resources and setting the stage for an ongoing cooperative relationship between Sero personnel and people from Intertrans."

"That sounds promising," said Reston. "Our biggest concern is how Intertrans will react to being a part of us. They already feel threatened and have built up further resentment since learning of our intended takeover. They have all the typical insecurities, doubts, and frustrations that go along with this kind of thing. How will the activity you propose help identify and resolve these issues, or will it?"

"That's the real strength of the merger problem-solving process," Williams replied. "When participants are able to be open and candid with one another across the interface, real issues can be surfaced and dealt with as problems to be solved. Otherwise they are too likely to remain hidden or to be played down or to be ignored because no one really wants to face being responsible for their existence. All of this is complicated by the fact that the organization being merged knows little or nothing beyond hearsay about the ways of work or even the politics of the acquiring organization. It's much better to play it safe rather than serving yourself up as a sacrificial lamb. We use the strategy of a theater in the round to initially expose the views and thinking of each group for study, understanding, and reaction by the other. The term *theater in the round* is a misnomer, because nothing is staged. There is no scenario and members are not acting out a part or constrained by assigned roles. Nonetheless, one group is asked to perform a task, while the other group observes. *Fishbowl* is an equivalent term but an inelegant way of picturing it."

Figure 8. Theater in the Round Promotes Shared Understanding.

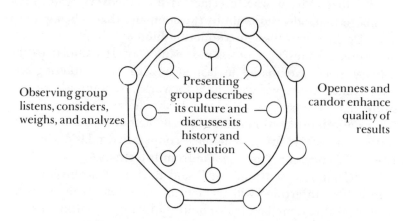

Observing group listens, considers, weighs, and analyzes

Presenting group describes its culture and discusses its history and evolution

Openness and candor enhance quality of results

"Do you mean one group makes some kind of presentation while members of the other group watch and listen?" Casper inquired.

"It's more freewheeling than that, but that's pretty much the idea," Williams answered. "Generally, we begin with one group's members reconstructing and discussing their history and organizational culture, while the other group's members listen. This gives everyone an idea of what each organization's traditions, precedents, and past practices are, the circumstances under which they came into being, and their evolution to the present. These factors significantly influence current action, and their appropriateness or compatibility relative to how things are done in the other group is important to know prior to designing a sound relationship. The observing team members also gain insight about how the other group members interact with one another, that is, whether leadership is open, autocratic, bureaucratic, laissez-faire, Machiavellian, whatever. Members of both groups must inevitably learn to deal with one another as persons, not as Xs in an organizational structure. This process of observing helps speed up that learning."

"Sounds like a good way of telescoping a year's experience of getting acquainted with the personalities involved in a few days," said Morton. "It will give us a chance to understand Intertrans's people and their problems, values, ways of thinking, and concerns, rather than blundering in and treading on them, only later to discover that we have been violating them in unknown ways."

Casper continued, "It's probably even more important because we already have a lot of preconceived notions about them, as undoubtedly they do about us. Unfortunately, we've known each other from a distance and as enemies rather than allies. We'll obviously need to work through old stereotypes, tense feelings, and long-held resentments before a new and sound relationship is truly possible."

"My God, I think if we'd really thought this through before we signed the papers, we might have given it a second thought," said Reston. "We may have just bought ourselves a bag of troubles. Unless we watch it, we stand a chance of alienating them more than we already have."

"That's why we think it's so important to share information about yourselves right from the beginning," Williams emphasized. "Group perceptions of each other may be based largely on hearsay impressions or third-party reports, and these sources often are faulty and biased. Getting the real story straight is critical. Since you two have been competitors, it's probably even more difficult to become one integrated whole within the Transway organization."

"I can see that clarifying our cultures and histories will be helpful," commented Morton. "What do we do after that?"

"Identify the specific issues that are of mutual concern or are of concern to one group or the other," said Williams. "Then you can begin to weigh divergent approaches for dealing with them on a strength-and-weakness basis. Concerns you'll hear probably will range all over the lot. Promotion practices, development opportunities, advancement, prospects of termination and transfer, the funding of retirement programs, and so on are likely to be priority items. While these issues may seem too detailed for higher-level executives, they are high priority to the security of members of the acquired group without regard for age, rank, or length of service. The future of members of the acquired organization is often in doubt or unknown, or the suspicion may exist that some people's numbers have been called. These preoccupations with personal issues may distract from working to solve broader problems, and they need to be brought out into the open and dealt with at the earliest possible time.

"After these discussions," Williams continued, "you evaluate and compare both organizations' reported concerns and identify questions and issues that need to be resolved. These discussions take place not as a theater in the round, but separately, so each side feels free to explore reservations and doubts without further escalating tensions and perceived threats."

"What comes next?" Casper inquired. "How do understanding and issue identification get translated into action?"

"The task is to develop a sound model for dealing with and resolving each of the major issues," replied Williams. "You'll work together to develop a basis for consummating the merger, then establishing and maintaining a healthy, productive relationship at this new interface. At that point, actual operations are examined to identify concrete changes that need to be initiated to gain advantages of scale, or of market segmentation, or of regrouping product lines for manufacture, or for developing an integrated purchasing operation, or warehousing, or whatever."

Reston's mind sped forward. "I'd like to see us end up with specific plans, task forces to implement them, schedules, and all the rest. Is that jumping too fast?"

"You can't predict. It depends on what develops and what is needed," Williams said in response. "If an unsolvable difficulty appears, something that wasn't even anticipated in the feasibility study, then the answer is, 'yes, too fast,' but," he continued, "that's the exception, not the rule. More often than not task forces or counterpart groups of personnel with similar functions from each group do the action planning. When this step is taken, the two presidents meet together, marketing meets with marketing, finance with finance, and so forth, so that firsthand expertise can be applied to testing the model on a function-by-function or area-by-area basis."

"I can speak for our group," Reston said, "and I think we're ready to take this step, though I'd like to run it by my group before making a final decision. Then, could you and I go to London and review this process with Intertrans about using the kind of Interface Conflict-Solving Model that we have been discussing? We can make the decision to do it jointly with them on the spot if it all works out."

"That sounds good," said Williams.

"But can you handle two groups of tough engineers alone?" asked Casper.

"I won't say that I can't, but I prefer not to," replied Williams. "It's better when there are two of us, myself and a colleague. What about inviting one of your plant managers from Fero or Pero to work with me? They're not involved in the merger, but I'm sure they're interested."

"Even more important than that," Reston ventured, "they themselves are likely to be involved in mergers in the period ahead, and they might find this one particularly interesting since they have no vested interests in how it comes out."

Williams replied, "The ball's in your court then."

"Do we get you and the other group gets the other person?" asked Casper. "If so, can we choose which one we want to sit with us?"

"No, that's not the way we do it," answered Williams. "Sometimes we both visit the same group. Sometimes I visit one and the other design administrator visits the other, and sometimes we reverse it. We can help one another most in conducting the session if we both know what's going on in each group. Then we can compare notes and check one another out. We have prejudices like everybody else, and this is the way we go about cutting down on our own biases."

Although Intertrans seemed unsure and concentrated their queries on risks rather than on how they might benefit,

they agreed that interface model building could potentially
strengthen their integration with Sero. Logistical considerations
were ironed out, and the Interface Conflict-Solving Model activity was scheduled for a neutral location. Participants shown
in Figure 9 are presented according to their positions prior to
the merger. Certain structural decisions regarding reporting relationships were finalized after the activity took place.

Figure 9. Merger Participants.

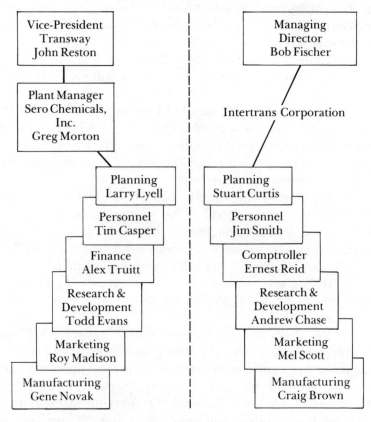

Reconstructing the Past

The two groups convened one Sunday in late spring about
six weeks after Transway and Damon had agreed on financial

terms. Williams, accompanied by Paul McBee, plant manager of Pero, managed the interface activity.

Williams introduced the design. "We're here," he began, "because your two organizations have become one, but as of now, this is true only from an ownership point of view. While it is relatively simple to accomplish a merger on paper, it is often much more difficult for people to shift their thinking and behavior to achieve the potential synergies in the merger."

"To clarify the objectives," said McBee, "they are to identify and resolve issues and concerns that might loom as barriers to successful, productive, mutually rewarding, and collaborative effort in the future. Reston's orientation prior to our convening outlined the process that we'll be following. So, unless you have questions at this time, let's get started with the first task of reconstructing the past. Are there questions?" Tension and suspense prevailed in the room. No one spoke.

Reston looked at Fischer and remarked, "Bob, we're anxious to get started."

"We're as ready now as later," Fischer replied tentatively.

The Acquired Organization in the Theater in the Round

People began milling around as the seating arrangement was shifted to ensure that everyone could hear. An inside circle was formed by members of Intertrans and the outer circle by executives of Sero.

"Okay," McBee said, "the ball is in Intertrans's court. As you start tracking Intertrans's history, it would be helpful to Sero's understanding for various members to contribute their views about significant events that have shaped your organization. Blind consistency is not to be expected as different people put their own interpretations on the same events."

"Brown, why don't you start?" Fischer suggested. "You're the oldest in terms of tenure."

"Right, Mr. Fischer, but I've only been here twenty-eight years, all in various manufacturing assignments, and we're a forty-year-old organization, so I don't know it all," Brown began. "I've heard reconstructions of our situation from earlier

times. Initially, this was a very tightly run entrepreneurial organization. That was before and following the last war, when
Britain's economy was by no means in good shape. It was a
highly risky venture and apparently great initiative was exercised to make our organization healthy. I only know that we
were unionized at that time. There were several strike threats
and a couple of walkouts during that era.

"Nonetheless," Brown continued, "we were profitable
almost from the beginning, but profit was measured in absolute
sterling, not in terms of return on investment as we try to do
these days.

"We suffered some effects from the London bombings,
but evidently the plant remained in pretty good shape. Within a
year and a half or so, I'm told it was restored to full operating
conditions. We moved along slowly as reconstruction in Britain
and Europe continued and became highly profitable. Market
conditions were excellent then, so we expanded and in several
years doubled production. Even though it was hard to get
equipment, we doubled plant size twice around 1950 to 1957. I
joined the company at the height of this expansion. At that
point we stabilized. Since the market was becoming saturated
we began looking for new opportunities. This led us into chemicals, and many of the products we specialize in now were developed throughout the 1960s."

"And how was the plant managed at that time?" asked
Fischer. "Was it still entrepreneurial, or how would you describe it?"

"Well," Brown began, "management had become quite
complacent by the 1970s. We'd known nothing but growth in
the aftermath of the war. We added a lot of people, the founder
died, and by then we made a successful transition from one major market into the two ancillary ones, which are our main lines
at the present time. With the increasing size, it was necessary to
establish working practices and procedures, clean up job descriptions, and that sort of thing. I expect we went a bit over-
board in the bureaucratic direction. Tough decisions regarding
cost control were deferred, and people were in the mode of
'produce more today and worry about operational details tomorrow.' We began to have a surplus of people. There was a

shift in the technical requirements of production, but we kept on the old-timers who had only rudimentary knowledge and skills and then added new people who had greater understanding of applied chemistry. By then we were severely overstaffed, so there were big personnel reductions in 1973 and 1974."

"Smith's area is personnel. What can you add, Jim?" Fischer inquired.

"Well, I'm not sure I have much to contribute," Smith responded. "I've been more of a policy and paper pusher than a member of management. My job is to enforce policy, not to create it. I know we've had difficult times with the union, but I don't really understand all the historical events that led up to them. I can speak to the mechanics of how we do things, but I'm only privy secondhand to the philosophy or rationale that guides our actions in the human resources area, because these decisions are made by Mr. Fischer and the people in Damon."

John Reston made a mental note, "At least as far as human resources policies are concerned, it sounds like Smith and Fischer are not on the same team."

After Smith's comments, Fischer addressed the members of Intertrans in turn, asking for a brief statement of anything pertinent from their perspective. Members of Intertrans reviewed their own tenures with the company, explaining their individual histories in different roles or job assignments. It was clear that no one had a comprehensive view of the organization's goals or values. When the review ended, Fischer said somewhat cautiously, "I'm not sure I can add much more," as he stood to complete the task, present a brief summary, and thank his group for their input. He then looked to Williams and McBee for further instructions, as Larry Lyell (Sero, planning) leaned over to whisper to Reston, "Did you hear any teamwork? Sounds like he manages them on a one-by-one basis."

Transway as the Presenting Group

"Transway is almost seventy-five years old," said Reston, "and its history is an interesting and varied one. From basically a one-man show operating on a shoestring, we've grown into a multinational corporation employing almost 100,000 people throughout the world. Transway's origins are in steel and metals, as are Fero's and Pero's, but we've diversified over the years, primarily by acquiring organizations with ancillary or complementary product lines such as Sero."

"As I recall," Alex Truitt, the financial officer, contributed, "our first move toward vertical expansion involved a major electronics firm."

"Right," nodded Evans (research and development). "That was said to be a really big step for us, because many of today's electronics applications hadn't even been envisioned then. We sold off the electronics arm of the company years later, but it turned out to be a very profitable venture."

"In the late 1950s and early 1960s, we really began to branch out in a number of other directions," observed Novak (manufacturing). "I wasn't around then, but I know that Transway acquired interests in petroleum products, space technology companies, magnetics firms, and finally chemicals."

"Yeah," Morton (plant manager) added. "That's when Sero was purchased. It was around 1965 when the merger with Transway was consummated. I remember only too well because I was working in Sero, in the manufacturing end at the time. We had just developed a new glue, which was far stronger than anything then on the market. Though it had not been recognized by Sero, Transway immediately saw the potential."

"And that's when I moved from headquarters' R&D to Sero," Evans recalled. "My background was applied physics, with some concentration in chemistry, so I came over to learn what I could about Sero's product lines . . . to head the R&D function not as a technical expert but more as a process manager."

"Except for Casper," Truitt noted, "all of us have been with Sero for ten years or more. I started out as an accountant in the early 1970s, and I've seen Sero more than double in size. As I see it, during that time our technical and financial record has been outstanding."

"Yes, the last several years have really been good," said Morton, "but we were pretty deeply troubled financially when Transway bought us. Our technical expertise kept us solvent, but it's been what we've learned about management that really turned us around."

"Sometimes we take our management philosophy and practices for granted, don't you think, Reston?" Madison (marketing) remarked. "Involvement and participation really have been the key to Sero's success. Our productivity and profit increased dramatically once we understood and began to apply principles of sound management."

"I saw a big difference in our organization when we really began to work together as a team," Lyell (planning) commented. "Before we developed good teamwork, I can remember how each of us protected our own turf, fought to gain a bigger share of the pie, and only concerned ourselves with our own little areas. If marketing had a problem, for example, it was their problem—no one else knew or seemed to care. Now we recognize we all have something to contribute to resolving critical problems or issues, regardless of the specific area."

Fischer observed to himself, "Reston gives them no leadership. They just seem to have a free-for-all. You can't really tell who's in charge. It's just like Americans. Everything is big and successful—no problems."

"That's something that really amazed me when I came in about three years ago," said Casper (personnel). "I was used to arbitrary, unilateral decision making. I didn't know what to think the first time somebody asked me what I thought about some concern outside of personnel, and they were really interested in my answer. I've learned a lot more about the chemicals business than I ever thought I wanted to know and about marketing, finance, and all the rest. Sure, good teamwork takes effort, but it's a lot more rewarding than operating out of a four-sided box on the organizational chart."

Smith, Intertrans's personnel manager, mused to himself, "My God. Casper's talking about the way we operate, and what's wrong with that?"

"Maybe what helped us the most organizationally was the strategic modeling process we implemented about five years ago," Lyell remarked. "Designing the model of what the company would ideally be in terms of financial success, talking about the nature of the business and its markets, then establishing goals and planning for further development and follow-up—these steps really gave us an overall direction and created the motivation for achievement."

"When we looked at our policies and structure in light of the strategic model, we began to reject the status quo as unsuitable for what we wanted to become," Evans explained. "That's when we changed some things around, freeing people to operate more naturally and productively, unconstrained by traditional organizational boundaries or rigid adherence to assigned roles."

"Let's see," said Reston as Evans trailed off. "Does that bring us pretty much up to date?"

"Seems so," Madison responded as the others nodded. "But, I want to add one thing to complete the picture. We re-evaluate our strategic model as we make our annual plans and introduce any needed changes. Critique is continuous and ongoing on an informal basis, with formal, planned critiques of individual, divisional, and company performances at regular intervals."

"Guess that's about it," Lyell summarized. "That's where we are and pretty much how we got here. Systematic organizational development is the crux of the issue, but I think we've made that clear."

"Just one more thing," Reston added, "and I think we'll be finished picturing our history and culture. Four of the seven of us were with Sero when Transway purchased it in 1965. I just want to say we've been through the Sero acquisition first-hand, and I know it can be very unsettling. I think I speak for all of us in saying we want this merger to be as constructive, involving, and productive as possible."

Critique of the Historical Review

Following the historical reviews, the groups from Sero and Intertrans separated to explore the implications of what had been heard and observed. Each group was asked to develop any further questions they might have and identify issues and concerns that might impede effective integration or serve as barriers to progress. A second aspect of the task called for a process critique. Both Sero and Intertrans were to describe how they had seen and interpreted one another's interaction during the history presentations. Excerpts of each team's discussion follow.

Intertrans's Discussion

"Well, we know more about Sero than we did before," Fischer commented, "but we still haven't learned the most important thing. Why did they really buy us out and what do they intend to do with us? As far as I'm concerned, I'm operating under the assumption that Transway wanted us not only because we're a viable economic unit and but also because we're in an excellent position to grow through expansions and the purchase of satellites. The only logical derivation is that I should have the same reporting relationship at the corporate level as Reston."

"That's the way we want it and that's the understanding all of us have," said Curtis (planning). "Otherwise we'd just be another plant and you, Mr. Fischer, would no longer be a managing director but a plant manager."

"I'd leave," snapped Fischer. "I'm not going to report to an American and take a step down in rank to do it." "Hear! Hear!" was exclaimed as people pounded on the table.

"I guess that's part of my main concern, too," offered Curtis. "They still don't understand how we think or what we're really like. It's pretty clear from hearing them talk and seeing how they act with one another that they have different ideas and different ways of doing things from the way we do them. I'm just worried that they'll try to make us adopt American practices and procedures that don't fit with our style or our people. We British are different."

"Even though they talked about strategic modeling, structure, and policy in general terms, it sounded ominous—like a fire bell. My guess is they'll try to control us through requirements and regulations," said Fischer. "I hate to see us lose the autonomy we've enjoyed all these years. We've never been subject to a higher authority—to being told what to do and how to do it. I always worked it out with the Damon people. Being second-class citizens will take some getting used to . . . and I'm not sure any of us are going to enjoy the transition. How about you, Smith? What's on your list of outstanding issues?"

"Most of my concerns are pretty specific," Smith (personnel) responded. "They talked philosophically about participation, involvement, and all that, but we need to know how they're going to pay us and evaluate our performance. What about our pension plan?" Smith continued. "Do we lose what we've already built, convert our vested interest to their system, or what? And how about transfers and promotions? How long will it be before they send someone over to us to 'run' things? Will they send in their troops and force us to lay off our own qualified staff?"

"Yes," Fischer nodded, "it's imperative to get these questions answered. Our people are afraid and justifiably so. It's the unknown that's so threatening. Let's try to get the kind of detailed responses we need to provide our staff some reassurance."

"What can you add from the technical side?" Fischer then inquired of Chase (research and development).

"It's clear to me," Chase answered, "that they're proud of their technical accomplishments. After all, technology has been their strength, their base of operations. Getting them to admit that we're more technologically advanced than they are may be an impossibility. We can cite quality and reliability statistics, but I think they'll dismiss our suggestions because they're supposedly the American experts in chemicals. If they'd let us, we might be able to teach them a thing or two."

"Scott," Fischer questioned, "what do you see from the marketing perspective?"

"Unfortunately," said Scott, "when we were first approached by Transway, one of the key reasons they gave for desiring a merger was that they want market separation—for us to concentrate on Europe and leave the American business to them. If we do, it'll be the kiss of death for us. Europe's economy is too depressed to support our entire operation. I hope they're willing to look at some alternative marketing plan, but I doubt they'll be receptive to our views. I think this issue deserves considerable attention, because the outcome is critical to our continued viability. If we're going to have any separate identity, we can't let them soak up our markets like a sponge."

"Okay," Fischer noted, "we've got to try to get them to see things our way. We'll have to be persuasive though. Maybe it's best if I take Reston aside and learn from him the corporate plans on this whole question of organizational structure and reporting relationships. I don't see the likelihood of progress unless that's cleared up. Are we talking to superiors or colleagues?"

"Hear! Hear! I second that motion," Brown said. "They're good in research and development, but we're better. Our operation may not be run as profitably by their measures, but we turn out a superior product. They had nothing but self-compliments and revealed no weaknesses. Therefore, I don't think they recognize our expertise or respect us for it, so I'm sure we'll never hear them admit that they could learn from us. All they seem to know about us is our bottom line and that's all they seem to care about."

"Well, Reid," Fischer sighed, "what can you add?"

"I've got a number of concerns," answered Reid (comptroller), "especially about the way they keep their accounts. In the accounting procedures manuals we've been given as guidelines, I feel they are demanding compliance with 'their' way and it doesn't make sense. Also, I'm confused over their terminology—'return on assets employed' as a measure of profitability. And while we're at it, how about getting a clear policy on capital expenditures? We've never needed spending authorization before, and, frankly, I think their $25,000 approval limit is absurd. At today's rates that's only £15,000, and that won't get us very much these days. They obviously don't trust us, or they don't think we can manage our own affairs."

"Let's see," Fischer paused. "Everyone's had his say and I think I've captured all your thoughts. Let's move on and describe the way they act with each other.

"I saw them as being very disorganized and kind of haphazard," Fischer continued. "Reston was never clearly in command."

Table 14. Summary of Intertrans's Reactions to Sero's Discussion.

Issue	Concerns	Questions
1. Autonomy	You want to impose your ways on us.	Will we have flexibility and self-determination?
2. Personnel	Your systems for bonuses and incentives differ from ours. You also appraise performance differently. What about promotions and transfers?	We have executive performance contracts. Will they continue? Must we adopt personnel practices that might not fit our situation?
3. Market separation	You want separate and identifiable markets—no overlap.	Can we do business in America? Will you do business in Europe?
4. Technology	You equate our low profit margin with poor technology.	Will we get a hearing and be respected for our technical expertise?
5. Finance	You want us to import your methods. Your system indicates a lack of trust.	Is unconditional compliance the expectation?
6. Authority and teamwork	You seem to operate as a team of equals without leadership.	Do you expect us to forego the way we prefer to operate or is how we operate as a team our own business?

"They seemed comfortable with the absence of authority," said Curtis. "Somehow they stayed on track, though, but it makes them seem so undisciplined."

"Anybody have anything else to add?" Fischer queried. When no one volunteered an alternative perspective, Fischer called the session to a close. People left the room singly or in pairs and the talk turned away from details of the merger, as though it were too painful to discuss further.

Sero's Discussion

"One thing seems certain," said Evans (research and development). "We've got a long way to go before integration with them becomes a reality. More than anything, their review of history revealed the depth of their concern, insecurity, and distrust."

"The perception that we're somehow 'out to get them' came through pretty clearly," Lyell (planning) agreed. "It wasn't so much what they said but their guardedness and hesitation."

"Yes," Reston added. "They seemed to weigh each comment so carefully. It seemed that their intent was to maintain distance rather than join with us, not to inform us. They turned to Fischer for permission to speak, much like children in school turn to the teacher."

"But we did hear some critical information," said Madison (marketing). "If we analyze what we heard and try to summarize their most pressing short-term concerns, I think they seem to revolve around specific personnel policies and practices."

"Let's start by listing the outstanding issues," Novak (manufacturing) suggested. Others agreed and asked Novak to write on the flip chart. "From what Smith said toward the end of their discussion, they're obviously concerned about salaries and benefits first."

"We'll need to explain the options for converting them to Sero's retirement plan and look at the best approach to dealing with their executive employment contracts," remarked Casper (personnel).

"And I detected some uncertainty about performance appraisals, promotions, and transfers," added Morton (plant manager), "particularly when it came to recognizing we may have overlap in sales representatives and duplication in the manufacturing operations."

"Maybe we need to outline our views of how personnel exchanges between them and us, as we envision them, might work to strengthen integration," suggested Truitt (finance). "The issue related to reporting relationships felt by Fischer remains unacknowledged by us."

As the discussion continued, Sero's members identified still other issues and concerns as indicated in Table 15.

In critiquing Intertrans's teamwork skills, Sero's comments centered around the feeling that a significant degree of

Table 15. Sero's Analysis of Intertrans's Concerns
Based on Their Presentation.

Issue	*Identified Concerns*
1. Personnel	Incentives Profits Pensions Performance appraisals Personnel transfers
2. Markets	Pricing policy Market definitions Strategies
3. Organization	Authority/responsibility Organization development Teamwork
4. Technology	Research and development Product development Data information sharing
5. Business/operations	Strategies (corporate) Focus and policies Priorities

reserve characterized the group's communication with one another. Fischer's manner of exercising authority led to discussions directed by Fischer in a formal manner, as if he were the hub of a wheel and the others were spokes radiating around him, but with no rim to tie them together. Reston pointed out, "It's as though Fischer's subordinates see themselves as responsible only to Fischer. Apparently they fail to regard themselves as equally responsible for helping one another and for operating the whole organization."

Isolating the Issues

Sero and Intertrans reconvened for the general session presentation of each group's separately prepared list of issues and concerns. Williams asked the groups to identify their designated spokesperson and McBee indicated that any exchange between the groups at this point should focus on questions seeking clarification.

"This session is intended to be informational," Williams explained, "not a debate relative to the merits or demerits of issues appearing on either list. After agreement is reached between you about what the most important items are, we can analyze and explore them systematically over the next several days."

Brown, the oldest in tenure, was chosen as spokesperson for his group. He spoke first, "I do wish to compliment my group who believe age is a source of wisdom." He continued, "We didn't prepare a newsprint summary; therefore, I will speak from my notes." He quickly reviewed his group's six-item list of outstanding concerns. In contrast with the more lively discussion that had taken place in their room, the Intertrans management group shifted back to their more muted, formal manner in the presence of the Sero group. Brown reflected this change as he spoke in quiet tones and with little enthusiasm, providing somewhat terse answers to Sero's few questions.

By comparison, Novak went to his team's newsprint summary taped on the wall and started with, "I was chosen because I can write." He then presented Sero's five-item list with considerable energy and enthusiasm. Intertrans listened attentively, but again asked no questions.

"Looking at the similarities and differences in our lists," Novak observed, "I see that the items fall into four or five major categories."

"If we take our list as it is," Brown suggested, "it seems that all your concerns are reflected in our six items, with the exception of 'business/operations' from your list."

"Maybe we can incorporate strategies, policies, focus, and priority into discussions of the autonomy issue," Novak suggested. "What do you think?" Novak asked the Sero table and found his view supported.

"That's all right with us, I suppose," Brown replied, searching Fischer's face for approval. Fischer was sitting passively with little expression on his face.

"Do you think your most pressing concerns will have been dealt with if we start with the Intertrans questions and then resolve how best to operate in each of the five areas of the

Sero analysis?" Novak asked, seeking agreement; he felt that both groups were in substantial accord regarding the outstanding issues.

"Well," Brown hesitated, "what do you think, Mr. Fischer?"

"Is there something else that should be discussed?" Williams probed, sensing Brown's reticence to speak up and noting Fischer's unresponsive look.

"Interrupting this orderly approach," Fischer started somewhat tentatively and then spoke more deliberately as he continued, "there is one thing we talked about, but didn't include on our list, and I'm the one who should ask it. We're not really sure you'll answer but, if you can, we'd appreciate learning why you bought us, and maybe something about what you intend to do with us now that you own us. We didn't exactly put those questions on our list but they are deep issues to us."

"That's clearly a legitimate topic," Reston smiled understandingly. "I recall how threatening the uncertainty was when Transway bought Sero. It was like looking into a darkened tunnel and wondering if the light at the other end was a promising future or an oncoming train. I'd like to suggest that we clear this issue away right now," he continued, "so that we're not slowed down by any obstacles that might arise because of misperceptions or faulty assumptions."

"That would be very helpful to us," Fischer said, obviously feeling the emotional strain from the doubts that already had arisen. The Intertrans group waited tensely, as though not sure what to expect. All eyes were on Reston as he began his explanation.

"First of all," said Reston, "I was in on this from the beginning since Sero's operation, which reports to me, was so similar in many respects to the Intertrans situation. Even though the ultimate decision made was further up in the Transway woodwork and required board approval, I participated in the study and recommendation phase. The 'powers that be' had pretty much decided that we should either own all of Intertrans or get out of it completely, so a study team was organized to consider and weigh the options.

"Morton and I were members of the team, along with three others from Transway headquarters. When we explored the various alternatives from a business perspective, we reached agreement to recommend the merger. The evidence we presented swayed the board in that direction," Reston concluded, turning to Morton.

"Two overriding considerations tipped the scales in favor of the merger," explained Morton (Sero plant manager). "The first was market share, and technology was the second. By combining Intertrans's market with Sero's, we will have almost 50 percent penetration of the United States and Western Europe. And, since your strength is industrial application and ours medical and pharmaceutical, it seemed we could both benefit by an exchange of technology."

"Are we to be an autonomous subsidiary?" Fischer asked, seeming somewhat reassured by what he'd heard so far. "Or are we going to be a manufacturing and distribution operation—an appendage of Sero? Are we going to be a dog or a tail?"

"We've made no decision to dismantle or supplant or supplement any part of your present operation. That's all to be determined based on business logic, and we intend to work with you in developing that logic," Reston replied. "If anything is already established, it's that we plan for you to grow, and to perhaps become more sophisticated as managers, as planners, and in other areas. The specifics should become self-evident as we work to create a sound relationship.

"One final point," said Reston. "My boss is waiting for a recommendation from me about how to put these two organizations together and that conclusion hasn't been reached yet. I was anticipating that out of this session we would develop the background knowledge and agreed-on rationale for making that decision."

"The most natural solution is to preserve the status quo, treating our two organizations as parallel and separate, possibly with some kind of transfer pricing arrangements for your products that can be marketed by Intertrans and Intertrans's products that can be marketed by Sero and limit any further collaboration to that," offered Fischer.

"But business logic says that when we have been in more or less direct competition in our markets, we should join rather than separate our forces. This way, we gain the efficiencies of scale that are possible and get the transfer of technologies that would strengthen both of us," suggested Reston.

Smith (Intertrans personnel) spoke up. "All kinds of problems can impede the development of an integrated approach. For example, how should we go about getting new personnel? Should we go to the open market to see what we can find? Should we consult with you to see if talent exists within your organization? If we do the latter and personnel are transferred, we've got an endless number of personnel problems, such as adjusting pay scales or whether exchanges are temporary or permanent. If permanent exchanges take place, that has implications for families, additional expenses associated with working in a different country, and so on."

"You're touching on the very issues that my boss will be wanting answers to," replied Reston. "We probably need a task force to get a handle on these and many other issues that will have to be resolved."

Williams said, "Look, I'd like to interrupt this situation. We have two persons interchanging and with an audience composed of the rest of you. In addition, we are jumping into problem solving pretty quickly before addressing the background concerns identified in depth. I propose that we need to shift away from the sequence of development we had been following and that each group, working separately, design an ideal model to integrate the two operations."

"Is the question we're to answer, 'Should Intertrans report into the corporation as a plant comparable with Sero or should it be a European subsidiary reporting in parallel with the domestic operations?' " asked Brown.

Fischer protested, "I'm not sure such a question should be discussed as an open question. It seems to me that it would be wiser for this to be discussed and resolved among Reston, myself, and William Smith, the executive vice-president. I don't feel that the Sero participants can see the full implications and benefits to the corporation of having a European subsidiary parallel with the domestic Transway operations."

Reston said, "These possibilities were discussed in the feasibility studies, and I think I can accurately reflect them to the Sero group, Bob. So let me give you the answer. The expectation was that, for the near future at least, the Sero and Intertrans operations are potentially capable of providing economies of scale, and it was anticipated that this could be brought about through some integration of joint efforts."

"Okay," said Fischer, with apparent reservation in his voice.

"Then, if the task is understood," said Truitt (finance), "let's break."

Intertrans's Discussion of the Ideal Merger Relationship

We can now follow the discussion that took place within the Intertrans group. In it we can see the beginning of the break up of what had appeared to be a solid front of resistance to the American takeover. The need to stick together for survival purposes did not seem realistic. Rather, their future as a competitive business appeared to rest on their cooperation with the larger organization. Also, Transway's openness to influence and their readiness to listen to Intertrans's concerns hastened the shift from suspicion to trust.

"As much as we would like to be a European subsidiary," said Curtis (planning), "the truth is that we are a plant with a small marketing organization. We've leaned on Damon for corporate services, and we literally don't have the strength to provide the corporate functions needed if we were to regard ourselves as a subsidiary."

"That's true," said Fischer, "but when are we going to get these things if we don't start now?"

"I'm not sure we want them or need them," suggested Brown (manufacturing). "Probably one of the things that made us attractive to Transway was that we didn't have all that overhead."

"One of the benefits of the combination is we don't have to suffer redundancies that might have created a number of surplus personnel. Anyway, those functions are available from Transway, if we are prepared to accept them," offered Smith (personnel).

"You're right," added Reid (comptroller). "Since Damon had provided headquarters services, this must mean that our personal jobs are reasonably secure since we are needed to head an overseas operation."

"Now we're talking best interest, not business logic," said Chase (research and development). "The compelling argument to me is the product and market overlap."

Scott (marketing) suggested, "If we take the responsibility for being the U.K. marketing arm for products manufactured in the United States, and they do likewise for ours in the United States, that fact would increase our manufacturing output and theirs as well without any significant increase in manufacturing or marketing costs."

"Add to that the stimulus we could get from an exchange of ideas," added Chase.

"I think we're two sister plants even though we reside in two different countries," said Brown, "and synergistic gains that Transway stands to realize compel us in that direction."

"I would like to hear your views on that matter, Mr. Fischer," said Curtis.

"What you say is true, at least for right now," Fischer replied, "but it ignores the possibility of using us as a staging base for expansion into the European Economic Community in the future."

"But does it?" questioned Curtis. "Wouldn't their thought be to use us for doing that anyway?"

"I guess you're right," responded Fischer. "To gain the stature of a subsidiary we've probably got to earn it. We need to show we can coordinate with Sero in coming up with some good ideas of our own about capital investment items involving European satellite operations that would naturally report to us. I'm afraid this discussion has about cost me my title," admitted Fischer.

"But not a whole lot else," ventured Curtis. "I think if we really commit ourselves to making it work we may be able to help you get it back in a bigger and more meaningful way."

"How would you feel, Mr. Fischer, about reporting to John Reston?" asked Brown.

"I think I'll just have to wait until I've had a chance to talk with Reston, and I'll tell you my reactions after that. Now we've got to see what they think," concluded Fischer.

After Sero also had completed its discussion, Williams reconvened the general session and asked Intertrans to review its conclusions.

Review of Conclusions

Brown, continuing to serve as spokesperson, summarized their conclusions as leaning in the direction of Intertrans being regarded as a sister plant to Sero, reporting into Transway through Reston.

Sero reviewed its conclusions, which were similar, leading Reston to say, "I hope I am not speaking out of vested interests, but I want to say it is gratifying that both groups weighed essentially the same arguments and reached similar conclusions. Logic has prevailed over preserving the status quo or playing politics for the sake of easing tensions, and so on. I hope I can supply the leadership that everyone seems to be asking for, and I look forward to the challenge of attempting to do so."

Williams suggested taking the agreements just realized as a new point of departure with one exception: they would start by exploring their implications in counterpart groups. Williams recommended, "Would it not be soundest to have a trilateral group consisting of Reston, Fischer, and Morton? This is the nucleus through which many of the needed decisions will have to be made. It may be natural for you three to begin exploring the implications of these decisions because they will affect how you work together."

Intertrans's executives looked at one another in apparent astonishment. The realization that they were, in fact, to have a "say" in their future seemed certain now that concrete steps were under consideration; they were to be part of the team rather than being told what to do next. Any reluctances or reservations appeared to vanish. Finally, Fischer commented, "I think we'll breathe a little easier now. From what you say, almost nothing of our future is predetermined, and we're actually going to be asked about shaping it rather than just being observers or recipients of what someone else thinks is best for us. I must say, it's surprising, but a welcome development that you really want our input. We'd feared the worst—that you'd impose yourselves on us in a coercive way. Even though we may have to face some negative consequences, at least we'll have a voice in how they are approached."

Designing a Sound Operating Model

The stage had now been set for developing a model to optimize the Sero-Intertrans interface. McBee introduced this activity by describing its purpose and reviewing the steps involved. Separate sessions in counterpart groups would address the sound operating conditions for each critical issue or concern needing resolution. These counterpart discussions would then be reviewed and discussed in a general session to obtain agreement on the specific proposals.

Snapshot views of the discussion among Reston, Fischer, and Morton and two counterpart discussions provide an indication of their inner workings.

Reston, Fischer, and Morton Meet Together

Morton said, "Let me welcome you aboard, Bob. Now that we are colleagues it occurs to me that you might find it useful for me to explain how John and I work together. This might provide a basis for you and John to discuss how you two might want to work together or even, for that matter, for all three of us."

"That would be informative," said Bob Fischer, "if it's all right with you, John."

"I would find it interesting to hear myself discussed in

front of myself," said John Reston jokingly. "But more seriously, I do think that's the point of getting started for us."

Reston, Fischer, and Morton proceeded to design specific
decision-making guidelines, proposing to make themselves an
operating committee responsible for receiving proposals by
other groups and for knitting the two organizations together, as
well as exercising their own initiatives for exploring new possibilities and ventures. Later, their analysis was presented to general session, where it was critiqued and modified but with only
minor revisions.

Scott and Madison: Marketing Counterparts

"What's your perspective on the best way to integrate the
marketing sides of the business?" asked Madison (Sero).

"Well, for one thing," Scott (Intertrans) responded, "we
have to think about the customers Sero already has in Europe
and the ones we've already established in America. How do we
make a smooth transition to market separation without sacrific-
ing good customer relations or creating undue confusion?"

"We've had a senior man who reports directly to me
going to Europe to deal with our customers. Would it be sound
to put him on temporary duty to train your reps and make the
transition with our customers personally?" Madison asked. "I
expect that wouldn't take more than a month or six weeks."

"That's just perfect. I wonder if we shouldn't just repeat
the process the other way around," replied Scott.

"Another advantage of that is we really need him back
home to concentrate his full attention on our own markets,"
added Madison.

"By this transfer of market responsibility, we'll each re-
gain the services of one full-time senior without having to add
to personnel," agreed Scott.

"But we can't solve this for ourselves because it has implications for at least warehousing, and it may even bear on
manufacturing," said Madison.

"All of this will have to get ironed out later on, but we
can agree in principle on the marketing aspects, pending a re-

view with the others of those parts that affect them," Scott agreed.

"You're on the site in Europe, but there has to be a transition in terms of inventory of our products, training account reps, and so on," noted Madison. "If we present the changeover in account representatives in a positive light, customers will perceive it that way. If we're negative about the change, we'll probably have difficulty bringing it off."

"What are some of the market separation benefits we could list, both for account representatives and for customers?" Scott inquired.

"One good thing that comes immediately to mind," said Madison, "is better, more responsive account servicing. Our European customers will probably welcome an on-site representative. They won't have to make a transatlantic call every time they want to place an order or request assistance. The same goes for your American customers."

"And our account reps probably won't miss the all-night flights to respond to a crisis or correct some mistake," Scott agreed. "It's clearly more cost effective to do business closer to home."

"Let's make a list of these points as we think of them," Madison offered, "then we'll present them in joint session. After our plan is critiqued and we see the solutions being developed by manufacturing and warehousing, and so on, we can design definite steps for implementation and specify individual responsibilities, time frames, and all the rest."

Chase and Evans: Research and Development
Counterparts

"Well," Evans (Sero) began, "as you learned in our presentation of history, I'm not an expert in chemistry. While I've learned a lot since I've been with Sero, I don't consider myself an expert chemist. My specialty is managing creative people in ways that maximize their potential. I have enough technical knowledge to converse intelligently, but my team members are the real problem solvers."

"How can we work together, then?" asked Chase (Intertrans). "Aren't we supposed to resolve technical issues between the two of us?"

"At our level," said Evans, "I think we should be concentrating on systems for coordination and mutual support, not on mechanics. The real issues, from my perspective, aren't in the nuts and bolts, but are part of the whole machine—how it's designed and what it's intended to do."

"You're saying we need to look at the broader issues, then," Chase noted. "I guess I'm as inexpert in managing from that perspective as you are in the specifics of chemistry. I've heard some of the management buzz words like *MBO* and *ZBB, strategic planning,* and so on, but I haven't developed a working knowledge of modern management theory and practice. My people and I function pretty independently of one another. We each have our own responsibilities, so we pretty much do what needs to be done, as individuals. I just try to keep everybody happy—my personal managerial philosophy is that you can't really lead an R&D group. You say 'manage' creative people. We say they can't be managed. We've either got a semantics problem, a real problem, or a learning problem. In any event, I must say we respect your technical prowess and you've expressed yourself favorably about ours so apparently we've both achieved strengths with opposite systems."

"I think you've put your finger on a kind of contradiction," Evans noted. "We'll need to do a lot more talking about this before thrashing things through. No matter how strong we are, it's still relative. I suspect we've got lots of opportunities to develop that neither of us has realized."

"If you're right," Chase said, "I could get excited too. It's so gratifying to see new ideas take form and grow into profitable, beneficial products. How can we make sure this happens in both our teams and that we share what we learn when it does?"

Chase and Evans discussed several ways for strengthening the technical interface between Sero and Intertrans. One of these centered on Sero's annual research and technology conference, which is based on internal presentations and special presentations by outside experts. The obvious first step was to enlarge this group to include the Intertrans technology personnel. Evans and Chase tentatively agreed to schedule this year's meeting four months earlier and to extend it by two days to maximize the interchange in collaborative planning now made possible by the merger. They developed additional steps for presentation to the general session, where they were reacted to favorably. Each R&D department agreed to designate one member to a task force to bring into focus the decisions before, during, and after the joint meeting. This task force would then develop a detailed implementation plan.

Final Steps

Each counterpart group reported on its meeting in the concluding general session. The subgroup discussions had established a bond of mutual interest between persons representing the same functional area. By this time, the participants were interchanging in a lively way as one organization, with the former we-they lines gone. Problems and possibilities were viewed from a functional perspective and in terms of what would be sound as an integrated effort. Discrepancies in the separate counterpart formulations of a sound interface relationship were thoroughly discussed. (See Table 16.) A number of specific major objectives essential to achieving the goal of constructive interaction were prepared to document agreed-on plans. A system to ensure ongoing critique was designed to measure progress and provide a gauge for change. Finally, time frames and individual and team responsibilities were assigned.

Impact

The merger described here took place two years ago. Since then, significant development activities have been undertaken with Intertrans. Numerous new operational efficiencies have reduced operating expenses for the merged organization below what they were for the two companies prior to the merger. Reducing the market overlap and improving products through shared technology and engineering contributed to this

Table 16. Consolidated Model for a Sound Merger Interface.

Element	Joint Agreements
1. Profit centers	Intertrans conducts its business as a profit center within guidelines consistent with Transway corporate policy.
2. Personnel	Promotion and remuneration are based on merit in the context of performance and measured in terms of mutually established objectives along with systematic organizational development and management development. Lateral mobility across functions facilitates career development between the United States and United Kingdom. Other things equal, preference for promotion is from within.
3. Market separation	Sero and Intertrans do not compete directly with one another but each markets the other's products. Sero's focus is the American market, and Intertrans concentrates on the market in Europe.
4. Technology	There is complete and open technical interchange between Sero and Intertrans.
5. Finance	Profitability is measured by return on assets employed. Accounting system of Intertrans is modified as necessary to accommodate Sero's record-keeping system.

savings. No senior personnel has left either organization. Fischer is now on Reston's direct staff in the United States and has been replaced by Brown from manufacturing. Plans are in place for significant product line expansions. Intertrans's personnel show no signs of feeling Americanized; the Sero group reports that their relations with Intertrans are open and healthy. Reston, who had previously been through a painful merger, concludes that six years of progress were condensed into six months of effort following this merger modeling process.

Dynamics of Change

The Interface Conflict-Solving Model used after Sero's acquisition of Intertrans illustrates how two previously competing groups can lay the foundation for ongoing synergistic integration. These groups were able to forge a relationship based on mutual trust and respect, achieve a level of candor conducive to effective conflict resolution, and secure members' commitment to making the merger a success.

Conflict at the Outset

During early phases, Sero and Intertrans demonstrated many of the "we-they" feelings and reactions that often typify merging groups. Intertrans's early participation was reluctant and guarded; not knowing what to expect from their new owners, Intertrans was understandably anxious about the future. Its members' initial comments to one another reflected doubt about Sero's intentions and a degree of suspicion and distrust surrounding underlying motivations for the purchase.

Sero's initial attitudes toward Intertrans generally avoided the feelings of superiority, dominance, and power that are characteristic of many acquiring groups at the outset of merger interface development. "We'll need to explain the options," "I detected some uncertainty," and other comments from Reston and Sero staff demonstrate genuine interest in dealing positively and constructively with Intertrans's concerns.

Learning from History

Intertrans's and Sero's reviews of history contributed significantly to their integration effort. Each group gained important information and critical insights about the other from hearing and observing the theater-in-the-round presentations. Not only does increased knowledge of one another enhance understanding but the review of history also prepares both the acquirer and acquired with data about divergent perspectives, values, methods, operations, and so on. Once these discrepancies in accustomed ways of thinking and acting are identified, conflict surrounding them can be resolved and the best strategy for the future found.

The Turning Point

With the reviews of history completed and outstanding issues identified, Sero took perhaps the most important step toward successful integration when Sero openly answered the acquired group's most pressing question. Reston's straightforward response to Fischer's urgent query about why Transway bought Intertrans assured Intertrans of its continued viability as a fully operational entity; it also alleviated members' deepest fears about ongoing employment and promised considerable autonomy to functions within broad corporate guidelines.

Further, and possibly more importantly, Intertrans learned from Reston's disclosure that almost nothing of their destiny would be predetermined—they would help shape their own future. By opening themselves to Intertrans's influence, Sero earned that group's trust and respect. At this point, Intertrans became committed to making a worthwhile contribution to the success of the merger venture.

Other Aspects

Several considerations help explain the successful results achieved from this application of the merger interface. One important aspect of this intervention's success relates to the participants themselves and to their responsibilities within their respective organizations. Both organizations were properly represented by their highest decision makers. Additionally, Reston had the authority to make major decisions affecting the merged organization. Heads of the operating components provided valuable participation in resolving issues and counterpart planning.

Positive effects of the sound merger model as a superordinate goal are clearly seen in the Sero and Intertrans integration. Once an agreed-on model was adopted, members of both groups focused their efforts on converting the model into a reality. Earlier doubts, antagonisms, suspicions, and tensions dissipated as both groups viewed the potential for a synergistic, mutually beneficial and potentially profitable merger relationship.

Resolution of differences, problem solving, and decision making were substantially improved through the exercise of good teamwork within and between the groups. The problem-solving skills demonstrated by Sero's top team in their theater-in-the-round interaction of open leadership, inquiry, advocacy, and critique served as a model of effective teamwork for Inter-

trans; the Intertrans members began to follow the model of
Sero's teamwork. As issues surfaced and were confronted between groups, each group member was able to contribute his
best resources toward resolving merger-related issues and concerns. Among these concerns addressed by counterpart pairs
were systems for the integration of personnel policies and procedures, plans for market separation, and ways of sharing tech-
nological expertise.

Success in this merger development session can be seen
in two ways. First, Sero came to view Intertrans, rather than itself, as the technical experts in special chemical applications and
to value the technical contribution Intertrans might make
through the merger. Secondly, Intertrans came to see Sero as
reasonable, even potentially helpful. Before the merger's conflict-solving interface, Sero's actions were interpreted from a
posture of fear and intimidation. As the interface progressed,
Intertrans came to regard Sero as a potential ally rather than as
a dangerous enemy. These new perceptions of one another were
not formed by individuals, but rather by each group. Past perceptions could be changed and new norms of cooperation and
collaboration adopted because members acted in concert, not in
isolation.

Sero's candor throughout the merger was an important
element of success. As the benefits of more open communication were seen firsthand, Intertrans's staff began to deal more
candidly with one another within their own group. Interaction
between the two groups also became more open and direct as
levels of trust and respect increased.

Summary

As the Sero-Intertrans merger demonstrates, previously
competing groups are not doomed to a future of disappointment, distrust, or despair or to a slow, reluctant integration,
each fearing a hostile reaction from the other for any miscue.
Although these and other negative feelings often apply to acquired and acquiring groups, they need not be permanent fix-
tures of merged organizations.

Merger applications of the Interface Conflict-Solving Model provide a constructive alternative to continued resentment, hostility, and unresolved conflict. Mergers can yield positive, synergistic results through the integration process outlined here. When truly successful, the new organization is stronger than either organization could have been without the other.

CHAPTER **10**

❧❧❧❧❧❧❧❧❧❧❧❧❧❧❧❧❧❧

Questions and Answers About Implementing the New Approach

The studies presented throughout this volume have provided numerous examples of the problems design administrators have had to solve in applying the Interface Conflict-Solving Model. This chapter highlights issues of how to use the model in an effective way. It states questions frequently asked and provides our answers to them.

Q: Are not problems between groups occasioned by difficulties of communication? If members on both sides of an interface were to communicate more fully, wouldn't this reduce or eliminate the tensions that exist at the interface?

A: Communication permits us to get at causes, but the cause is not in communication. The causes that underlie interface conflict are more than simply telling people the rationale of decisions reached or how expensive it is for them not to cooperate or sitting them down in a room to work it out for themselves. The key involves communication between the contending groups, but far more than just communication.

   By "more than just communication," we mean the

values that people embrace regarding what is right and what is wrong, good and bad, sound and unsound, and fair or unfair. If the situation at the interface violates any of these underlying bases of judgment, communication between the contending groups is likely to further the conflict rather than to bring about resolution. Vested interests, territory, status, prestige, or rivalry can operate as insidiously as can values.

It may be that win-lose has come to dominate thinking and emotions. Entertaining the idea of resolving the dispute amicably is equivalent to selling out or swallowing righteous indignation, and this is extremely difficult for anyone or any group to do; such change suggests that members are rejecting their group as "no good" and want out of it.

Behind all of these influences may be historical behavior that has led to mutual disrespect, lack of confidence, and suspicion. Under these conditions, if people were to communicate, which is another way of saying "open up," they would communicate incendiary emotions at the risk of escalating, not diminishing, the conflict.

Q: Are there other causes of interface disputes?

A: In addition to conflicts whose primary roots are in the loss of trust and respect, other causes of conflict at the interface are found in belief systems that have roots external to the situation itself. For example, differences in religious values often result in people from different groupings seeing one another in terms of differences rather than similarities.

Conflicts that originate in belief systems are among the more difficult to relieve by techniques of conflict resolution because belief systems generate their own versions of righteous indignation toward groups that are in opposition. The distrust and lack of respect are not caused by the functional working arrangements between groups and they do not originate in issues of territory or prestige.

The Interface Conflict-Solving Model has utility in settings when belief systems are in conflict, but in a somewhat different way than when the interface problem is rooted in distrust or lack of cooperation and teamwork. It is used not to change the belief systems but rather to discover conditions of agreement on operational relationships and engineer the tactics for solving those issues unrelated to the belief systems themselves.

As an example, belief systems that can come into conflict may be at the root of tensions between research and development (R&D) and a user organization. R&D personnel may have a tendency toward perfection, wanting to reach conclusions based on high levels of probability, not reaching final resolution until an experiment has been replicated, and so on. The degree of certainty required by a researcher to stand behind conclusions may be very great in comparison with a user group.

Users may be more accustomed to approximate solutions or making an attempt at solving a problem and, if it fails to work, trying something else. This attitude toward problem solutions may cause the user to see R&D attitudes toward certainty as esoteric and unrealistic, while the R&D attitude toward shallow evidence may cause them to see the user as risky. This interface conflict is reinforced by belief systems concerned with the canons of science as contrasted with empiricism and pragmatism. Under these conditions, the model can be used to establish better operational relationships within the constraints created by the belief systems.

Q: Are there other limitations in using the design beside groups in conflict because of contradictory belief systems?

A: Another limitation relates to differences between sociological groups and intact groups. An interface conflict between intact groups is one in which everyone who is involved in the situation can regard himself or herself as a member—someone who shares norms for behavior and conduct. He or she is subject to pressures from other members if departure in any significant manner from the norms is evidenced. Furthermore, the others are immediately present, usually engaging in day-to-day contact, and the norms of conduct and the punishments for deviation are subject to reinforcement, more or less on a daily basis. Other characteristics of intact groups are more important from the standpoint of applying the interface design.

Sociological groupings are of a different character. There is little likelihood the design can be employed to resolve differences that exist between them. A sociological grouping places people into classes based on religion, nationality, socioeconomic status, and so on, but often such persons do not have day-by-day contact with other members of their sociological group. These sociological categories exist in researchers' minds, but people do not have a sufficient membership within the primary group for members to be able to collaborate in the induction of change. Thus, sociological groupings generally are not a sound basis for trying to solve interface conflicts through the design.

Q: Are there any other barriers to its use?

A: The Interface Conflict-Solving Model does not work in a situation where one group is bent on executing a power play on another—unless this can be stopped. Power has to be suspended as the basis for problem solving. Both groups must be committed to an appeal to reason and analysis as the basis for finding solutions, rather than cutting off thinking by imposing a solution. This is a limitation in the use of the design, of course, because many power-oriented groups are committed to power as the means of control.

Q: Isn't there a different Blake-Mouton Interface Conflict-Solving Model than the one in Chapter Three and, if so, why did you change?

A: Yes, there is. It was the basis of our 1964 book, *Managing Intergroup Conflict in Business and Industry*. It had four perspectives: "how we see ourselves," "how we think they see us," "how we see them," and "how we think they see themselves." Although it is quite a good model, so far as it goes, it lacks an ideal formulation and the double perspective is not always necessary.

Q: Doesn't the federal mediation service in the Department of

Labor offer a service similar to the Interface Conflict-Solving Model?

A:　Yes and no. The approach we designed for the federal government in the 1960s was based on an earlier version, the one depicted in our 1964 book.

Q:　Are there other ways to resolve disputes at the interface?

A:　Yes, at least three. One is the Interpersonal Facilitator Model in Chapter Four. Structural solutions also are a possibility. The project or product manager solution creates a new group to deal with a complex problem rather than to deal with it through cooperation by intact groups. Either one, the project or product manager, is a good solution where it can be applied. The matrix organization, another structural solution, sets up multiple reporting lines in a way that may reduce group-anchored vested interests.

Q:　Those statements about ideal relationships in the study sound like heaven on earth; they appear too good to be true.

A:　There is a risk that ideal thinking may be misinterpreted as idealistic. This misunderstanding is possible from some of the tables that describe ideal models. Since the reader was not there when the models were written, some of them may seem abstract. If readers were to adopt the frame of reference of the participants who created these ideal models, they would realize that the ideal models have significant meanings to those who have experienced the phenomena. For example, trust and respect mean a great deal to a department that has routinely been promised actions by another department only to be disappointed each time because the other department failed to deliver.

　　"Reward based on merit" also has significant meaning to those who have been operating in organizations that base rewards on seniority. It means even more in organizations characterized by political conspiracies with the spoils going to the winners, without measuring whether actions are sound in the light of long-term perspectives and criteria. "Ideal thinking" should be regarded for what it is: a statement of possibilities subject to achievement within measurable periods in the future.

Q: I think I've got an approximate understanding of the inter-
     face process, but it worries me and I'll tell you why. It
     feels rigid and predetermined. It does not seem to deal
     with the unique features of situations or exploit break-
     throughs of the kind that happen when they are least ex-
     pected. It seems technocratic, imposing a structure on peo-
     ple, and it violates the traditions of the sensitivity move-
     ment, with the trainer as a catalyst or facilitator. Society
     has been moving away from form and standardization, and
     it seems to me that this design is moving against that direc-
     tion. Doesn't it go against the traditions that have been
     building now for a century and at a rapid pace since the
     end of World War II?

A: These concerns have been expressed over the years by peo-
     ple who have been acquainted with the sensitivity training
     movement and with androgogy and other forms of educa-
     tion where the person in charge takes a facilitator role. Our
     design for problem solving does depart from the facilitator
     model and from the sensitivity training movement, which
     started in the late 1940s. The sensitivity mechanism is use-
     ful, as far as it goes, for learning something about one's
     own reactions to ambiguity and uncertainty. It also is use-
     ful as a way of learning about one's own reactions to per-
     sonal efforts to contribute structure to an otherwise un-
     structured situation and to frustrations at finding others
     unwilling to accept what one has recommended. Further-
     more, it is useful for getting feedback from other people
     about one's own behavior. When several people share the
     same basic emotional reactions to a person, he or she
     knows that such shared reactions are likely to be genuine
     and objective; then, what others have to say may have im-
     plications for one's own effectiveness and how it might be
     increased.

         The next consideration is, "How might one use the
     sensitivity mechanism for dealing with an actual situation
     in which people have a vital stake in the outcome?" One
     cannot presume the absence of a task, as in the sensitivity
     situation, because the task is the reason for people asso-
     ciating in the first place. It is a basis for separating them

into subgroups to gain the efficiencies that can come from people with similar objectives sharing a common effort; people with a different objective can be segregated into another group to achieve that objective.

Take operations and maintenance, for example. The operations people cannot work when equipment is out for repair. The maintenance people cannot get their job done if the equipment is so badly damaged that it is impossible to repair it in anything approaching a reasonable time frame. The primacy of the task is the issue, not the primacy of the feelings of individuals relative to one another. Frustrations and hostilities are stimulated when two separate groups seek to do an interdependent task. When working with a group that shares a primary concern for being effective in executing a definable task, the sensitivity arrangement simply keeps people away from the problem to be solved by placing primary emphasis on person-based emotions and feelings rather than performance-based emotions and feelings.

The sensitivity mechanism is insufficient for use in structures when participants must confront their tensions related to performing significant tasks. When both groups approach the activity by designing an ideal strategic model for their relationship, the result is an expanded imagination, creating vistas that may have previously never been examined and, in several different ways, creating positive and constructive attitudes, rather than taking the existing frustrations that are sources of antagonism as the starting point.

After repetition followed by repetition of the basic design, the foremost common problem, regardless of the particular kinds of groups having difficulty, is their loss of mutual trust and respect; this diminished trust is the difficulty to be overcome. Other considerations seem to be of lesser importance, relative to this one. The way to get at this core issue is to track its causes in history and to plot the changes necessary to restore problem solving based on trust and respect.

Q: If trust and respect are at the root of the interface relationship problem, why not start directly with that issue? For example, say to the groups, "Look, through the interviews, we have come to know some of the difficulties experienced as you try to work together. In our view, the top problem to tackle is 'trust and respect.' Do you have sufficient mutual trust and respect to be able to work together effectively? If not, what causes the deficit and what can be done to restore it?"

A: Telling participants what their problem is does nothing to gain their involvement in discovering that lack of trust and respect is the problem. Rarely is the problem of trust recognized in the interviews in this clear way. Although it can be inferred from many things that are said in interviews, for a line manager or internal or external consultant to make such a judgment from interviews conducted before an interface activity is to ask participants to accept more than can reasonably be expected. Even if it is possible to identify the trust and respect issue as the primary problem, this identification does nothing to create the conditions of its restoration.

It is important to provide a hollow framework for participants to use in self-diagnosis—that is, the ideal-actual discrepancy, which allows the trust and respect issue to appear. This provides participants with an opportunity to discover it on their own initiative.

Q: But how do you know that distrust and disrespect will always be the dominant underlying problem?

A: No one can ever say "always," but in the many repetitions of this design it has been found to be the most likely common denominator. Nothing in the Interface Conflict-Solving Model tilts group diagnosis in the direction of identifying distrust and disrespect as the issue. Again, the design is a hollow strategy; it permits an unfolding of dynamics that are there. It does not tell people what specific emotions are more likely to be present and which less likely.

Q: You've given eight or ten examples of problems that involve the breakdown of trust and respect or issues of rivalry that have been approached in this manner. Any more?

A: An interesting application, one that has important implications in many companies, involves a core executive group at the top that has become insulated and isolated from operations beneath it. These executives may be interacting in a harmonious manner among themselves while they are unaware of their loss of contact with department heads or managers who report to them.

The Interface Conflict-Solving Model has proven to be very useful in such situations. The first group is the core executive level and the second group is made up of department or division heads. Each group working separately describes the ideal relationship between these two levels and then pictures the actual relationship, matched on an element-by-element basis. Once both of these formulations have been consolidated with both groups together, then it's possible to plot specific steps of change.

This is a particularly fruitful application of the design because it permits those at the second level who feel the problem to express themselves about the relationship and its consequences as they see it while protecting any individual from accusations of complaining or disloyalty.

Q: Got another example?

A: Often an interface problem among several plants that report to the same headquarters does not appear as such because they have little or no direct dealings with one another. Under these conditions, the plants may be competing for funds, location of new units, and so on. This competition can become intense; we know of a situation where one plant arranged to find out the other plant's proposed budget for a new unit so that the first plant's budget for the same new plant would be competitive. Once this underhanded maneuver became more widely known, it promoted a heightened secrecy about improvements in standard production processes and occasioned extensive and expensive efforts with one plant protecting itself from being taken advantage of by the other.

We used a three-way interface design with the relevant personnel from headquarters in one group, one plant as a second group, and the other plant a third. The modeling involved designing optimal relations between the headquarters and each plant and between the plants. As it turned out, the headquarters group acknowledged that its attitudes particularly about capital items had been biased in favor of one plant over the other. Once it became apparent that the headquarters was a key contributor to the feelings of rivalry between the two plants, steps could then be taken to rectify the circumstances that had brought it about and to restore a basis of greater objectivity in plant development.

Q: Is there an upper limit in terms of how many should participate?

A: Not really. The minimum interface consisted of two people on one side and seven on the other; this worked well. The maximum was twenty-four from each side. In the latter case, participation within each group was likely to be unequal because some persons had a broader grasp of the problem than others and could contribute more. Additionally, some people were there to provide specialized background and information and were not in a position to participate evenly in a give-and-take. The discussions themselves were of such keen interest even to those who had only special contributions to make that they rarely found it boring.

Q: By the way, do you have any thoughts about where a session like this ought to be undertaken and about the facilities that are needed?

A: The matter of singular importance is to arrange for this activity to take place where distractions either from operations or from the outside are at a minimum. That often means away from the facility and preferably at something like a retreat location. This aspect of the total programming is calculated to maximize the likelihood of success. That means that operational responsibilities are handed over to others while attendees are at the session, and the place where the model is undertaken is a relaxed one where people can thoughtfully analyze and reflect on the fundamental problem confronting them.

As far as facilities are concerned, the only requirements are three rooms when there are two groups, four rooms when there are three groups, and so on. Each group needs to have a home base where it can carry out its discussions in private, and the interface also requires a general session room that can be set up so that each group retains its integrity by sitting together at tables. It is preferable in general sessions for the group character to be maintained rather than for people to sit randomly. Often the groups need to have a private discussion of some point that has just been made to inform their spokesperson how best to respond. This can be done most effectively when group members are all seated together.

The only equipment needed are flip charts with stands so that each group can formulate its thoughts in written form as the basis for exchanging viewpoints through the spokespeople. Felt pens make it easier to see what is written from a distance.

Q: What is a "task paragraph"? Is it the same as the "instructions to participants"?

A: The Interface Conflict-Solving Model is formal, not formal in the sense of "coat and tie" but in the sense that the procedures have been extensively tested and reasons for relying on them in comparison with alternative possibilities have become clear. The task paragraphs or questions express in written form each activity the groups undertake. They make concise and specific what is and what is not entailed and this increases understanding of the purpose of the activity and how to go about accomplishing it. Frequently, when groups have discussions within their group, they consult the task paragraph to test whether the activity they are undertaking is congruent with it.

Q: Can a universal task paragraph be employed, or is it sometimes necessary to design tailor-made task paragraphs?

A: The best answer is "both." Standardized task paragraphs provide structure and direction devoid of content with regard to the issues under examination. This has proven effective because groups can fit their own content to it without difficulty. Yet, on some occasions, as exemplified particularly in the Consolidated Utilities case, it is desirable to write task paragraphs specific to the particular interface situation. Sometimes this strengthens the design administrator's understanding of the underlying dynamics in the relationship.

There is another reason for writing specific tasks. By engaging participants of both groups in thinking aloud about the initial task paragraph, their understanding of the process to be employed may be increased, and this usually heightens readiness to participate.

Q: Of what relevance are the background qualifications of the internal or external consultant?

A: A possible concern is that many organizational consultants, whose experience has been in a different tradition concerned with helping individuals and with team building, may see the formal character of the design as constraining. They may interpret the set of steps as preventing a free flow of ideas rather than see it as a way of channeling resources while containing the conflict and preventing it from getting out of hand. Then they may break the design and deal with the relationship in their own way.

A prerequisite is that internal or external consultants be aware of this and be prepared to apply the design in the recommended ways before attempting to change it. This helps the consultant gain a deeper comprehension of the power of the design.

Q: Beyond equal or higher rank, neutrality, and a person who is respected from both sides of the interface, are there any unique qualifications for the person, either internal or external, who administers the design?

A: The design administrator's contributions are more than simply administering the design in a mechanical manner, but the additional contributions require no exceptional or unique skills beyond those on which mature managers rely in their day-to-day actions. The critical difference that makes it possible is that the line manager is neutral while the other line managers who are participating in the activity are involved. As a neutral participant, the administrator

can readily see, for example, that wisecracks and snide remarks spoken across the cleavage provoke responses in
kind that can escalate efforts on each side to belittle the
other. What participants may consider a legitimate and
clever "put down" can be seen by the neutral administrator as contradictory to the purpose of the meetings. The
line manager/administrator can ask participants to live by
the expressed guidelines as well as an outsider can. No
unique skill is involved.

The same generalization holds when, out of impa-
tience, participants from either side may propose to break
the program design in joint sessions and bypass the spokesperson. No special skill is required by the design administrator to ask both groups to restore the arrangements that
call for presentations through spokespersons.

The important feature is that design administrators
clearly understand why the design has been programmed
according to the sequence described; they must also recognize and resist the pulls and tugs to shift from an administrator role in the direction of a facilitator model.

Q: What about issues of candor—don't participants frequently
"pull their punches"?

A: An additional benefit from interviewing is that it puts the
design administrator in a position of being able to assess
openness and candor in the sessions themselves. If there is
a discrepancy between what is being said in the interface
seminar and what participants discussed in the interviews,
the design administrator is in a position to confront the
discrepancy. This kind of intervention is probably more
successful when done with individual groups as appropriate
rather than as a general session topic. Sometimes it is
posed more effectively as a question such as, "Is this group
dealing with the fundamental issues of the problem, or are
they being glossed over? From what I learned in interviews, I think it might be well to critique the candor in the
team and see if it can be improved."

Q: But can a design administrator expect a successful outcome
starting from scratch, that is, with no prior experience?

A: Lack of prior experience is a barrier to effectiveness re-
     gardless of the area of activity; experience per se is no sure-
     fire qualification for success, but the more of it the better.

Q: Then how can experience be acquired by someone who
     needs it?

A: There are several ways. One is through participating in an
     interface seminar conducted by an experienced design ad-
     ministrator. Another is to understudy an experienced de-
     sign administrator while the design is being implemented in
     some other setting. A third is through attendance at semi-
     nars designed specifically for giving attendees a simulated
     experience of the design and opportunities to explore its
     dimensions and more subtle aspects. These public seminars
     are conducted at various locations on a scheduled basis,
     and attendance is open to line and staff insiders as well as
     interested external consultants.

Q: Are interface situations predisposed to explode like a time
     bomb?

A: Yes, many interface situations that are emotionally charged
     are particularly likely to erupt unless the design is admin-
     istered in a sound way. The Interface Conflict-Solving
     Model defuses these conditions, particularly by abiding
     groups to develop, exchange, and consolidate their ideal
     formulations, a step that reveals to both groups that con-
     structive motivations are operating not only in themselves
     but in the other group as well.

Q: In many interface situations, a deep win-lose orientation
     between groups can promote remarks between groups that
     arouse feelings of hostility and antagonism. The ground
     rules of the Interface Conflict-Solving Model are that these
     remarks are discouraged. Isn't it better to let them be
     spoken, and in this way to allow participants to ventilate
     their frustrations? Discouraging such remarks prevents free
     expression of feelings. It creates artificial constraints,
     doesn't it?

A: This question focuses a key aspect of implementing the In-
     terface Conflict-Solving Model. The rationale is that such
     remarks stimulate replies that also are hostile, and such ex-

changes activate tensions, reignite old feelings of antagonism, and steel participants for further fighting. They serve
to reinforce and to inflame the adversary relationship.
However, those who make such remarks are often unaware
of the tensions revealed in such comments. Once attention
is focused upon them, the unhealthiness is sensed.

Q: After the need for trust has been identified, why require
participants to dig into the actual situation? It seems that
progress could be made by directing attention to what
must be done to strengthen trust and respect. Shortcuts
are valuable these days when time pressures are so great.

A: There is a certain logic in that route. You just described
what has been done by saying, "If the absence of trust and
respect is what needs to be corrected, let's get to it and
find ways to bring it back into existence." The troubles encountered in this direct approach are numerous. People
tend generally to bypass an accurate and thorough examination of what is true in the actual situation—the here and
now as it is occurring. It is important for participants to
identify, line and verse, the specifics on what they do at
the interface that reveals the erosive effect of distrust and
suspicion. Without being specific, they find it difficult to
take steps to make changes. Many groups simply do not
know what it is that they do or fail to do at the interface
that causes suspicions and doubts. Only through active
diagnosis by participants, with validating feedback from
the other group, are members in a position to know what it
is they do or fail to do that has adverse effects on the
other group; this puts them in a position to change. The
bypass may improve the situation momentarily, but change
is accelerated when participants have become precise, concrete, and specific about what has to be changed.

Q: What steps can be taken to be specific, particularly with
the ideal model?

A: There are at least two. One involves producing word pictures of concrete action describing what each behavior
would result in when converted into an actual practice.
Another is in creating a flow chart diagram of the optimal

procedures to govern the interchanges between groups
when cooperation is needed, such as we presented in Chapter Five where the basis for plant participation in engineering was pictured as a series of choices.

Q: Is one intervention by the design administrator sufficient
to produce a norm against hostile remarks?

A: Usually, but not necessarily. Two or three interventions
may be required, but ordinarily it is unnecessary to deal
with the issue as a major topic again. It is always possible
for the design administrator to smile at a person who is
making such a remark or to wave a hand and say "uh-huh"
in a friendly manner. If continued, it is even possible to
deal with that person in a humorous way by asking, "Now,
how helpful do you think that was?" Such a question
helps a person see that he or she is not contributing to constructive consequences. When such remarks continue, it is
not unusual for other members of their own group to ask
them to "knock it off."

Q: What additional steps can be taken if they do persist?

A: Here is another possibility. Let's say the circumstance is
one where a group reports its conclusions regarding the description of the actual. The other group does the same. At
this point there may be large discrepancies between the
two descriptions. Members need to react to the other
group; someone might say, "There's no way you could see
the situation as it is. You are just looking at it through
prejudiced eyeballs." Then it may be useful to ask each
group to discuss among themselves their reactions to the
other group's presentation. In this way, participants are
able to discharge their tensions and feelings within their
group rather than across group lines.

Q: Many times group members ask the design administrator
how they are doing, as though for confirmation that they
are moving in the right direction. How do you deal with
that?

A: This is not something to be discouraged by saying to participants, "Don't ask us how you are doing. This is your
problem to determine from your own judgment." The de-

sign administrator does avoid evaluative remarks because encouragement can produce a sense of dependency; participants may then work to please the design administrator rather than to solve their real problems with the other group.

Still such questions are asked. There are several ways to react when called on to give an evaluation. When the question is asked close to the beginning, the administrator might say, "Well, I'm not in any better position than anyone else to answer that," or, "That remains to be seen. The quality is in results and those can only be known at a later time."

"How are we doing?" may also be asked with the hope that the situation will open up to allow personal opinions to be expressed. If this is the case, the expected response is, "How do you think you are doing?" The anticipated answer then is, "Well, that brings up a point I want to talk about," or, "That brings up something I think we as a group should talk about."

When the question indicates a degree of concern that progress is not being made, the design administrator might reverse it and say, "That's a good question to turn into a critique. Why not answer the question as a group. What *is* the quality of the work? What kind of accomplishment is being achieved? Is it satisfactory? Should the discussion be changed to make it more effective?" This response permits group members to step away from what they have been doing to consider how well they have been doing and to make changes if necessary.

When the same concern continues to exist, then the design administrator might ask a still different question, such as, "Why is this question being asked? What makes this question an important one to ask? Do you want reassurance or are you concerned that you really aren't putting out the total effort and want encouragement that what is happening is good enough?"

Q: It seems to me that this is awkward and that little is lost by being more informal and casual in dealing with these questions at face value. If people want to ask them, then why not answer them?

A: The purpose of dealing with them in these ways is to keep responsibility for accomplishment centered on participants who need to resolve their conflicts rather than the design administrator taking responsibility for offering false encouragement or by measuring out punishment by making members feel guilty.

Q: What about chatting with people outside the sessions about the sessions themselves? This is an opportunity for the design administrator to suggest ideas or open up alternatives that may not have been considered during the sessions. It's also an opportunity to provide personal encouragement.

A: The design administrator may see such outside conversations as ways of influencing the progress being made in implementing the design, but by and large it is unwise to make suggestions in this informal manner. There are several reasons for this. One is that whatever the design administrator says may be used by one faction within a group against another to create pressure for getting agreement rather than relying on working differences through and resolving them directly. Another reason is that not all parties to the activity know really what's going on between the design administrator and one member or a clique, and they may sense influences being brought to bear by colleagues that they don't understand and may disagree with. A third reason is that this way of influencing the process is susceptible to design administrator manipulation through a few cleverly placed suggestions. The administrator may get the process to go in a direction that he or she thinks is in the best interest of success, and yet it may be that he or she is failing to sense deeper tensions being experienced by the groups that need to be worked through rather than bypassed or disregarded. If the design administrator has suggestions to offer, it is probably better to offer them in the joint session if they are pertinent to its effectiveness or to one entire group so that everyone is in a position to know what has been proposed and to give their reactions to the wisdom of doing what has been suggested.

Q: Many times group members can feel concerned about their own performance or what's happening in the situation, and they approach the design administrator to ask questions of clarification or to get the design administrator's point of view about a problem of relationship under discussion. How should the design administrator deal with these kinds of queries?

A: Sometimes people seek outside discussions to get reinforcement of their points of view and to relieve personal tensions. If the design administrator agrees, or if a question is asked in a way that puts the design administrator into disagreement with another, that member can then use the design administrator's remark as reinforcement for his or her convictions in future group discussions.

Sometimes these questions are asked for other reasons. Since the design administrator doesn't participate in the content, offering a minimum of procedural help, this can suggest remoteness. Such questions may be posed to reduce the anxiety that the design administrator may be making harsh or negative judgments but not revealing them. If questions are posed for this reason, the design administrator might respond in a friendly manner but not to the question as asked. In other words, the design administrator might be more open and congenial but still avoid a direct answer to the question.

Q: In reading these case reports, I am impressed with how little explicit help the design administrator provides. For example, I did not see examples of the design administrator assisting the groups by making lists and summarizing remarks made by members. Wouldn't this help by allowing participants to concentrate on the discussion? Did you forget to mention this, or don't you help groups in this way?

A: The latter. One reason is that participants are experts about their own problems. Often they understand subtleties and nuances that a person monitoring the discussions misses, at least to some degree. The result is that any writing by the administrator is not as representative a picture as might have been produced if one member had taken the responsibility of doing so directly.

Secondly, if one of the members takes responsibility for recording suggestions or if various members share the task, the newsprint record serves as a focus for attention so that the thinking that is going on is crystallized as the newsprint recording is made. When participants themselves do the recording, they become more involved in "owning" the record. It is not a product produced by outsiders.

Another reason is that to offer help in this way can produce a dependent relationship by making the design administrator more important and central to the activity than he or she needs to be. The less contribution he or she makes in these procedural ways, the more attention is focused on the group's own activities, not on analyzing why the design administrator stated things the way he or she did. When this kind of procedural control remains with the group, members are more responsible for their own "product" and more involved in creating it.

Q: In the illustration of the interventions in the interpersonal facilitator model (Chapter Four), process interventions such as rephrasing, reflecting, or clarifying helped people to say something they were struggling with in a more expressive manner. I see little or nothing of this kind of contribution by the design administrator in the other studies. Many consultants consider such contributions important. Is my understanding correct?

A: Yes, with one possible exception. Ordinarily a design administrator avoids doing the things you suggest because if he or she does them, the group comes to expect them. Members start to rely on the administrator rather than exercise responsibility for helping one another to be clear and concise.

An exception is when people are talking past one another, or where different meanings are being assigned to the same expressions without the group recognizing or acknowledging that words are being used in vague and sometimes contradictory ways. If the design administrator recognizes that this is happening and the group is not taking responsibility for a higher standard of speaking and listening, then he or she might intervene, saying something like, "You may be talking past one another or you might be understanding something that may not be what the other hoped to communicate. Bill, would you repeat what Tom said to be sure your understanding is what he intended to convey? Let's hear what you think Tom had in mind."

If the need continues, then the administrator should ask, "Why are vague statements and misunderstandings allowed to continue? Why is no one taking the initiative to ensure fuller understanding of what the speakers are saying?" In this way the design administrator tries to get a discussion of the problem going. He or she might even ask, "What steps can be taken to reduce the communication problems these blockages produce?" In other words, the design administrator does not take responsibility for clarifying contradictions or confusions, but he or she may aid the group in establishing higher norms of member responsibility for reducing communication blocks and confusion under their own initiative.

Q: A point was made about retesting the priority of elements in the ideal and actual formulations as a function of ongoing discussions. When both groups have dealt with their highest priority and the discussion has been completed, they are asked to reexamine the priorities of the remaining items to determine the next discussion. Why repeat this when priorities have already been set?

A: To presume that the second element continues to have the same priority after the first discussion has been completed is unjustified. When the first element has been satisfactorily dealt with, it may make several, and occasionally all, of the remaining elements obsolete. For this reason, it is important to reexamine the priority of elements after the first has been discussed, after the second, and so on. Sometimes the originally established priorities remain, but as often as not, the priorities shift. Other elements take on a different character in the aftermath of a successful discussion of trust and respect.

Q: If the problem solving takes place at lower levels in the organization, how are the bosses involved in learning about what happened and in approving the solutions?

A: This is the closing-the-loop step between those who engage in the interface problem solving and those above them who are responsible for supervision. Higher levels need to know and sometimes to approve the total plan and the steps of implementation that are developed in the Interface Conflict-Solving Model. This loop closing can be undertaken in one of two ways. One is to arrange for significant higher-level persons to join the activity group for the last two hours or so to hear directly from participants what has transpired and to learn about steps that are being recommended through a joint presentation by spokespersons. Another way is for the design administrators to retain the initiative of meeting with each group's boss, either in separate sessions or together to review the problems encountered, progress made, and recommended steps. This latter step may be taken during the interface if a critical decision is needed before consideration is given to implementation.

The other loop closing is how those who engaged in the Interface Conflict-Solving Model communicate activities, conclusions reached, and program steps for implementation to those who report to them. These are likely to be either technically qualified personnel, persons responsible for supervision, or, on occasion, subordinates actually doing the work. In any event, it is important for them to be informed so they can begin to build expectations for the changes that are about to take place.

Two different possibilities need to be evaluated before the answer to this question can be considered. One is, do "they"—that is, subordinate levels—share the same basic attitudes toward the other group as were evidenced during the Interface Conflict-Solving Model session? If the answer is yes, then they need more than just being provided information about what happened. They also need to be aware of their own attitudes toward the other group. A group can do this by experiencing significant aspects of the design, possibly thinking through two or three elements of an ideal relationship, and continuing with descriptions of the actual relationship for the same elements. Once these steps have been experienced, participants are more able to understand and interpret information offered to them about what happened in the interface.

If those to whom communication is directed do not hold the same negative attitudes of distrust and suspicion, then the communication can center on operational implications.

Q: Why is follow-up necessary, particularly if the tensions are broken and participants see what needs to be done?

A: It is important to program into planning on a scheduled basis some time at which participants reconvene to study whether the steps for solving the problem were sound and to identify any barriers to implementation that may have been encountered. Fade-out of interest and involvement may result without this step.

Q: Can you give any other guidelines for an inexperienced design administrator?

A: A first-time design administrator might consult the Design Administrator's Procedural Index at the back of the book whenever certain points are being approached. Page numbers are given for the various cases that illustrate how any particular decision has been dealt with in other situations. Referring to this index can help clarify the procedure, suggest next steps, or give the design administrator confidence that the process is unfolding according to expectations.

Q: How effective is the Interface Conflict-Solving Model in resolving differences between groups?

A: This question is difficult to answer in any simple way. Part of the difficulty arises from differences in the origins or causes of interface conflict. Some differences stem from belief systems and some differences are rooted in structural arrangements or in process. Some interface problems are between intact groups while others are between sociological groupings.

When these origins are considered in relation with one another, the model has been found most effective in applications when the difficulty is a "bad" process; its next highest rate of success is when structural origins of interface difficulties are the cause. It is least effective when the differences arise from deeply held belief systems like religion.

Q: Have there been any failures?

A: Failure can be looked at as relative to the degree of success or as an outright flat failure. Flat failure has been experienced two or three times in thirty years. The causes are easily found in the incorrect conclusions drawn by those directly at the interface when they have assumed that they are autonomous with respect to solving the interface problem. That is, the people who have the problem feel that it is within their own authority to resolve the issues. The failure has occurred when others higher up in the hierarchy vetoed agreements reached during the Interface Conflict-Solving Model.

Q: Anything more on flat failures?

A: Yes. Some groups consider the process and then decide not to go ahead. This may have happened because the model either was not understood or sufficient attention was not placed on gaining commitment to take a step. In such cases, the problem is likely to persist with the resultant tensions and losses from the breakdown of collaboration.

Q: What are some conclusions regarding the likelihood of achieving a successful outcome from this approach?

A: Certain possible generalizations include the following:

1. The more intense the tensions at the interface, the greater the likelihood of success.
2. The fewer the participants whose lives are affected by the interface conflict, the greater the likelihood of success.
3. The greater the reliance on power for coercing solutions, the less the likelihood of success.
4. The greater the gain by each group from resolving the

differences at the interface, the greater the likelihood of success.

5. The more dedicated to organizational excellence, the greater the likelihood of success.

Applications of the Interface Conflict-Solving Model that have resulted in complete failures are rare. Interface situations have characteristically undergone improvement, some more and some less than others.

Q: The illustrations provided are concentrated in business and industry. Is the Interface Conflict-Solving Model restricted to these areas?

A: By now the uses and limitations of the Interface Conflict-Solving Model in industry, government, and academic and medical institutions are quite well understood. It constitutes an approach that allows many conflicts to be resolved that otherwise persist because they are not subject to resolution by more conventional procedures. Basic to the effective results that it produces is recognition and resolution of two underlying motivational dynamics that account for so many intergroup conflicts. One is the erosion of trust, which induces suspicion. The other entails feelings of rivalry related to vested interests of numerous kinds. Both cause either withdrawal or withholding of cooperation or even efforts to reduce the effectiveness on the other side of the interface.

Q: Are the present situations between hostile countries inevitable or might they too be subject to resolution through application of the Interface Conflict-Solving Model or variations of it?

A: The question is too important to the future to ask it and leave the possibility unexamined and unevaluated. The alternative is to permit the expansion of win-lose positions and to extend the existing stalemates indefinitely. One of the remaining applications of the Interface Conflict-Solving Model that is of signal importance is in relations between governments. The urgency of finding better solutions to these conflicts is evident in the almost unbelievable drains on effective international problem solving and the consequent feelings of fear resulting from these rivalries and distrusts.

Relieving the present antagonisms between the United States and the Soviet Union is certainly of singular importance. A step toward bridging some of these differences might be initiated by using the model with key governmental representatives from the two sides. At the least this variation might produce more fresh alternatives for higher levels to consider than the conventional reliance on power that has characterized historical relationships. The basic model appears to be a viable approach and how it might be applied is suggested by the examples provided here.

The practicality of this step is suggested by examining the alternative as implemented by President Jimmy Carter at the Camp David discussions between Israel and Egypt and involving active participation limited to Carter, Anwar Sadat, and Menachim Begin. However, the other attendees at Camp David (who did not attend joint sessions) were the proper ones, the location was right, and the time available sufficient. All that seems to have been lacking was Carter's lack of familiarity with the Interface Conflict-Solving Model.

The possibility of such a first step between the United States and the Soviet Union being undertaken seems highly remote, but, on the other hand, nothing can be more unrealistic than perpetuating and extending the antagonisms and defensive reactions that have been produced over the past half century. It is difficult to feel that much would be lost even if failure were to result, but it is easy to see that much would be gained were success to be realized.

Annotated Bibliography

This annotated bibliography identifies sources pertinent for further study of intergroup relations and how they may be strengthened.

Austin, W. G., and Worchel, S. *The Social Psychology of Intergroup Relations*. Belmont, Calif.: Wadsworth, 1979.

This review of the research basis for studying intergroup relations by numerous authors is primarily for an academic audience.

Blake, R. R. "Psychology and the Crisis of Statesmanship." *The American Psychologist*, 1959, *14*, 87-94.

This article is of interest from an historical perspective because it introduces the idea that an organized and systematic approach to resolving conflicts between groups is a possibility.

Blake, R. R., and Mouton, J. S. "Intergroup Therapy." *International Journal of Social Psychiatry*, 1962, *8* (3), 196-198.

An organized approach to conflict between groups is elaborated in this article.

Blake, R. R., Shepard, H. A., and Mouton, J. S. *Managing Intergroup Conflict in Industry*. Houston: Gulf Publishing Company, 1964.

This is a comprehensive framework of intergroup relations within industry and of alternative possibilities for solving conflicts between groups. It contains original experiments with industrial managers as subjects, dealing with the underlying dynamics of intergroup frictions induced by temporary membership.

Brown, L. D. *Managing Conflict at Organizational Interfaces.* Reading, Mass.: Addison-Wesley, 1982.

This book is a basic sociological analysis of relations between groups and it offers many structural ways of strengthening intergroup relations. The dynamics of conflict as they relate to intergroup cooperation are briefly mentioned.

Coser, L. A. *Continuities in the Study of Social Conflict.* New York: Free Press, 1967.

Coser's conceptual analysis of relations between groups in conflict is among the best available for seeing issues of conflict in historical perspective approached from several different academic disciplines.

Deutsch, M. *The Resolution of Conflict.* New Haven, Conn.: Yale University Press, 1973.

This text is among the most often quoted in the field of conflict. Some of it is directly pertinent to the analysis of conflict between organized groups.

Fisher, R., and Ury, W. *Getting to Yes: Negotiating Agreement Without Giving In.* Boston: Houghton Mifflin, 1981.

Rules for successful negotiation are presented in this book, but no significant distinction is drawn between how to proceed when the parties negotiating are two people as contrasted with two groups.

Fordyce, J. K., and Weil, R. *Managing with People.* Reading, Mass.: Addison-Wesley, 1971.

Fordyce and Weil use the term *organization mirror* to describe a way of giving an intact group input for how representatives of outside groups see it. This process is unrelated to resolving conflicts in the relationship or to rebuilding trust.

Lawrence, P. R., and Lorsch, J. W. *Developing Organizations: Diagnosis and Action.* Reading, Mass.: Addison-Wesley, 1969.

The descriptions in this volume are concerned with group-to-group interfaces and utilize an action research model for the induction of change. External consultants, using interviews and questionnaires, diagnose the organization, report results, and design structural or educational interventions to resolve specific blockages in communication and decision making.

Lawrence, P. R., and Lorsch, J. W. *Organization and Environment: Managing Differentiation and Integration.* Homewood, Ill.: Richard D. Irwin, 1969.

This series of case studies compares high- and low-performing departments or units within organizations for the manner in which they solve interdepartmental conflicts.

Nierenberg, G. I. *The Art of Negotiating: Psychological Strategies for Gaining Advantageous Bargains.* New York: Hawthorn Books, 1968.

Many issues arise about whether individuals are dealing with one another as a pair or as group representatives. Nierenberg does not make this important distinction explicit.

Sherif, M., and others. *Intergroup Cooperation and Competition: The Robbers Cave Experiment.* Norman, Okla.: University Book Exchange, 1961.

This is an important and original investigation of how groups of youngsters establish their intergroup relations under camping conditions. It stimulated further interest and is considered a classic in the field.

Tjosvold, D., and Johnson, D. W. *Productive Conflict Management.* New York: Irvington Publishers, 1983.

This collection of articles by well-known authors provides a number of interesting generalizations about organized intergroup relations.

Walton, R. E. *Interpersonal Peacemaking: Confrontations and Third Party Consultation.* Reading, Mass.: Addison-Wesley, 1969.

Treating peacemaking as the resolution of differences between individuals, Walton summarizes an Interpersonal Facilitator Model approach similar to that presented in Chapter Four in which a neutral or third party helps pairs of individuals reach resolution of their differences. The book does not give attention to differences between groups that are related to issues of membership and where, if cooperation is induced, conflict may be increased and the cohesion reduced.

Design Administrator's Procedural Index

This index is for use by design administrators in planning and conducting Interface Conflict-Solving sessions. It is organized in the normal sequence of activities; page numbers indicate where the topic is discussed or illustrated. Chapter Ten, pages 286–311, provides a series of questions and answers regarding background information and issues of concern to design administrators.

Background Considerations

Exploring Possibilities

Planning for Conducting
an Interface Conflict-Solving Design

Orientation of Participants

Step 1: Developing the Optimal Model

Step 2: Consolidating the Optimal Relationship

Step 3: Describing the Actual Relationship

Step 4: Consolidating the Actual Relationship

Step 5: Planning for Change

Step 6: Progress Review and Replanning

Interventions

Interventions by the design administrator have been separated from other categories and provided below since any one or more of them may occur at each step of the Interface Conflict-Solving sequence.

Name and Subject Index

A

A.M. Castle, use of Interface Conflict-Solving Model in, xi

Actual relationship, description of: by corporate-field, 194-196, 202; in Interface Conflict-Solving Model, 18; by line and staff, 109-116; by operations and maintenance, 42, 49-50; by parent-subsidiary, 237-238

Administrators, design, 19. *See also* Design administrator

Androgogy, 291. *See also* Synergogy

Antagonisms: between line and staff, 109; between parent-subsidiary, 211; between union and management, 144

Approaches, conventional for resolving differences, 10-17

Arbitration: disadvantages of, 15; role of arbitrator in, 15

Austin, W. G., 313

Authority, power and, 207

Autonomy, as issue in merger, 269

B

Behavioral dynamics: historical role in, 287; in mergers, 251

Belief systems, 287-288

Blake, R. R., x, xix, 23, 101-104, 106, 107, 108, 109, 117, 119, 120, 132-135, 137, 143, 208, 209, 313

Blake-Mouton Interface Conflict-Solving Model, x. *See also* Interface Conflict-Solving Model

Brown, L. D., 314

C

Candor: described, 49-50, 113, 123, 150, 191-192, 202, 226-227, 237-238, 266; lack of, between international and headquarters (Comtradco), 197-198; between parent-subsidiary, 231. *See also* Openness

Change: and behavior, 19; differences between evolutionary and planned, 162-163; dynamics of, 52, 140, 169, 204, 247, 281;